✠

COPTIC ORTHODOX
PATRIARCHATE

See of St. Mark

GOD AND MAN

BY
H. H. POPE SHENOUDA III

Title   : GOD AND MAN

Author   : H. H. Pope Shenouda III

Translated By   :Dr. Wedad Abbas

Illustrated By   : Sister Sawsan

Typesetting   : Y. M. Ekladios

Press   :Dar El Tebaa El Kawmia, Cairo

Edition   : First Edition – December 2000

Legal Deposit No. : 14299 / 2000

H.H. Pope Shenouda III
117th Pope and Patriarch of Alexandria and
the See of St Mark

Table of Contents

****

INTRODUCTION

This book is the fruit of a series of more than forty lectures delivered from 1976 till the eighties.

The main topic of these lectures is God -blessed be His name- in His relationship with His creation, particularly with man. Some other lectures can be classified as theoretical theology.

The lectures could be divided into three sections under the following titles:

1. God's exclusive attributes.

2. God's relationship with man.

3. Man's relationship with God.

The three sections are correlated even in their details and could not be completely separated.

This correlation resulted in some unavoidable repetition to keep the whole structure of the subject.

Take for example a topic like Love and Giving in God's relationship with man: This topic is included in two sections" "God's Relationship with Man Is a Love History" and "God's Relationship with Man Starts with Giving". The first section concentrates on "Love", and the second on "Giving". However, some interrelation exists between both, as we cannot separate God's love from God's giving. The repetition in both, therefore, was necessary to achieve perfection of each subject.

Likewise, most of God's attributes could only be understood within this relationship with His creation.

We cannot speak separately about some attributes of God, like His wisdom, goodness, compassion, dispensation, ... etc., but we should mention how such attributes appear in the relationship between God and His creation. This is what we have done.

Now, dear reader, in this book you have almost the forty subjects

The lectures are a mixture of theological and spiritual tackling, and as a whole depend almost completely on the Holy Bible where the history of God's relationship with mankind existed even before man's creation.

We present you this book for your meditation.

Let it be a cause for deepening your relationship with God so that His love in your heart may grow and your knowledge of Him may increase. Put before you the beautiful words in the Gospel according to St. John:

"And this is eternal life, that they may know You, the only true God ..."(Jn. 17: 3)

Now we have to leave you to live with this Beloved Almighty God through the words of the book

Pope Shenouda III

SECTION 1

GOD'S ATTRIBUTES

Contents of this Section:

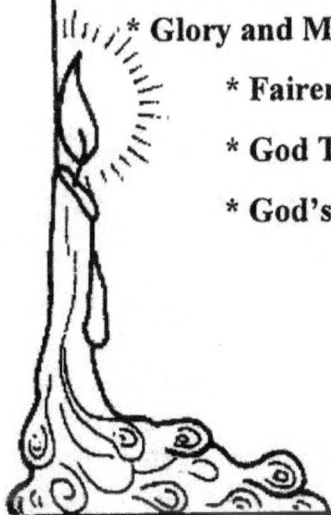

GOD'S EXCLUSIVE ATTRIBUTES

Some of God's attributes are shared by His creation, but these attributes are in God exclusive and unlimited whereas in His creation they are relative and limited. This applies to some attributes such as power, wisdom, knowledge, love, forgiveness, beauty and splendor, mercy, giving ... etc.

God is Wise, and many people are wise. But God's wisdom is exclusive and unlimited, whereas the wisdom of the people is limited and proportional with the intelligence and prudence endowed them by God.

On the other hand, some attributes belong to God solely and no creature whatsoever share them. They are exclusive attributes, among which are the following:

* God is Eternal:

God alone is Eternal, with no beginning. No other creation is described as eternal because all creation is made by God, hence having a beginning which is that of its emergence into existence. No creation existed before being brought into existence by God.

The universe with all its continents, countries and nations, oceans, rivers and seas, suns, moons and stars, all of this universe has been created in a certain time and nothing in it can be described as eternal. Even the light is not eternal, for there had been a time when no light existed until God said, "*Let there be light"*(Gen. 1: 3) and light came into existence. The whole nature likewise is created and not eternal, and its beginning is the day God made it and brought it into existence.

* God's Existence is Imperative:

God's existence is imperative as some describe it. His existence is very necessary because all things testify to the existence of a higher Being, an Omnipotent Being who brought these things into existence and was the cause of their existence.

Some philosophers call God "The First Cause", that is the first cause of the existence of all existent things.

No being, other than God, his existence can be described as imperative or indispensable because all other beings are created and have a beginning before which they had not been. Thus some time had passed before such created things existed, therefore, their existence is not a necessity.

* God is the Creator:

He alone is the Creator who created everything. The term "create" means making from nothing, which is a matter belonging solely to God.

The farthest extent attained by the human mind is making marvellous things, but this cannot be called creation.

This is not creation because man, with his marvellous intelligence made them from the material created by God. Truly man achieved wonderful things in the field of industry and technology as we see in the present days, but even the human mind itself is created by God, and man's intelligence is a gift from God.

God then has created material and has created intellect and mental acuteness. Then the mind made use of the material and of such mental acuteness in making all marvellous products. But God remained the sole Creator.

God has not only created material and every material thing, but He created also the spirit and the soul.

God created the spirit of man, and created His angels as spirits (Ps. 104: 4). He created life, and as a creator He can take off the life He had given. Therefore He gives life and causes death; life and death are in His hand. He also created nature and can put an end to it.

---

* God is Almighty:

None but God is almighty. Some beings have power but not omnipotence; the angles for example are described as excelling in strength (Ps. 103: 20), yet they are not almighty. Even humans: some have great power whether in body, intellect, will or authority, but no human is almighty.

Suffice to remember that no human has ever been able to overcome death.

All humans are overcome by death and no one could conquer it. All people die even though very aged, and the rest will also die, because before death all stand helpless!

No human also has ever been more powerful than sin, for sin has cast down many wounded, and all who were slain by her were strong (Prov. 7: 26). It is also said, *"They have all turned aside, they have together become corrupt; there is none who does good, no not one"*(Ps. 14: 3); *"No one is good but One, that is, God"*(Mt. 19: 17). Everyone has certain weaknesses which differ in kind and extent from one person to another. This means that no one is almighty or omnipotent.

Even Satan, with all his power, is not all powerful

He could not conquer everyone, but was many times conquered by saints. Though he ruled over some persons and dwelt in them, yet many righteous persons possessed the power of casting out devils.

---

* God is Omni-present:

God is everywhere: in heaven, on earth, and in between. No place is vacant from Him, and no place can contain Him. This Omni-presence is an attribute of God alone. No one can be present in two places at the same time, but God is present in all places at the same time. And while He is present everywhere, He observes what happens everywhere. He sees, hears, and watches everything, and nothing is hidden from Him. This is a special power belonging solely to God.

When we say everywhere, we mean even the visible and the invisible things.

Since God is everywhere, and no place can contain Him, He is even in the heart and mind. Therefore He alone examines the hearts and reads the thoughts.

The Omni-presence of God makes us contemplate on movement with regard to God.

God does not ascend or descend, because He is present everywhere, which means in the place where He is said to ascend or descend. He is present high above and underneath. He does not leave one place to another because no place is vacant from Him. Therefore He does not go or come, for He fills all and fills every place. It is an attribute confined to God alone.

* God Knows Everything:

God alone knows everything about everything. He knows things before happening, for He knows the future, the transcendental, and the realities. He knows the past, the present, and the future; for everything is before Him at the same time. He knows the visible and the invisible things, and knows the nature of all beings because it is He who gave them this nature. God's knowledge is complete and inclusive, and at the same time certain and firm. He knows everything by Himself without a medium, and immediately not gradually. This is the divine knowledge which is distinct from the type of knowledge the humans acquire.

* God is Boundless:

God is not limited by place; for He is in every place and not contained in any place.

God is not limited by time; for He has no beginning nor end.

God is not limited in knowledge; for He knows everything about everything.

God is not limited in His attributes. And in all this He is distinguished from all other beings.

God is the Living and the Immortal (1 Tim. 6: 16, 15)

* God is Unchangeable:

The human beings change in form, intellect and age. Their knowledge increases and sometimes decreases by forgetfulness. They change by growing, by becoming disabled, or by collapsing. They change in power, health, and position. But God never changes; He does not increase because there is no more to attain, being Himself perfect in everything. He does not decrease because that does not suit His divinity. He does not change because there is no better state than His to acquire.

Some may wonder how we say God is unchangeable while He once for example wanted to destroy the people of Nineveh then He forgave them and extended His mercy to them!

We explain to those that it is the people of Nineveh themselves who had changed from sin to repentance. In their sin they deserved God's punishment, but in their repentance they deserved God's mercy and forgiveness. God's scales remained unchanged.

This is only a hint about God's attributes, for no language can ever fully cover the subject.

GOD THE CREATOR

The creation process is very amazing; it is beyond the human intellect and can only be understood through faith and inspiration. For in fact the Creator is not merely a maker because a maker makes things from an existing material, whereas the creator creates a thing from nothing!

Amazing indeed that God made everything from nothing!

This creation work by God implies types of power, wisdom, art, order, beauty, and humbleness. God, in His humbleness, has not willed to be alone existent, so He brought to existence other beings to be with Him.

God's goodness, benevolence, and love are the cause that made Him create the things existing now.

God was not in need for the universe, but the universe rather is in need for God as we say in the Liturgy of St. Gregory: [You were not in need for my servitude, but I rather am in need for Your Lordship]. God did not create man to be glorified by him; for before man God had been glorified by His angles. God even was not in need to be glorified by the angles nor by the nature because He is glorified in His own attributes, in His own nature which is boundless and beyond understanding. Thus He created the world out of His benevolence.

But when has God created everything?

The time is unknown, which the Scriptures called "*in the beginning*" "*In the beginning God created the heavens and the earth*"(Gen. 1: 1). He created the heavens with everything in it, and the earth with everything in it. He created the spirit and the material; He made His angles spirits (Ps. 104: 4) and from the material He made all material beings.

God even gave some of the creation the gift of life.

He gave life to plants, animals, and man; and before that to the angles. Out of His love He granted man, and the angles, an immortal spirit. To the animals He gave life that ends by death. The type of life given by God to plants is different from that given to animals, and from the life given man.

God created all classes of creation, even what seems tiny or little!

It is an evidence of God's humbleness that He created the rational and the irrational creation, the animate and inanimate beings. He created the huge elephant as well as the worm that creeps under the stone, the strong lion and the weak frightened rabbit, the monkey and the gazelle, the high mountain and the deep valley. He created heat and cold, light and darkness; everything is made by His hands.

Some would ask: Did God create Satan?

Yes, Satan also is God's creation, but God did not create him a devil. God created Satan an angel, with the great wonderful nature of angels. But this angel turned through his deviating will into a devil. Satan was a Cherub, and was described in the Book of Ezekiel as *"covering cherub"*(Ezek. 28: 14, 16). When he was created, as God says, he was the seal of perfection *"full of wisdom and perfect in beauty"*(Ezek. 28: 12)

God's power appears also in the great number and variety of His creation.

Millions and millions of creatures are repeated every generation. Some of these creatures are repeated every year or a couple of years, and some are innumerable such as the sand of the sea and the stars and planets in heaven.

We know only the visible of God's creation and know nothing about the invisible.

We exert much effort to know about the invisible. For instance we do not know the secrets contained underground, but we exert effort through excavations to know, for example, the sources of water or petroleum under ground, or the volcanoes emitted. Much more can be known by excavations about gold, precious stones and metals existing inside the mountains. The deep waters of seas contain even more and more, therefore institutes have been established for sea sciences as well as for geological research. At present studies are being conducted for space sciences where phenomena are studied, such as the non-gravity of some zones where spacemen can walk in space! Indeed we only know in part as St. Paul the Apostle says (1 Cor. 13: 12), not only of the other world but also of this world, of the earth on which we live. Little only is that which we know of the earth and of what surrounds it.

We are amazed at the wonderful order and system in which God created the world with its beings.

Suffice to look at the celestial bodies with its wonderful system.

See what laws govern these celestial bodies and keep them standing in their place and organizing their interrelation which affects also our lives! The earth, for example, turns around itself in front of the sun once every 24 hours without failing along ages and ages, causing the night and the day. And the moon turns around the earth once a month causing the lunar phases: crescent, lunar quarter, full moon, convex, and wanning moon. All this happens in a fixed order which proves that the heavenly laws are set by a great engineer whom the ancient philosophers called the Greatest Engineer.

Noticeable also is the amazing system of the weather.

God has set a system for hot and cold weather, for winds and rain, for air pressure, for sequence of night and day, darkness and light, for humidity and dryness ... etc. All this is set in so wonderful order that man can expect what would happen afterwards. God organized everything; He made light for work and darkness for rest. What an organized harmonious universe indeed!

Another amazing organized and harmonious system like that of heaven and earth is the system of the human body.

Man is called a Micro Cosmos; for whoever considers the human body systems and their functions will find wonderful evidence of the power of the Creator. Take for example the human brain with its structure and work. See how it gives orders to the other members of the body, and what powers of movement, sight, hearing, memory ... etc it contains, so that any destruction of such powers cannot be restored at all. See also the heart and the circulation of the blood in the body affecting blood pressure, pumping, and distribution. See how the blood groups differ from one person to the other and how blood is generated in the body. There are also the wonderful body tissues, nerves, and body systems like the digestive system and reproductive system, genetics ... etc. Even the teeth, these small bones which are not like other big parts of the body such as the vertebral column and the bones of the arms, legs and feet. Each tooth is an amazing world by itself, connected with the other teeth with nerves and blood and are structured so wonderfully and harmoniously that no artificial teeth can match.

God's wonders appear clearly in the human fingerprint.

God created for every person a certain fingerprint which is different and distinguished from that of the others. We stand astonished at the millions and hundreds of millions of fingerprints that differ from each other !! What engineer or artist –however skilful- can draw such varied shapes of fingerprints as

God has done for His creation!! There is also the voice which differs from one person to the other, so that one can distinguish the voice of a person even through telephone from very far distances!

Add to this the human features God created.

From one man and one woman there came varied and distinguished features for millions of people whether in the shape of the face, the eyes, the looks ... etc. If one would say this is due to genetics, we say that genetics is also set by God. All this will appear simple if compared to the world of the spirits!

The world of the spirits is an evidence of the existence of a wonderful omnipotent Creator

Let us contemplate first on the angles who are called *"angles of light"*(2 Cor. 11: 14). The Psalmist said about them, *"Who makes His angels spirits, His ministers a flame of fire"*(Ps. 104: 4). The angels are varied in rank, for there are the Archangels, the Cherubim and Seraphim, and the thrones, principalities, dominions and powers. They move from heaven to the earth in a glimpse of an eye, and work powerfully whether for help or punishment. Examples are the angle who shut the lions' mouths for Daniel the Prophet (Da. 6: 22), and the angel who had stricken all the firstborn of the Egyptians in the days of Moses the Prophet (Ex. 12).God has given the angels the power to work miracles.

If we descend from the world of the angels we shall see also the wondrous work of the Creator in the human spirit.

The human spirit is really a wonder in its connection with the body, the mind and the conscience, and with life and death. This immortal rational articulate spirit, its destiny after death and return to the body in the general resurrection reveal amazing power of the Creator. Spiritualists have attained much knowledge, however, they ought after all to say "we do not know".

Let us descend farther to the smallest creatures: the insects, like the bee and the ant.

In these insects we see the wonders of the Great Creator. This is evident in the very wise system the bee follows, and how it produces the honey and the queen's food from the flowers nectar and keep them in tiny cells! The ant likewise has a wonderful system as it is very active and never stops work. The ants co-operate and communicate with each other and store their food in a wonderful way.

Many and innumerable indeed are God's wonders apparent in His creation; no books can contain them.

God created the whole world in an amazing order

God created man last, on the sixth day, after having prepared everything for him as we say in the Liturgy of St. Gregory: [You have set heaven a ceiling for me and paved the earth for me to walk on. For me You calmed down the sea and tamed the beasts. You left me in need of nothing of Your honorable works.] God made the whole nature in man's service; created light, heat, food and drink, trees, fruits and birds for him. For the beasts God created plants and herbs for food, water for drink, and place to live in. Then God created beasts with His wisdom and in a certain order, and lastly He created man.

Some would ask about the six days of creation.

On these six days many saints have written calling them (Hexameros), like the Hexameros of Basil, of Epiphanios, and of John Chrysostom. These six days of creation raised argument between the scholars of religion and geologists, for the latter say that the earth dates back to millions of years!

Our explanation is that the days of creation are not solar days of 24 hours each day.

God created the sun on the fourth day; which means that the first four days were not solar days. Moreover, the Scriptures do not mention that the seventh day has ended. So, since Adam and Eve we have been living in the seventh day which ends only by the general resurrection and the end of ages. The days of creation are therefore unlimited periods of time where one day can be a moment or millions of years. But in all cases the beginning and the end of such an unlimited period are called *"the evening and the morning"*

GOD THE UNLIMITED

Man shares God some attributes, but these attributes are limited in man and unlimited in God

A person might be wise, but God's wisdom is unlimited whether in kind or extent. One might be powerful, but God's power is unlimited. Knowledge likewise can be an attribute of man, but with God it is unlimited. The same applies to all shared attributes. This leads us to a theological rule:

Among God's attributes belonging to Him alone is His being unlimited.

God is unlimited with regard to space and time, with regard to power, to knowledge and wisdom, to holiness and justice, to greatness and glory, and with regard to everything.

* God is unlimited in space and time:

God is unlimited with regard to space. He is Omnipresent, not bound by any space nor contained in any place. He is present in the whole universe.

He is present in heaven, on earth, and in between. He is in the space and in the deep waters. That is why David the Prophet said, *"Where can I go from Your Spirit? Or where can I flee from Your presence? If I ascend into heaven, You are there; If I make my bed in hell, behold, You are there. If I take the wings of the morning, and dwell in the uttermost parts of the sea, even there Your hand shall lead me, and Your right hand shall hold me.*"(Ps. 139: 7-10). It is thus said that **heaven is God's throne and earth is His footstool** (Mt. 5: 34, 35). He is present in Paradise, the third heaven (2 Cor. 12: 2, 4) (Lk. 23: 43), and in the heaven of heavens. Solomon said of God when consecrating the Temple, *"Behold, heaven and the heaven of heavens cannot contain You. How much less this temple which I have built!"*(1 Kgs. 8: 27)

God is everywhere, He sees what people do and hears what they say.

Everybody is under God's control. No one can deny what one has done, for God is Almighty. Therefore Elijah the Prophet said, *"As the Lord lives, before whom I stand ..."*(1 Kgs. 18: 15). As the human beings stand before God while on the earth, the angels stand before Him in heaven.

God is everywhere and is not affected by anything anywhere.

He is present where saints praise Him with pure hearts, and where the wicked are, watching their wickedness or rebuking them and urging them to return. He says to some of them, *"Behold, I stand at the door and knock"*(Rev. 3: 20). As the sun rays enter into the dirty places, cleans them and kill microbes therein without being affected by their dirtiness, God likewise enters every place, changes it and is not affected.

God is everywhere, so we cannot say that He ascends or descends, nor that He walks or moves.

If we say that God ascends, where can He ascend since He is actually in the place where He is said to ascend! And if we say that God descends somewhere, He is certainly there in that place. He does not walk nor move, because He is everywhere. He does not quit a place to another, because He fills all places. Any verses in the Holy Scriptures contain such terms are just included to make the meaning comprehensible. Such terms can also be understood to mean that He appeared in the place where He is said to have ascended, descended or worked. God does not go to a certain place, quit it, or move from one place to another; He is present in all the places all the time. He just appears in that place or announces His presence there.

When God gave Moses the Law on the mount, He was in heaven and on the earth at the same time, and likewise when He was talking to our Father Abraham and called him. The same can be said of all other encounters between God and people since our forefather Adam and throughout the ages. He is unlimited with regard to place.

God is also unlimited with regard to time.

God is eternal, has no beginning. This attribute belongs to God alone and no one shares in it; for all beings are created. Any created being has a beginning, that in which God has made this being, before which this being had no existence. God alone is eternal as He Himself said in the Book of Isaiah the Prophet, *"Before Me there was no God formed, nor shall there be after Me"*(Isa. 43: 10).

God, being eternal, is necessarily existent.

God's existence is a necessity behind the existence of other beings, for since these beings have existed at a certain time, there must be a creator who brought them into existence, that is God. No other being is necessarily existent because every being is created and had no existence before that time. Hence the existence of any being is not necessary.

God, besides being eternal, is also everlasting.

He is unlimited with regard to time; He has no beginning nor end; He is beyond time; being the Creator of time. The same applies to God's wisdom and Spirit. His Spirit is everywhere and existing even before any creation, the same as His wisdom, *"All things were made through Him, and without Him nothing was made that was made"*(Jn. 1: 3).

God is likewise unlimited in power.

---

* God is Unlimited in Power:

God is Almighty or Omnipotent, and Job the Righteous described this attribute of God, saying, *"I know that You can do everything, and that no purpose of Yours can be withheld from You"*(Job. 42: 2).

God alone is Almighty because *"with God all things are possible"*(Mt. 19: 26); *"The things which are impossible with men are possible with God"*(Lk. 18: 27). Therefore we believe in miracles and the Holy Scriptures are full of miracles. The miracles are beyond the understanding of the human mind but not against it. The miracles fall within the scope of God's unlimited power.

God's power of creation is an example of His unlimited power.

God's power created various types of creation; He made His angles spirits (Ps. 104: 4), and made the inanimate things material. He made man of material and spirit, and made other animate beings like plants and animals of innumerable species ascending from the insects up to the huge animals like the lion and elephant. Some of these live on earth, others in the sea, or in space.

Another example of God's unlimited power is His power of raising the dead.

This does not refer only to raising some people from the dead such as Lazarus who had been dead four days (Jn. 11: 39), but also to the general resurrection at the end of the ages. How all the human beings will rise, those who have been dead since Adam and Eve; those who have turned into dust, eaten by beasts or consumed by fire; those eaten up by worms, and those whose bodies dissolved and were absorbed in the earth! How they all will rise and stand before God on the Day of Judgement with their spirits and bodies! What an unlimited power before which the human mind stands amazed or rather breathless.

God is not only Omnipotent but He is also the source of all power.

God gives power to the angels who are described in Psalm (103: 20) as excelling in strength. They can move from heaven to the earth in a glimpse of an eye implementing God's commands. These commands might be a merciful act as Daniel said when he was cast in the den of lions, "*My God sent His angel and shut the lions' mouths*", or a punishment as when two angels struck the men who were at the doorway of Lot's house with blindness (Gen. 19: 11)

God gave His saints the power to work miracles.

God gave Moses power to divide the Red Sea with his rod (Ex. 14: 16), and to bring out water from the rock, by merely striking it, so that the people might drink (Ex. 17: 6). God gave power to Elijah to raise the son of the widow in Zerephath from the dead (1 Kgs. 17: 22). He gave power to Elisha to raise the son of the Shunammite woman from the dead (2 Kgs. 4: 36)

Such miracles were not worked by the power of those holy men throughout generations, but by God's power, and were preceded by prayers and promises from God. Therefore St. Peter the Apostle, after healing the lame person at the gate of the temple which was called "Beautiful", said to the Jews, "*Why do you marvel at this? Or why look so intently at us, as though by our own power or godliness we had made this man walk? The God of our fathers ... has made this man strong*"(Acts 3: 12-16). He thus ascribed the power of the miracle to the Lord.

It is God the Almighty who gave the human mind amazing powers as will be expounded afterwards.

However, God who gives power, is capable also of taking it away whenever He wills.

God gave the valiant Samson indescribable physical power, but when Samson broke his vow after telling Delilah about it God withdrew that power from him and delivered him into the hands of his enemies (Jud. 16). And when Samson shook himself free as he used to do he could not because he did not know that the Lord had departed from him.

God gave power even to the fire to burn, but in the story of the three holy young men who were cast by the Persians into fire God did not allow the fire to harm them as we read, "*on whose bodies the fire had no power; the hair of their head was not signed ...*" (Da. 3: 27).

He gave a great power to the sea so that its rising waves can drown the greatest ships. However, He calms it whenever He wills as the psalmist says, "*O Lord God of hosts, who is mighty like You, O Lord? ... You rule the raging of the sea; when its waves rise, You still them*"(Ps. 89: 8, 9). We remember here the Lord's miracle of rebuking the wind when He said to the sea, "*Peace, be still!*" And the wind ceased and there was a great calm (Mk. 4: 39). A similar miracle is that of walking on the sea (Mt. 14: 25-32)

Some might inquire about the power of Satan!

Satan is not a god of evil, but just God's creation. God created Satan an angel with all the powers of the angels, but he turned himself into a devil and lost his holiness. However he retained the power of the angels but still under God's control.

In the story of Job the Righteous, God gave permission to Satan only within certain limits (Job 1: 12; 2: 6). God first permitted Satan to stretch out his hand to all Job had, but not to his person. Satan could not go beyond this limit. The second time God permitted Satan to touch his bones and his flesh but to spare his life. And Satan did so but his power was limited with God's power. God allowed Satan to tempt Job so that Job might be an example of patience (Jas. 5: 10, 11) and obtain the reward of his patience (Job 42: 12-16).

In the temptation on the mount the Lord said to Satan, *"Away with you, Satan!"*(Mt. 4: 10), and Satan departed and could not disobey.

We cannot forget the numerous miracles of casting out the devils. Among these miracles is that of the Legion of the many demons. The demons went out but asked the Lord's permission to let them enter the swine, and He permitted them (Lk. 8: 32). Some times the demons cried out in fear of being destroyed by the Lord (Mk. 1: 24). The people were amazed and spoke among themselves, saying, *"With authority and power He commands the unclean spirits, and they come out"*(Lk. 4: 36)

The end of Satan is certainly in the hand of God the Almighty who will destroy him.

God bound Satan for a thousand years (Rev. 20: 2), which punishment is a clear evidence of God's power. Finally God will cast him with his supporters in the lake of fire and brimstone where they will be tormented day and night forever and ever (Rev. 20: 10). Even the wicked will be also cast into the everlasting fire prepared for the devil and his angels (Mt. 25: 41).

God The Holy

God alone is the Holy.

The Seraphim praised Him with this song, saying, *"Holy, holy, holy is the Lord of Hosts"*(Isa. 6: 3). And in the Book of Revelation, those who have victory sing to Him, saying, *"Who shall not fear You, O Lord, and glorify Your name? For You alone are holy"*(Rev. 15: 4). The holy Virgin Mary also, in her wonderful praise song, said, *"For He who is mighty has done great things for me, and holy is His name"* (Lk. 1: 49)

Indeed God's name is holy as the holy virgin said.

The Third Commandment therefore commands, *"You shall not take the name of the Lord your God in vain, for the Lord will not hold him guiltless who takes His name in vain"*(Ex. 20: 7). God's name should be uttered with all reverence. Therefore the first supplication in the Lord's prayer is *"Hallowed be Your name"*. The Lord prevented us from swearing by God's name or by anything related to Him; He said, *"do not swear at all: neither by heaven, for it is God's throne nor by the earth, for it is His footstool; nor by Jerusalem, for it is the city of the great king"*(Mt. 5: 34, 35). We should rather use God's name in our worship with awe fit for His holiness.

God is Holy, and His Spirit is the Holy Spirit.

The Son also is Holy, as the angel announced to the Virgin, *"that Holy One who is to be born will be called the Son of God"*(Lk. 1: 35). Since holiness is the attribute of the three Persons, we describe them as the Holy Trinity. We pray in the praise song, saying, *"O You Holy Trinity, have mercy on us"* "Agia Treiyas, Elison Emas".

We sing the praise of God's holiness in our prayers every day.

We praise His holiness in the Lord's Prayer, in the seven hourly prayers, in the Trisagion, *"Holy God, Holy Almighty, Holy Immortal"*, and in the holys, *"Holy, Holy, Holy is the Lord of hosts. Heaven and earth are full of Your glory and honor"*. These praise songs we sing in all ritual prayers. There is also the long hymn "Agios" –that is "Holy" which is said in the Good Friday and in the consecration of monks, in the funeral service, and on many occasions. The same hymn is said, combined with many other hymns such as "Ommonogenis", that is "You the Only-begotten". In the Preparation Prayer, the priest starts with the words *"O Lord, who knows the hearts of all, who is Holy, and who finds rest in His saints; who alone is without sin, and who is mighty to forgive sins; You, O Lord, know that I am not worthy, deserving, nor fit for this Your holy ministry"*

God's holiness is personal, belonging to Him, and existing in His nature before times.

God's holiness is permanent and everlasting, unchangeable, and absolute. With human beings, if anyone is described as holy, this will be through struggling and through the work of the Holy Spirit within him to a certain extent. The human holiness may change or decrease, and the human beings even lost the holiness they had when first created in God's image and after His likeness (Gen. 1: 26, 27). All people are said to have turned aside, *"They have together become corrupt; there is none who does good, no, not one"*(Ps. 14: 3). But God alone remained Holy.

What then is this holiness of God? What does it signify?

God's holiness signifies complete purity and utter righteousness. It signifies the whole and absolute meaning of all virtues and good attributes, and furthermore signifies truth and goodness. For God alone is good as it is written, *"No one is good but One, that is, God"*(Mt. 19: 17). God is all good, and all His works are good deserving our thankfulness and gratitude as well as absolute commitment to God's good will in confidence. God's holiness refuses sin and is not pleased with it because sin is against God's nature. Men themselves, though sinful, abhor sin and impurity, how much rather does God who is the light itself and whose nature rejects darkness!

Strange indeed that we remember God's love and forget His holiness and goodness, and forget that through sin we are separated from God.

God is the Light (1 Jn. 1: 5), even the true Light (Jn. 1: 9), whereas sin is darkness (1 Pet. 2: 9). Whoever lives in the darkness of sin will have diverted from the light of God the Holy. As the Scripture says, *"For what fellowship has righteousness with lawlessness? And what communion has light with darkness? And what accord has Christ with Belial?"*(2 Cor. 6: 14, 15)

God is holy and whatever surrounds Him or belongs to Him is also holy.

His heaven is a holy heaven. The angels who serve Him in heaven are the holy angels. Likewise the priesthood ministering to Him on the earth is holy priesthood, of which the Psalmist says, *"Let Your priests be clothed with righteousness, and let Your saints shout for joy"* (Ps. 132: 9). Therefore God commanded Moses the Prophet to anoint Aaron his brother with the holy ointment to minister to Him with his sons; He said, *"Then you shall bring to the door of the tabernacle of meeting and wash them with water. You shall put the holy garments on Aaron, and anoint him and consecrate him, that he may minister to Me as priest"*(Ex. 40: 12-14). Thus Moses did, *"And he poured some of the anointing oil on Aaron's head and anointed him, to consecrate him*" (Lev. 8: 12). He did the same to Aaron's sons, anointing them alike.

The sacraments in which God's Holy Spirit works are called the Holy Sacraments.

Wherefore we say the Holy Baptism Sacrament, the Holy Chrismation Sacrament. For the Holy Eucharist Sacrament, it is administered on the holy altar through the holy liturgy which we call "the Mass of the holy". Regarding the worthiness to partake of the Sacrament, the priest says "the holies for the holy". All this exhorts us to walk in complete holiness so as to be worthy to partake of the Holy Flesh and Blood. Therefore the Holy Sacraments can only be offered on an altar previously consecrated, that is sanctified with the holy ointment. This consecration takes place by the descending of God's Holy Spirit to sanctify the altar through the holy priesthood. In case there is no holy altar, a holy board shall be sufficient, which is also previously consecrated and sanctified with the Holy Myron ointment.

As God is Holy, any place He dwells in becomes a holy place.

When God showed Himself to Moses the Prophet in the burning bush, He said to him, *"Take your sandals off your feet, for the place where you stand is holy ground"*(Ex. 3: 5). And when He appeared to Jacob the father of fathers above the ladder reaching to heaven, our father Jacob said, *"How awesome is the place! This is none other than the house of God, and this is the gate of heaven!"*(Gen. 28: 17, 18). Then Jacob consecrated the place.

Hence, we look to the house of God as very holy, and we say to the Lord with the psalmist, *"Holiness adorns Your house, O Lord, forever"* (Ps. 93: 5). And when we enter into the house of God we say with David the Prophet, *"But as for me, I will*

34

come into Your house in the multitude of Your mercy; in fear of You I will worship toward Your holy temple" (Ps. 5: 7).

All places of God are holy places, therefore we say, *"His foundation is in the holy mountains"* (Ps. 87: 1). We also call God's city Jerusalem *"the holy city"* (Mt. 4: 5)(Rev. 21: 1). Even the tabernacle of meeting was holy, being consecrated by Moses the Prophet. It contained the holy and the most holy places. Everything therein was consecrated and was called holy, such as the vessels of ministry and the priestly garments which the Lord God commanded Moses to make, *"And you shall make holy garments for Aaron your brother, for glory and for beauty"* (Ex. 28: 2). Even the human body, being a temple of God as God's Spirit dwells in it, is a holy body *"For the temple of God is holy, which temple you are"* (1 Cor. 3: 17).

The believers are thus called saints and a holy people.

The Scripture says, *"The Lord will establish you as a holy people to Himself"* (Deut. 28: 9). St. Peter the Apostle calls this people *"a holy nation"* (1 Pet. 2: 9). In the epistles of St. Paul, he calls the believers "saints", *"Greet every saint in Christ Jesus ... All the saints greet you, but especially those who are of Caesar's household "* (Phil. 4: 21, 22); *"Therefore, holy brethren, partakers of the heavenly calling ... "* (Heb. 3: 1). In his epistles, St. Paul often starts with the words, *"To all the saints in ... "*

The believers are called saints because they are the children of God the Holy.

They are born of God's Holy Spirit in the baptism water (Jn. 3: 5)(Tit. 3: 5). They are saints because He loved them and washed them from their sins in His own blood (Rev. 1: 5). They are saints because they are members of His body (Eph. 5: 30) (1 Cor. 6: 15). They are saints because they have been anointed with the holy ointment, and because the Holy Spirit dwells in them (1 Cor. 3: 16)(1 Jn. 2: 20). Thus all those in whom God the Holy dwells become holy.

Holiness, however, is not a mere title, but a life.

As St. Peter the Apostle says, *"as He who called you is holy, you also be holy in all your conduct, because it is written 'Be holy, for I am holy'"*(1 Pet. 1: 15, 16). And as St. Paul the Apostle says, *"For this is the will of God, your sanctification"* (1 Thess. 4: 3); *"perfecting holiness in the fear of God"* (2 Cor. 7: 1); *"that we may be partakers of His holiness"* (Heb. 12: 10). Such holiness is one without which no one can see the Lord.

In the life of holiness we obey God's holy commandments.

Because God is holy, every word from Him is holy. His scripture is called the Holy Scripture, as St. Paul the Apostle said to his disciple Timothy, *"and that from childhood you have known the Holy Scriptures, which are able to make you wise for salvation ... "* (2 Tim. 3: 15).

As we should be keen on obeying God's Holy Scriptures, we should also be keen on keeping the Lord's day Holy. The Scripture thus commands, *"Remember the Sabbath day, to keep it holy"* (Ex. 20: 8). This day of the Lord should be kept holy as well as all the Lord's feasts and convocations (Lev. 23).

The fasts also are holy days for the Lord, therefore a fast is called a holy fast, for we fast to God the Holy. The Passion Week likewise is called the Holy Week or the Holy Pascha, because in it we remember the Holy Lord.

Whatever we do for God the Holy is thus holy to Him and sanctified by Him.

Vows, offerings, and firstlings are all holy to the Lord. Our covenants with Him and His covenant with us are all holy. Even the books used in His worship are holy, such as the Holy

Euchologion and the Holy Psalmody. The icons reminding us of
the saints are as well holy, being consecrated by the holy church.

**If we want to live with God the Holy, we should lead a
holy life.**

Such a life can be holy through His work within us and
through our love towards Him; wherefore those who live in
holiness in this world will live with God in eternity. This eternal
life will witness only God the Holy with His holy angels and
saintly human beings.

GOD THE ALMIGHTY

We praise God's might every hour of the day in the Trisagion:

Holy God, Holy Mighty, Holy Immortal.

God's might is amazing for it is a self-power; that is not acquired from an external source. Unlike this is the human power or the angels' power, for those obtain their power from God the Creator. Even the human mind with its wonderful power that could reach the space and produce astonishing inventions, this mind is God's gift to the human beings. The same applies to the angels, whereas God's power belongs to Him. Moreover, any being may lose his power or have it decreased, competed or turned inactive temporarily. But God's power is firm, unmatched, and unchangeable.

God's might is distinguished from any others', as God alone is Almighty.

There might be a creature with power from a certain aspect, but no creature is all powerful. This is an attribute of God alone (Gen. 48: 3); He said of Himself, " *'I am the Alpha and the Omega, the Beginning and the End'*, *says the Lord who is and who was and who is to come, the Almighty"* (Rev. 1: 8). This attribute is mentioned in many places in the Book of Revelation, as in (Rev. 16: 7, 14; 21: 22).

The angels are described as excelling in strength (Ps. 103: 20). However, they are not omnipotent. Man as well may be mighty in some aspects, but undoubtedly not in everything. The nature likewise: an earthquake might destroy some buildings but not all. This is applicable to all creatures, but God has everything within His power as Job the Righteous said, "*I know that You can do everything, and that no purpose of Yours can be withheld from You*"(Job 42: 2).

However, as some youth once said to his teacher in Sunday Schools while discussing this point:

There is one thing which God cannot do, that is sin, because it is against God's holiness!

But in explanation of this point, we say that sin is not a power but rather a weakness. An arrogant person, for instance, cannot be humble, and the unjust cannot be just, and the adulterer cannot be chaste. On the other hand, we cannot say that the just has no power to do injustice, for injustice is a passive attribute. We rather say that a just person has the power to do justice. Likewise, we say that God the Holy has the absolute power to do righteousness. But we cannot say that He has no power to do wrong, because a wrong doing is a weakness not a power.

God is also unmatched in His power and might.

Primitive nations believed in two gods: one for good, and the other for evil. Such faith is against God's might; for we do not believe at all that Satan is God's rival or a god of evil because he is God's creation. However, God has not created him a devil, but an angel, and with his free will, which deviated, he became a devil; an opponent of God's will. There are some people also who resist God's will, but God is long-suffering with them. Yet:

1. God will cast the devil into the lake of fire and brimstone (Rev. 20: 10).

God --in the last days- will consume with the breath of His mouth him who opposes and exalts himself above all that is called God (2 Thess. 2: 4, 8). God will also reward all who resisted Him according to their work. He will say to them on the Day of Judgement, *"Depart from Me, you cursed, into the everlasting fire prepared for the devil and his angels"*, *"And these will go away into everlasting punishment"*(Mt. 25: 41, 46)

2. God interferes also on the earth whenever He wills to stop the devil and prevent him from doing his will.

This is clear in the story of Job the Righteous. At the beginning, God allowed Satan only to tempt Job by touching his possessions and his children. Afterwards, God allowed Satan to touch Job's body, but prevented him from touching his person (Job 1: 12; 2: 6).

In the temptation on the mount as well, God permitted Satan to tempt the Lord to a certain extent only. And when the Lord said to him, *"Away with you, Satan!"*, he left not daring to do anything more (Mt. 4: 11).

We cannot forget also the miracles of casting out demons which the Lord and His disciples worked.

This shows how weak the demons are before the Lord. Suffice that they cried out to Him, saying, *"Let us alone! What have we to do with You, Jesus of Nazareth? Did You come to destroy us?"*(Lk. 4: 34)(Mk. 1: 24). In the miracle of the Legion cast out by Him, they begged Him that He would permit them to enter the swine, and He permitted them (Lk. 8: 22). Hence demons are not God's rivals.

God's power appears also in His creation

Man cannot go farther than being a maker or inventor, who explores the nature and properties of the things and makes of them whatever his mind can make. As to creating, that is bringing into existence from nihilism, it is within God's sole power. No one can do it, not to mention God's amazing power of creating these numbers and kinds of creation, visible and invisible, which no human mind can count.

Another astonishing miracle is the raising of the dead.

We read in the Holy Scripture about miracles of raising the dead by God's power, but the incredible miracles beyond the human mind is that of raising all the dead on the Last Day. Millions and millions from all over the world, whose bodies and bones have dissolved and turned into dust, will rise at the same time. Their spirits will enter them again and they will stand before God in that awful Day of Judgement to receive each according to his works (Jn. 5: 28, 29). They are the most powerful miracles beyond the human mind.

Many other miracles and wonders are within God's power.

The Holy Scripture contains so many examples of similar innumerable miracles and wonders. Among these examples are the miracles of restoring sight to the blind, healing of irremediable diseases, dividing the Red Sea, bringing down manna and quails from heaven and water from the rock, the wonderful manifestations, the descending of the Holy Spirit as tongues of fire, the numerous gifts of the Spirit, the inspiration the signs of the last times, dreams to human beings, and many other wonders beyond human power.

God in His power, being humble, gave power to some of His creation.

Examples of this are the powers given to the angels, to the human beings and to the nature, besides natural powers and supernatural powers that come under wonders and miracles.

To the angels God gave wonderful powers so that they can move between heaven and earth in the glimpse of an eye and do miraculous works entrusted to them.

Likewise, God endowed the human mind with certain powers. By these powers scientists could invent and make things beyond imagination and so many that they appear now as normal. Among these inventions are the facsimile, the computer, long distance telephone, aeroplanes, atom and laser used in the field of medication and industry, space and water sciences ... etc.

God gave also His beloved among men to work miracles in His name and by His power: *"Behold, I give you the authority to trample on serpents and scorpions, and over all the power of the enemy"*(Lk. 10: 19). He endowed them the power to heal the sick, raise the dead, and cast out demons (Mt. 10: 1). He said to His disciples, *"But you shall receive power when the Holy Spirit has come upon you"*(Acts 1: 8).

It is a great power, that which is given men, yet it is not their own power but God's power working in them.

Of this St. Paul the Apostle said, *"But by the grace of God I am what I am ... not I, but the grace of God which was with me"* (1 Cor. 15: 10); *"I can do all things through Christ who strengthens me"*(Phil. 4: 13).

It is a superior power indeed, not human, but divine, granted men by God. Of this the Lord Christ said,

"without Me, you can do nothing" (Jn. 15: 5)

It is true that we can do many things, but through faith in God's power working in us and with us. It is so written in the Gospel, *"all things are possible to him who believes"*(Mk. 9: 23). If one believes that God is able to do all things, God will do everything through him, and through his prayers God interferes and works.

God is likewise powerful in His work.

This power appears in the miracles done by His word or by the impact of His word on teaching. God said, *"Let there be light"*, and there was light (Gen. 1: 3). This happened on the first day of creation, and in all the days of creation, God commanded and the creation came into existence.

The Lord said to the man with the withered hand, *"Stretch out your hand"*(Mt. 12: 13), and it was restored as whole as the other. His words were a command issued to the nerves, tissues, veins, and bones that each would return to its place and work normally. The words were a command to the disorder to get away. And when He said to the son of the widow in the city of Nain, *"Young man, I say to you, arise"*(Lk. 7: 14), this word was a command to the spirit to come and reunite with the body, and a command to the body to return to its normal work. And both were restored. All the miracles likewise were worked by a mere word.

The power of the Lord's word is apparent also in the teaching, as the Scripture says, *"For the word of God is living and powerful, and sharper than any two-edged sword, piercing even to the division of soul and spirit"*(Heb. 4: 12). How beautiful also what was said about the impact of the Lord's words in the Sermon on the Mount, *"He taught them as one having authority, and not as the scribes"*(Mt. 7: 29).

Let us talk also of God's power in His love.

The Scriptures say, *"having loved His own who were in the world, He loved them to the end"*(Jn.13: 1); *"For God so loved the world that He gave His only begotten Son, that whoever believes in Him should not perish but have everlasting life"*(Jn. 3: 16). Thus His love is demonstrated in the Redemption of which He said to His disciples, *"Greater love has no one than this to lay down one's life for his friends"*(Jn. 15: 13).

God's powerful love is manifest in His giving, for He gives to all liberally and without reproach (Jas. 1: 5). He gives without being asked, and gives more than we ask for, without measure (Jn. 3: 34). He opens the windows of heaven and pours out of His love and blessing so much that we say enough! enough!

God's power is apparent in the help and deliverance.

God's deliverance appears where there is no hope nor rescue, as the psalmist said, "*Many are they who say of me 'There is no help for him in God'*"(Ps. 3: 2). Then he says, "*The right hand of the Lord does valiantly. The right hand of the Lord is exalted. The right hand of the Lord does valiantly. I shall not die, but live*"(Ps. 118: 15, 16). For this power he sang, "*If it had not been the Lord who was on our side, when men rose up against us, then they would have swallowed us alive ... Our soul has escaped as a bird from the snares of the fowlers. The snare is broken, and we have escaped. Our help is in the name of the Lord, who made heaven and earth*"(Ps. 124). In his trust in God's power, the Psalmist said, "*Yea, though I walk through the valley of the shadow of death, I will fear no evil. For You are with me, Your rod and Your staff, they comfort me*"(Ps. 23: 4).

God's delivering power appears in dividing the Red Sea (Ex. 14). It appears also in the words of Daniel the Prophet, "*My God sent His angel and shut the lions' mouths*"(Da. 6: 22), and in rescuing the three young youths from the furnace of fire (Da. 3). God's power is clear in supporting young David to overcome Goliath the valiant when David said to Goliath, "*This day the Lord will deliver you into my hand*"(1 Sam. 17: 46). It is clear in His sending an angel to save Paul and Silas from the prison, "*Suddenly there was a great earthquake, so that the foundations of the prison were shaken; and immediately all the doors were opened and everyone's chains were loosed*"(Acts 16: 26). God's power is evident in His promise for the church, "*the gates of Hades shall not prevail against it*"(Mt. 16: 18), and in His word through Moses the Prophet to the people, "*The Lord will fight for you, and you shall hold your peace*"(Ex. 14: 14).

We rejoice in being under the protection of the powerful God who is capable of saving us.

Indeed, but for God Almighty who puts limits to the harm done by the wicked, they would prevail against the others and destroy them! And had not God put a limit to Satan and bound him, he would have destroyed the whole world!!

This power God gives His church whom He describes in the Song as, *"Fair as the moon, clear as the sun, awesome as an army with banners"*(Song 6: 10).

God's power is wonderfully apparent in His long-suffering

He endured the people's blasphemy, apostasy, disobedience, iniquity, and corruption though He was able to destroy them. He did not do that because the long-suffering is certainly more powerful than the offensive. That is why Paul the Apostle said, *"We then who are strong ought to bear with the scruples of the weak"*(Rom. 15: 1).

God endured much and powerfully, with long-suffering, until they repented.

He endured Saul of Tarsus who persecuted the church long until he repented and became a great apostle. Likewise He endured Irianus the Governor of Ensena - the most hard-hearted governor under Diocletian – till he repented and became a martyr. And God bore also with Longinus the soldier who pierced the side of the Lord with the spear and made him believe and become a martyr.

God bore with Augustine in his sins and corruption when young, and led him to repentance. Thus Augustine became a monk, a saint, and a source of spirituality and contemplation.

With the same power, the Lord endured all the sins of Zacchaeus the tax collector, the adultery of the woman who was caught in the very act, the sins of Mary the Coptic, and the hard-heartedness of Moses the Black. And all those, as well as others, He turned into saints!

On the contrary are the human beings; for we are weak in our forbearance, we are easily affected, we rage and become angry, and we even avenge ourselves. But God forbears with all, and is longsuffering and patient. He endured the blasphemy of the communists in Russia for seventy years till Russia repented and turned to faith.

God is not only powerful in His forbearance, but also in His forgiveness.

Human beings can hardly forgive, and if they forgive they cannot forget. Even if they think they have forgiven, they may remember all previous offences whenever they are subject to a new offence. But God is powerful in His forgiveness as He himself said, *"For I will forgive their iniquity, and their sin I will remember no more"*(Ps. 32: 1, 2). And it is written of His reconciliation with mankind, *"not imputing their trespasses to them"*(2 Cor. 5: 19). The Psalmist tells us about God's forgiveness, *"Blessed is he whose transgression is forgiven, whose sin is covered. Blessed is the man to whom the Lord does not impute iniquity."*(Ps. 32: 1, 2). St. Paul the Apostle, admiring these two verses, repeated them in his Epistle to the Romans (Rom. 4: 7, 8).

In his forgiveness, it is said, *"the Son of Man has come to seek and to save that which was lost"*(Lk. 19: 10); and, *"the Son of Man did not come to destroy men's lives but to save them"*(Lk. 9: 56). God does not only forgive His people but also washes them and they become whiter than snow (Ps. 51: 7).

Many are the aspects of God's wonderful power.

Examples of God's power are: His power of knowledge, of punishment, of dispensation, and many other aspects of power for which here is not the place to mention.

GLORY AND MAJESTY
BELONG TO GOD

Great is God in His glory, and *"great is the glory of the Lord"*(Ps. 138: 5). For this greatness the Psalmist sings, *"O Lord, our Lord, how excellent is Your name in all the earth, who have set Your glory above the heavens!"*(Ps. 8: 1, 2).

And in the Book of Job, Elihu said, *"Behold, God is exalted by His power; who teaches like Him? ... Behold, God is great, and we do not know Him."*(Job. 26: 22, 26). Moreover, the fathers compared between Him and the gods of the Gentiles; they said, *"Declare His glory among the nations, His wonders among all peoples. For the Lord is great and greatly to be praised; He is also to be feared above all gods. For all the gods of the peoples are idols"* (1 Chr. 16: 24-26)(Ps.96: 3-5)

David the Prophet, speaking about God's greatness, said:

"His lightnings light the world; the earth sees and trembles. The mountains melt like wax at the presence of the Lord, at the presence of the Lord of the whole earth. The heavens declare His righteousness, and all the peoples see His glory"(Ps. 97: 4-6); *"Great is our Lord, and mighty in power; His understanding is infinite"*(Ps. 147: 5); *"Among the gods there is none like You, O Lord, nor are there any works like Your works. All the nations You have made shell come and worship before You, O Lord, and shall glorify Your name. For You are great, and do wonderous things; You alone are God"*(Ps. 86: 8-10)

Many have praised the Lord's wonders and great works.

While crossing the Red Sea, Miriam the prophetess, the sister of Aaron, took the timbrel in her hand; and all the women went out after her with timbrels and with dances. And Miriam answered them, *"Sing to the Lord, for He has triumphed gloriously! The horse and its rider He has thrown into the sea"* (Ex. 15: 20, 21). Moses the prophet and the whole people sang the same song (Ex. 15: 1)

Eliho the son of Barachel the Buzite, likewise, said, *"Stand still and consider the wondrous works of God"*; *"He does great things which we cannot comprehend"* (Job 37: 14, 5). And David the prophet said, *"The works of the Lord are great"* (Ps. 111: 2); *"O Lord, how great are Your works! Your thoughts are very deep"* (Ps. 92: 5); *"O Lord, how manifold are Your works! In wisdom You have made them all."*(Ps. 104: 24); *"For I know that the Lord is great, and our Lord is above all gods. Whatever the Lord pleases He does, in heaven and in earth, in the seas and in all deep places"*(Ps. 135: 5, 6)

Indeed, God is great, and all His works and attributes are great.

God is great in His power (Nh. 1: 3); great in His mercy (Ps. 86: 13); great in His wonders and His goodness (Ps. 31: 19); great in His care (Heb. 13: 20); great is He amidst His people, and His name is great among the Gentiles (Mal. 1: 11). Daniel calls upon Him in the land of captivity, saying, *"O Lord, great and awesome God"*(Da. 9: 4). Even king Darius gave the command, *"I make a decree that in every dominion of my kingdom men must tremble and fear before the God of Daniel. For He is the living God, and steadfast forever, His kingdom is the one which shall not be destroyed, and His dominion shall endure to the end. He delivers and rescues, and He works signs and wonders in heaven and on earth, who has delivered Daniel from the power of the lions."*(Da. 6: 26, 27).

Therefore those who experienced the Lord, used always to magnify Him.

David the prophet said cheerfully, *"Oh, magnify the Lord with me, and let us exalt His name together"*(Ps. 34: 3); *"I will extol You, O Lord, for You have lifted me up, and have not let my foes rejoice over me"*(Ps. 30: 1). And St. Virgin Mary, in her praise song, said, *"My soul magnifies the Lord ... For He who is mighty has done great things for me, and holy is His name"*(Lk. 1: 46, 49).

The psalmist repeats in many psalms, *"Let all those who seek You rejoice and be glad in You; and let those who love Your salvation say continuously: Let God be magnified!"* (Ps. 70: 4; 40: 16; 35: 27). Malachi the prophet also said, *"Your eyes shall see, and you shall say: The Lord is magnified"* (Mal. 1: 5). Truly, *"Great is the Lord, and greatly to be praised; and His greatness is unsearchable"*(Ps. 145: 3; 48: 1).

God's greatness is accompanied with His glory and honor

The Psalm says, *"Give unto the Lord, O you mighty ones, give unto the Lord glory and strength. Give unto the Lord the glory due to His name; worship the Lord in the beauty of holiness"*(Ps. 29: 1, 2); *"Declare His glory among the nations, His wonders among all peoples"* (Ps. 96: 3). And all the ministers of the Lord say cheerfully, *"Not unto us, O Lord, not unto us, but to Your name give glory"*(Ps. 115: 1).

The angels also say this glory, *"Glory to God in the highest"*(Lk. 2: 14).

God is glorified in heaven by His holy angels. This is described by Isaiah the prophet, *"I saw the Lord sitting on a throne, high and lifted up ... above it stood seraphim; each one has six wings ... and one cried to another and said: Holy, holy, holy is the Lord of hosts; the whole earth is full of His glory!"*(Isa. 6: 1-3). Ezekiel the prophet also gave us another picture about *"the likeness of the glory of the Lord"*(Ezek. 1: 28) with the four living creatures.

God's glory is intrinsic; it is the glory of His essence.

It is the glory of this Unlimited God, the Invisible, the incomprehensible, the Omnipotent, the Omnipresent, existing before ages, who tests the mind and the heart (Jer. 11: 20) (Rev. 2: 23). He is all wisdom, *"How unsearchable are His judgments and His ways past finding out!"*(Rom. 11: 33).

True indeed are the words of one of the holy fathers, who said: Any time I proceeded to talk about the Godhead, the language failed me! We stand before His divinity astounded, for the Godhead is invisible, no man can see Him and live (Ex. 33: 20), *"whom no man has seen or can see, to whom be honor and everlasting power"*, *"the king of kings and the Lord of lords, who alone has immortality, dwelling in unapproachable light"*(1 Tim. 6: 15, 16).

God is glorified in His eternity and oneness, and in His being the Creator of all.

God has no beginning of days, before Him there was no God formed, nor shall there be after Him (Isa. 43: 10). Since eternity, before any creation, and before ages, He was present, alone, the cause of every existing thing. In His goodness and grace He willed to bring into existence other things giving them this grace. So He created everything, *"All things were made through Him, and without Him nothing was made that was made"*(Jn. 1: 3). He said, *"Let there be light"*, and there was light (Jn. 1: 3). The same happened with all other creation. Then God saw everything that He had made, *"and indeed it was very good"*(Gen. 1: 31).

God is the cause of existence, of blessing, and of life, and the source of all power.

God's glory is in His own nature; in Himself, for He is *"the true Light which gives light to every man"*(Jn. 1: 9). He called us out of darkness into His marvelous light (1 Pet. 2: 9). *"God is a consuming fire"*(Heb. 12: 29), so the fire of the burnt sacrifice was a symbol of Him (Lev. 1: 3, 13). Likewise, the fire in the censer is a symbol of His divinity.

Heaven is God's throne, and the earth is His footstool (Mt. 5: 34, 35).

That is why Solomon the Wise said to Him on the day of the consecration of the Temple, *"Behold, heaven and the heaven of heavens cannot contain You. How much less this temple which I have built"*(1 Kgs. 8: 27); *"He bowed the heavens also, and came down with darkness under His feet"*(Ps. 18: 9); *"He rode upon a cherub, and flew; and He was seen upon the wings of the wind"*(2 Sam. 22: 11).

The power of God's glory was manifested in creation and in His resurrection.

He created everything from nothing; He is the resurrection and the life (Jn. 11: 25). As He said, *"He who believes in Me, though he may die, he shall live"*, and also, *"I have the keys of Hades and of death"*(Rev. 1: 18). His glory appears also in His power to raise the dead who died since Adam till the end of the ages, though they have turned into dust, as He says; *"all who are in the graves will hear His voice and come forth – those who have done good, to the resurrection of life, and those who have done evil, to the resurrection of condemnation"*(Jn. 5: 28, 29).

God's glory was manifested in the Transfiguration, the Resurrection, and the Ascension.

The Lord was greatly glorified in the Transfiguration, as He was surrounded by light, Moses and Elijah with Him, and His clothes shining, exceedingly white (Mk. 9: 1-5). In the glorious resurrection, He overcame death, came out of the tomb while closed, and entered the upper room to the disciples while the doors were shut (Jn. 20: 19). And in His glorious ascension, He could go up into heaven with the glorious body, where a cloud received Him out of the sight of the disciples (Acts 1: 9). Out of His love, He granted us to rise with our bodies transformed to conform to His glorious body (Phil. 3: 21).

There is also the glory of His Second Coming.

In His second coming, He will come, "*in the glory of His father with His angels, and then He will reward each according to his works*"(Mt. 16: 27), and as written in another place, "*He comes in His own glory and in His Father's, and of the holy angels*"(Lk. 9: 26); and "*When the Son of Man comes in His glory, and all the holy angels with Him, then He will sit on the throne of His glory. All the nations will be gathered before Him, and He will separate them one from another, as a shepherd divides his sheep from the goat ... will say to those on His right hand: Come, you blessed of My Father, inherit the kingdom prepared for you from the foundation of the world ...*"(Mt. 25: 31-34).

We glorify Him, not only for such terrible judgement, but we also glorify Him in His crucifixion when we say to Him throughout the Passion Week, "**Thine is the power, the glory, the blessing and honor, forever. Amen.**" For on the cross He is glorified in His love, in His sacrifice and forgiveness, in His giving and reconciliation, and in His obedience to God the Father.

After His crucifixion and resurrection, the Lord revealed to us how He will appear in His glory. He appeared to St. John the visionary, *"His eyes like a flame of fire ... and His countenances was like the sun shining in its strength ... and His voice as the sound of many waters"*(Rev. 1: 14-16). St. John the Beloved, describing this wonderful sight, said, *"When I saw Him, I fell at His feet as dead, but He laid His right hand on me, saying to me: Do not be afraid; I am the First and the Last ..."*(Rev. 1: 17)

All the above is only a hint about God's glory, but what is the attitude of the creation towards this?

How should we glorify God

First of all, we shall believe that glory belongs to God alone.

This will make one aware not to glorify oneself, but to give all glory to God, as the psalmist said:

"Not unto us, O Lord, not unto us, but to Your name give glory"(Ps. 115: 1)

Whatever good you do, be sure that it is not from you, but God did it through you, by the power He gave you and by the divine grace that worked in you and with you. That is why Paul the apostle said, *"But by the grace of God I am what I am, and His grace toward me was not in vain; but I labored more abundantly than they all, yet not I, but the grace of God which was with me"*(1 Cor. 15: 10). King Herod accepted to be glorified by the people, so the angel of the Lord struck him immediately because he did not give glory to God, *"And he was eaten by worms and died"*(Acts 12: 23).

Before God, the angels and all the heavenly hosts stand in awe.

The Cherubim and Seraphim stand in awe before His glory; with two wings they cover their face, with two they cover their feet, and with two they fly (Isa. 6: 2). Because of God's awe, *"every knee should bow, of those in heaven, and of those on earth, and of those under the earth"*(Phil. 2: 10).

St. John the visionary, likewise, saw *"the twenty-four elders fall down before Him who sits on the throne and worship Him who lives forever and ever, and cast their crowns before thr throne, saying: You are worthy, O Lord, to receive glory and honor and power; for You created all things, and by Your will they exist and were created"*(Rev. 4: 10, 11). St John saw also those who had the   victory, singing, *"Great and marvelous are Your works, Lord God Almighty! Just and true are Your ways, O King of the saints! Who shall not fear You, O Lord, and glorify Your name? For You alone are holy."*(Rev. 15: 3, 4).

We all should awe Him, for He is King of kings and Lord of lords (Rev. 19: 16)

We shall awe His name and not use it in vain, *"for the Lord will not hold him guiltless who takes His name in vain"* (Ex. 20: 7). We should bow our heads when we sing to Him, *"Holy, holy, holy"*, and when we pray we should stand in awe, kneel down, or prostrate ourselves. So said the psalmist, *"Exalt the Lord our God, and worship at His footstool- He is holy."*; *"Exalt the Lord our God, and worship at His holy hill"*(Ps. 99: 5, 9).

In awe we should deal with God and with whatever relates to Him: His house, His Scriptures, His Holy Sacraments ... etc.

As to God's house, we say to Him in the psalm, *"But as for me, I will come into Your house in the multitude of Your mercy; in fear of You I will worship toward Your holy temple"*(Ps. 5: 7); *"Holiness adorns Your house, O Lord"*(Ps. 93: 5). Did the Lord not defend the dignity of His house, saying, *"For My house shall be called a house of prayer"*(Isa. 56: 7). This reverence of God's house, Jacob, the father of fathers, said, *"How awesome is this place! This is none other than the house of God, and this is the gate of heaven!"*(Gen. 28: 17).

As an expression of glorifying God, we take off our shoes when in His holy places

Thus said God to Moses when calling him out of the burning bush, "Take your sandals off your feet, for the place where you stand is holy ground" (Ex. 3: 5). The same words were also said to Joshua the successor of Moses (Josh. 5: 15). That is why we take off our shoes in awe when we enter into the holy sanctuary, and in monasteries, we take off our shoes even before going into the church. This makes us feel how awful and holy the place is, and so we glorify the Lord and owner of the place.

The more one awes God's house, the more one benefits spiritually.

On the other hand, whoever enters God's house without fear or awe cannot feel God's presence in it nor can glorify God in His house. He cannot also have a contrite heart nor benefit spiritually. In olden times, the people dwelt far from the Tabernacle of Meeting which was surrounded by the tents of the priests and Levites who served God's house.

With the same awe we hold God's Holy Scriptures.

When the Gospel is being read in the chusrch, the deacon cries out, "Stand in awe of God, and listen to the Holy Gospel". And the Patriarch takes off his crown in reverence for the word of God being read, all the people stand in awe, and all the priests kiss the Gospel. In glorifying God, we glorify His word and His Scripture, and the more we do that in awe, the more we benefit.

In the Holy Mass, as well, the same happens

Before the divine mysteries, when the Holy Spirit descends the deacon calls upon the congregation, saying, "Worship God in awe and fear". All the people kneel down and praise God while kneeling, prostrating, or at least standing, giving glory to God. In the Holy Mass, we often repeat the Greek words, "Zoxa Patri ... " which mean "Glory be to the Father, the Son, and the Holy Spirit". And in the Midnight Praise Song we repeat the words "Glory be to You, O Lord, the lover of mankind"

In the Holy Mass, we say to God:

Before You stand thousands of thousands and myriads of myriads ministering to You.

We awe Him whom all these millions and billions of heavenly hosts awe, of whom an angel flying in the midst of heaven said, "Fear God and give glory to Him"(Rev. 14: 7). The psalmist likewise said, "Give unto the Lord glory and strength. Give unto the Lord the glory due to His name"(Ps. 29: 1). When He spoke to our father Abraham the father of fathers, Abraham felt contrite, and humbly said, "I who am but dust and ashes have taken it upon myself to speak to the Lord"(Gen. 18: 27). Before Him the tax-collector stood afar off not daring to raise his eyes to heaven, and beat his breast, saying, "God, be merciful to me a sinner!"(Lk. 18: 13)

But why should we awe God? And why kneeling and prostrating?

It is because we do feel God's majesty and glory, and our contrition and unworthiness. Truly, O Lord, who are we to stand before You though dust and ashes? Before You, all greatness and all presence diminish. We do not worship You merely by our bodies or by bowing our heads even to the dust, but rather by bowing with our souls and minds, by humbleness of heart, and by contrition of spirit.

We glorify God by obeying Him and doing His will.

Walking in the path of sin is disobedience to God and to His commandments. It is revolting against Him and rejection of His Kingdom. A sinner is one who does not glorify God in his own life nor cause others to glorify Him. The Lord thus says in His sermon on the mount, *"Let your light so shine before men, that they may see your good works and glorify your Father in heaven"*(Mt. 5: 16). By this you can glorify God, by making people glorify Him because of your conduct.

You can also glorify God by your repentance and obedience to Him, as the Book of Revelation, speaking about some sinners, says, *"they did not repent and give Him glory"* (Rev. 16: 9).

Every part of us should glorify God, as St. Paul the apostle says,

" ... glorify God in your body and in your spirit, which are God's"(1 Cor. 6: 20)

Not only should we glorify God by our tongues, saying "Glory be to You, O Lord.", but rather more by our spirits that should submit to God's Spirit, *"For as many as are led by the Spirit of God, these are sons of God"*(Rom. 8: 14). We should also glorify God in our bodies when these bodies live as temples of God's Holy Spirit dwelling in them (1 Cor. 6: 19; 3: 16). We do not glorify God at all when we make of our bodies tools of sin, as the apostle says, "*Do you not know that your bodies are members of Christ? Shall I then take the members of Christ and make them members of a harlot? Certainly not!*"(1 Cor. 6: 15). On the other hand, we glorify God when we lead an ideal life as ideal persons or families. In this case, people will love God because of us, and will love religion and spirituality because of us, thus they glorify God.

We also glorify God by spreading His Kingdom on the earth

Our Lord Jesus Christ gave us the example when He said to the Father, "*I have glorified You on the earth. I have finished the work which You have given Me to do ... I have manifested Your name to the men whom You have given Me ... I have given to them the words which You have given Me ... Those whom You gave Me I have kept, and none of them is lost ... I have declared to them Your name, and will declare it, that the love with which You loved Me may be in them, and I in them*"(Jn. 17: 4, 6, 8, 12, 26). Can we, likewise, say this? Have we witnessed to the Lord with our lives and our preaching? Have we spread His Kingdom on the earth? Have we been a cause of glorifying His name?

The preceding is the positive aspect of glorifying God, but if we cannot attain that, we should at least keep away from passivity.

We should keep away from grumbling against God, and from blaspheming His name. We should avoid disobedience and transgression. We should avoid pride, by which we ascribe to ourselves what God has done through us. We should be aware not to defile God's holy Temple, which is our bodies, and

58

should not suffer that people blaspheme against God's name because of us (Rom. 2: 24)

We should, in the first place, put God's glorification as our goal continually.

If we concentrate on this goal, we shall seek the means leading to that. Moreover we should know that **if we glorify God, God will also glorify us**. How wondrous that God glorifies His creation, give them glory from His own! What great humbleness is this!

God glorifies His creation:

Great indeed is God in His glory; to Him alone is glory and honor. The heavens declare the glory of God; and the firmament shows His handwork (Ps. 19: 1). Yet, He gives glory and honor to His creation!!

Not only to the rational creatures, but also to the irrational, You give glory.

As the apostle says, "*the glory of the celestial (bodies) is one, and the glory of the terrestrial is another. There is one glory of the sun, another glory of the moon, and another glory of the stars; for one star differs from another star in glory*"(1 Cor. 15: 40, 41). God even described the sun and the moon as great; for the divine inspiration said in the history of creation, "*Then God made two great lights: the greater light to rule the day, and the lesser light to rule the night*"(Gen. 1: 16). Likewise the Lord said about the flowers in their beauty and adornment, "*even Solomon in all his glory was not arrayed like one of these*"(Mt. 6: 28, 29). God even gave glory to the irrational things like gold, silver, emerald and pearls, which He called precious stones (Rev. 21: 19-21).

God gave man glory since He created him.

The first glory God gave man was creating him in God's image and likeness (Gen. 1: 26, 27). The second glory given man by God was endowing him with power. He empowered him to subdue the earth and have dominion over everything that moves on it (Gen. 1: 28). The same blessing was given again to our father Noah after the landing of the ark (Gen. 9: 1, 2).

It's God's pleasure to glorify man, because His pleasure is in man's offspring. God does not consider man's glory rivalling Him.

But, what then is the meaning of God's words, "*I am the Lord, that is My name; and My glory I will not give to another*" (Isa. 42: 8)?

The glory which God does not give to another is the glory of His divinity.

The preceding words were said on the occasion of His rejection of other gods and of worshipping idols. Therefore, He followed these words by the phrase, "*nor My praise to carved images*". Other than this glory of divinity, God gave many kinds of glory to His creation.

See what splendid and great glory God gave to the angels!

The psalmist described the angels as excelling in strength (Ps. 103: 20), and St. Paul described them as angels of light (2 Cor. 11: 14). St. Paul tells us that they are classified into thrones, dominions, principalities, and powers (Col. 1: 16). God gave the angels a glorious nature by which they can move from heaven to earth in a glimpse of an eye, besides a power by which they do wonders.

Even to human beings God gave the power to work signs and wonders.

How amazing is that which God gave Moses the prophet to do: to stretch out his hand with the rod over the sea and divide it so that the people go on dry ground through the midst of the sea, and the waters were a wall to them on their right and on their left (Ex. 14: 22), then to stretch out his hand over the sea that the waters may come back and the Egyptians be overthrown in the midst of the sea (Ex. 14: 26, 27). Furthermore, God gave Moses the power to strike the rock with his rod and water comes out of it (Ex. 17: 5, 6). God even said about Moses, *"He is faithful in all My house. I speak with him face to face, even plainly, and not in dark sayings; and he sees the form of the Lord"* (Num. 12: 7, 8).

See also the wonderful miracles with which God glorified His apostles of the New Testament.

The Lord Christ said to His disciples, *"Heal the sick, cleanse the lepers, raise the dead, cast out demons"*(Mt. 10: 8). We are amazed at what is written in the Book of Acts about St. Paul the apostle that *"even handkerchiefs or aprons were brought from his body to the sick, and diseases left them and the evil spirits went out of them"*(Acts 19: 12). We cannot count the signs and wonders worked by the father apostles that were the cause of spreading faith. Suffice to mention the words of the Lord:

"he who believes in Me, the works that I do he will do also; and greater works than these he will do"(Jn. 14: 12).

We feel startled at this verse and at the power with which God glorified those who believed in him, not only in the Apostolic Era, but also throughout ages and ages by the hands of

His saints whether martyrs, priests, or hermits whom He gave power of prayer and intercession. Thus He said before His ascension, *"And these signs will follow those who believe"*(Mk. 16: 17, 18)

God glorified man by making him a temple of His Holy Spirit (1 Cor. 3: 16), and by endowing him with the gifts of the Holy Spirit.

God gave man various gifts which St. Paul the apostle defined in his First Epistle to the Corinthians (1 Cor. 12), among which are: wisdom, faith, knowledge, gifts of healings, the working of miracles, prophecy, discerning of spirits, tongues, interpretation ... etc. And as St. James the apostle said, *"Every good gift and every perfect gift is from above, and comes down from the Father of lights"*(Jas. 1: 17)

God glorified man also by the grace of calling, election, and justification.

For it is written, *"For whom He foreknew, He also predestined to be conformed to the image of His Son ... whom He predestined these He also called; whom He called, these He also justified, and whom He justified, these He also glorified"* (Rom. 8: 17)

Some glory God granted man is the glory of priesthood.

Priesthood makes man a steward of God (Tit. 1: 7), and a steward of the mysteries of God (1 Cor. 4: 1), and even an ambassador for Christ (2 Cor. 5: 20). With this work of stewardship or embassy, God grants man the authority to forgive sins, as the Lord did when He breathed on His holy disciples, and said to them, *"Receive the Holy Spirit. If you forgive the sins of any, they are forgiven them; if you retain the sins of any, they are retained"*(Jn. 20: 22, 23); and also, *"Whatever you bind on earth will be bound in heaven, and whatever you loose on earth will be loosed in heaven"*(Mt. 18: 18)

Through this authority, they were given to grant the Holy Spirit.

In the apostolic era, the father apostles used to lay their hands on the baptized and the Holy Spirit descend on the baptized. This happened to the Samaritans when Peter and John laid their hands on them, they received the Holy Spirit (Acts 8: 17, 18). And the Ephesians, *"when Paul laid hands on them, the Holy Spirit came upon them, and they spoke with tongues and prophesied"*(Acts 19: 6)

God glorified His priests as we see in the case of Aaron.

For the Lord God commanded Moses, *"And you shall make holy garments for Aaron your brother, for glory and for beauty. So you shall speak to all who are gifted artisans, whom I have filled with the spirit of wisdom, that they make Aaron's garments, to consecrate him that he may minister to Me as priest"*(Ex. 28: 2, 3).God commanded also, *"You shall also make a plate of pure gold and engrave on it, like the engraving of a signet: Holiness to the Lord ... So it shall be on Aaron's forehead"*(Ex. 28: 36-38). For Aaron's sons, the Lord God commanded Moses, *"You shall make tunics ... sashes ... hats for them, for glory and beauty"*(Ex. 28: 40). What amazing words are these *"for glory and beauty"*!

What amazing glory is that which God gave Moses when appointing the seventy elders!

God said to Moses, *"Gather to Me seventy men of the elders of Israel, whom you know to be the elders of the people and officers of them ... Then I will come down and talk with you there 'I will take of the Spirit that is upon you and will put the same upon them; and they shall bear the burden of the people with you '"*(Num. 11: 16, 17). How strange that God takes of the Spirit that is on Moses and give others! But it happened! Moses gathered the seventy men ... placed them around the tabernacle,

"Then the Lord came down in the cloud and spoke to him, and took of the Spirit that was upon him, and placed the same upon the seventy elders; and it happened, when the Spirit rested upon them, that they prophesied"(Num. 11: 24, 25). Thus God glorified Moses, His prophet and priest, before all the people.

This is evident in the words the Lord Christ said to the Fathr about His holy disciples:

"The glory which You gave Me I have given them"(Jn. 17: 22)

What glory is that which the Lord gave His disciples? Is it that glory given Him by the Father? How is that? This reminds us of the words in the Book of Revelation, *"To him who overcomes I will grant to sit with Me on My throne, as I also overcame and sat with My Father on His throne"*(Rev. 3: 21). St. John tells us that He saw God's throne in heaven, and what else? He says, *"Around the throne were twenty-four thrones, and on the thrones I saw twenty-four elders sitting, clothed in white robes; and they had crowns of gold on their heads"*(Rev. 4: 2-4). What a wonderful scene! Humans sitting on thrones beside God and having gold crowns on their heads! It is the glory which God – in His humbleness – gives to His beloved servants.

God gave Elijah another kind of glory:

He gave him the power to shut and open heaven. So Elijah said, *"As the Lord God of Israel lives, before whom I stand, there shall not be dew nor rain these years, except at·my word"* (1 Kgs. 17: 1). Elijah prayed earnestly that it would not rain; and it did not rain on the land for three years and six months. And he prayed again, and the heaven gave rain, and the earth produced its fruit (Jas. 5: 17, 18). Another time, Elijah ordered that fire come down from heaven and consume fifty men of the army, and it happened so. This he repeated again and his word came true (2 Kgs. 1: 10-12).

God glorified Elijah bey bringing him up into heaven by a chariot of fire (2 Kgs. 2: 11)

Among the ways in which God glorified His children is the transfiguration.

When the Lord transfigured on mountain Tabor before three of His disciples, *"His face shone like the sun, and His clothes became as white as the light"*(Mt. 17: 2), and He permitted that Moses and Elijah appear with Him on the mountain. They appeared in glory and spoke with Him (Lk. 9: 31).

The greatest glory still which God gives His children is the everlasting glory.

The glory of the resurrection will come first when He will transform our lowly body that it may be conformed to His glorious body (Phil. 3: 21). Then the corruptible body will be raised in incorruption, *"It is sown in dishonor, it is raised in honor. It is sown a natural body, it is raised a spiritual body"*, *"And as we have borne the image of the man of dust, we shall also bear the image of the heavenly Man"*(1 Cor. 15: 43, 49); and we are transformed into the same image from glory to glory (2 Cor. 3: 18)

We will be delivered from the bondage of corruption into the glorious liberty of the children of God (Rom. 8: 21)

Thus said St. Paul the apostle, *"The sufferings of this present time are not worthy to be compared with the glory which shall be revealed in us"*(Rom. 8: 18). And St. Peter the apostle, likewise, spoke about *"the glory that will be revealed"*(1 Pet. 5: 1). He said, *"and when the Chief Shepherd appears, you will receive the crown of glory that does not fade away"*(1 Pet. 5: 4). This is because, *"the God of all grace ... called us to His eternal glory by Christ Jesus"*(1 Pet. 5: 10). Then we will be caught up in the clouds to meet the Lord in the air in His second coming, *"thus we shall always be with the Lord"*(1 Thess. 4: 17).

FAIRER THAN THE SONS OF MEN
(Ps. 45: 2)
GOD THE BEAUTIFUL AND THE BEAUTY LOVING

God is perfect in everything, and beauty is an aspect of His perfection.

God is beautiful in His perfection, and perfect in His beauty.

The psalmist describe Him as *"fairer than the sons of men"* (Ps. 45: 2). He is described also as *"unapproachable light"* (1 Tim. 6: 16), and as *"the true Light"* (Jn. 1: 9). David desired this beauty of the Lord; He said, *"One thing I have desired of the lord. That I will seek. That I may dwell in the house of the Lord all the days of my life, to behold the beauty of the Lord and to inquire in His temple"* (Ps. 27: 4). How dazzling was the Lord's beauty on the Mount of Transfiguration (Mk. 9)! And when He revealed Himself to St. John the apostle, *"His countenance was like the sun shining in its strength"* (Rev. 1: 16)

See what beautiful words are said of our Lord Jesus Christ in the Song of Songs:

"His countenance is like Lebanon, excellent as the cedars. His mouth is most sweet, yes, he is altogether lovely" (Song 5: 15, 16). *"His head is like the finest gold ... His eyes are like doves by the rivers of waters, washed with milk"* (Song 5: 11, 12). And the church describes Him, saying, *"My beloved is white and ruddy"* (Song 5: 10); that is white in the purity of His heart, and ruddy in the precious blood poured for us.

God's beauty and love of beauty appears in His creation.

If we start with the beauty of the angels, we can truly say that even Satan before his fall was *"full of wisdom and perfect in beauty"* (Ezek. 28: 12). The heaven was beautiful, and the earth as well, and God saw everything that He had made, and indeed it was very good (Gen. 1: 31).

Look at the moon in heaven and how beautiful it is when full. It is so beautiful that people used to describe a beautiful person as being like the moon. The sun is even prettier and the moon derives its light and beauty from it. The virgin of the Song was described *"as the morning, fair as the moon, clear as the sun"* (Song 6: 10). The beauty of the stars are said to be different from each other in glory (1 Cor. 15: 41).

The earth is also created very beautiful

The earth will all its seas, lakes and rivers, with its trees, fruits and flowers, with its mountains, valleys and plain, all these wonderful scenes demonstrate the Creator's marvelous work and love of beauty. This beautiful nature made poets sing its praise, like the great poet Ahmed Shawki (surnamed the prince of poets) who said:

Stop sailing, O ship mast, and see,
This nature which the Creator made marvelously.

Indeed, how beautiful the scenery is at sunset time and sunrise time! How beautiful the rainbow is with its varied colors! How beautiful the colors and harmony of flowers, roses, and sweet basils are! They are pretty in their variety and their beautiful scent, that no artificial flowers can be compared to them however accurately made, for these remain lifeless and without odour or softness.

God loves beauty so much that He put the man He created in a garden!

See what a garden contains of beauty, of tenderness, of flowers, of birds, of trees, of fruits, and in all, of fascinating scenery that gives happiness!

Man himself is created beautiful.

Suffice what the Scripture says that God created man in His own image according to His likeness (Gen. 1: 26, 27). Eve was very pretty, the prettiest in the whole world. No other woman deserved to be described as the prettiest except the holy Virgin Mary. Adam also was beautiful, but this beauty was afterwards deformed by sin.

Many prophets and saints were described in the Scripture as beautiful or handsome.

Joseph the righteous was described as *"handsome in form and appearance"* (Gen. 39: 6). Moses also was a beautiful child (Acts 7: 20) (Heb. 11: 23). Probably this was the cause that Pharaoh's daughter took him and he became her son (Heb. 11: 24). Likewise David the Prophet was beautiful, *"he was ruddy, with bright eyes, and good looking"* (1 Sam. 16: 12, 18). Sarah the wife of our father Abraham continued very beautiful till the age of ninety that Abimalech king of Gerar took her to be his wife (Gen. 20: 2). There are also Job's daughters who were born to him after the temptation he underwent. They were described in the Scripture by the words, *"In all the land were found no women so beautiful as the daughters of Job"* (Job 42: 15)

All those were beautiful in the spirit as in the body.

An example of this is Esther who was the most beautiful of all women at that time, so they chose here to be the wife of king Ahasuerus, *"The young woman was lovely and beautiful"*, *"Esther obtained favor in the sight of all who saw her"* (Esth. 2: 7, 9, 15). This saint fasted and called upon the whole people to fast. God was with her and she saved her people (Esth. 4: 16).

The greatest example of beauty of body and spirit is that of St. Virgin Mary

The holy Virgin looks beautiful in her picture. Her beauty is not ordinary beauty, for the beauty of the spirit gives certain spiritual beauty to the features. Her features reveal the meekness, gentleness, chastity, calmness, and peace of heart, besides all other beautiful virtues.

Beauty is a gift from God, which becomes more glorious by the beauty of spiritual virtues.

The features usually reveal the condition of the spirit whether good or evil, and reveal also the heart feelings. The eye - in particular – is a mirror of man's inner emotions, whether love, lust, anger, envy, desire to avenge, cruelty, kindness, fear, courage, or any other emotions.

Holiness, chastity, and purity as well appear in one's features and looks. How beautiful are the words of St. Joseph to St. Anthony the Great, when he said, [It is sufficient for me to look at your face, my father].

When God created man, He created him beautiful in body and spirit.

Through sin man lost this beauty. But the Lord Christ came and presented to us the divine picture which man had lost. For the Lord Christ is *"the image of the invisible God"* (Col. 1: 15); *"being the brightness of His glory and the express image of His person"* (Heb. 1: 3). He presented to us the perfection of beauty in form and spirit.

God, as beauty-loving, granted beauty to various creatures.

The birds, for example, with their various kinds and shapes, with their beautiful voices and varied tones, play for the universe wonderful beautiful and joyful music. The butterflies with their beautiful and varied colors reveal the marvelous work of the Creator who gave them such beauty in hundreds of shapes before which any artist stands astonished and unable to imitate them. The colored fish, likewise, with the hundreds of shapes and wonderful colors give us an idea about the beauty-loving creator. See the flowers, roses, and basil of which beauty the Lord said, *"Consider the lilies of the field ... even Solomon in all his glory was not arrayed like one of these"* (Mt. 6: 28-30)

God has not confined beauty to females, but He gave beauty to males also.

Some people say that the lion is more beautiful than the lioness, and the cock than the hen, and the horse than the she-horse.

Even things that have no male or female are endowed with beauty by God, such as the natural scenery.

If the bodies have such beauty while on the earth, what can we say about the bodies after the resurrection?

St. Paul said the human bodies will be raised in glory and in power. They will be raised spiritual bodies and heavenly bodies (1 Cor. 15: 43-49). What a beautiful image our beauty-loving God will give us in the resurrection! Remember the wonderful words of St. Paul the apostle when he said about the Lord Christ, *"Who will transform our lowly body that it may be conformed to His glorious body"* (Phil. 3: 21). How beautiful and how marvelous is the image of His glorious body!

God, the beauty-lover, was concerned about the beauty of His house.

God set a model of the Tent of Meeting before Moses the Prophet *"Thus Moses did according to all the Lord had commanded him."* This phrase is repeated many times in Chapter (40) of the Book of Exodus. Moreover, God called

Bezalel, a great artist and filled him with the Spirit of God, in wisdom, in understanding, in knowledge, and in all manner of workmanship. God chose him *"to design artistic works, to work in gold, in silver, in bronze, in cutting jewels for setting, in carving wood, and to work in all manner of workmanship"* (Ex. 31: 2-5).

God was not satisfied with all this, but He even chose the materials for the work which the gifted artisans with Bezalel and Aholiab were to do, *"a veil of blue, purple, and scarlet thread, and fine woven linen ... with an artistic design of cherubim"* (Ex. 36: 35). He chose also the acacia wood, the pure gold and silver, and the precious stones for His house. He commanded that the utensils of the altar, the lampstand and the cover of the ark (the mercy seat), all be made of pure gold. He ordered also that the two Cherubim be made of beaten gold, spreading their wings above and covering the mercy seat with them (Ex. 37)!

Not only the Tent of Meeting that was so beautiful, but also the garments of Aaron the high priest were very beautiful.

They made the holy garments for Aaron as the Lord commanded Moses, *"Of the blue, purple, and scarlet thread ... the ephod of gold, blue, purple, and scarlet thread, and of fine woven linen"* (Ex. 39). So beautiful and wonderful were the garments of ministry for Aaron and his sons, garments for glory and beauty (Ex. 28: 40)! Upon the hems of Aaron's garments were pomegranates all around and bells of gold between them all around, *"a golden bell and a pomegranate upon the hem of the robe all around"* (Ex. 28: 34). On the turban was put a plate of pure gold on which was engraved - like the engraving of a signet – *"Holiness to the Lord"*. Thus the Lord God commanded Moses, saying, *"And you shall make holy garments for Aaron your brother, for glory and for beauty. So you shall speak to all who are gifted artisans, whom I have filled with the spirit of wisdom, that they may make Aaron's garments, to consecrate him, that he may minister to Me as priest"* (Ex. 28: 2, 3).

See how God who loves beauty dressed Aaron such beautiful garments which He defined exactly by Himself!

What was done for the Tent of Meeting was also done, and much more, for the Temple.

"Thus Solomon had all the furnishings made for the house of the Lord: the altar of gold; and the table of gold ... the lampstand of pure gold ... the lamps and the wick – trimmers of gold ... and the censers of pure gold ..." (1 Kgs. 7: 48-50).

Much more beauty was in the pillars and their capitals in the shape of lilies, for which Solomon called Huram who was filled with wisdom and understanding and skill (1 Kgs. 7: 13, 14).

Some would think that simplicity is required in everything whether in the building or in the garments. But God who loves beauty so willed that His house be marvelous in beauty and magnificence. This wonderful beauty with which Solomon finished the work made the queen of Sheba astounded, *"there was no more spirit in her"* (1 Kgs. 10: 5).

Thus was God's house a curiosity in beauty, in building, in decorations, and in prayers as well.

Not only the Temple was so beautiful, but the Tent also which was described as a dome. In the Hymn of Praise we say [You adorned our souls, O Moses the Prophet, with the honor of the Dome which you had adorned]. For all this the believers praise God saying, *"How lovely is Your tabernacle, O Lord of hosts!"* (Ps. 84: 1)

The Church likewise God made beautiful in everything.

The Church is indeed beautiful with her pretty icons, lights, candles and incense. She is beautiful with its twelve pillars, representing the twelve disciples, and with the capitals representing the crowns of the disciples. She is beautiful with her meaningful and symbolical rituals, and with her beautiful hymns, music, anthems, and songs.

God so loves beauty that He gave us music and singing in our worship.

St. Paul the apostle mentioned this type of worship in his epistles. He said, *"... in psalms and hymns and spiritual songs, singing with grace in your hearts to the Lord"* (Col. 3: 16). How beautiful it is to pray and sing to the Lord! David the Prophet used to pray his psalms accompanied by a big band of musicians. He himself used to pray while playing lute, flute, cithara, or the ten-strings giving beautiful harmonious music and hymns. Up till now our prayers in the Holy Mass are sung with tunes, even the Gospel is read in the same way, and also all the anthems. David defined such musical instruments used in praising the Lord, saying,

"Praise Him with the sound of the trumpet;
Praise Him with the lute and harp!
Praise Him with the timbrel and dance;
Praise Him with stringed instruments and flutes!
Praise Him with loud cymbals;
Praise Him with clashing cymbals!
Let everything that has breath praise the Lord." (Ps. 150: 3-6)

Music used in worship has its beauty and influence.

Therefore I urge the father priests in the church abroad to say the prayers of the translated liturgy with tune because the prayers said without musical tune often lose their spirituality and influence.

Many of the books of the Scripture, especially the peotic ones, have certain rhythm. Examples of these are the book of Job, the Psalms, the Song of Songs, some of Solomon's Books.

Moreover, some of the anthems included in many books were sung.

The beauty of music in the church is not the only beauty, for God granted us the beauty of art in His house.

Besides the beautiful music in the church, there is the beautiful architectural art with the inscriptions and symbols, and the art of icons. All these have spiritual impression. In the Tent of Meeting there were also other arts such as the art of textile, the art of designing and working gold, silver, bronze and wood. God who loves beauty endowed some people with such artistic gifts such as Bezalel the son of Uri, He said, *"I have filled him with the Spirit of God, in wisdom, in understanding, in knowledge, and in all manner of workmanship"* (Ex. 31: 3)

Among the types of beauty which God loves in His church is the beauty of order.

Everything in the church is organized in a divine way as it is written, *"Let all things be done decently and in order"* (1 Cor. 14: 40). And in the miracle of the five loaves and two fish the Lord commanded His disciples to make the people sit down in groups in ranks, in hundreds and in fifties (Mk. 6: 40). Therefore the church is like heaven in its beauty and order, and the earth likewise as we say in the Lord's Prayer, *"On earth as it is in heaven"*. God loves order and loves everything to be organized, so the divine inspiration commands, *"you withdraw from every brother who walks disorderly"*(2 Thess. 3: 6).

See also the beauty of style as in the Gospel and the Epistles of St. John.

The sentences are organized in wonderful rhythm, as in (Jn. 1), *"In the beginning was the Word, and the Word was with God, and the Word was God ... In Him was life, and the life was the light of men ... "* (Jn. 1: 1-4). And in John's first epistle, he said, *"They went out from us, but they were not of us; for if they had been of us, they would have continued with us"*(1 Jn. 2: 19).

It is evident also that the beauty of words in dealing with others and in communicating or talking with them creates love and gives influence. It may lead also to friendship. A beautiful word is impressive, and a beautiful smile is unfluential.

But the most important beauty God requires from mankind is the beauty of the spirit.

God desires us to have a beautiful spirit perfumed with purity and holiness, of which the spirit said in the Song of Songs, *"Perfumed with myrrh and frankincense, with all the merchant's fragrant powders"* (Song 3: 6). Of such spirit St. Peter the apostle also said, *"the incorruptible beauty of a gentle and quiet spirit, which is very precious in sight of God"* (1 Pet. 3: 4)

God, the Beautiful and Beauty-Loving, has treasured much more beauty in eternity.

St. Paul the apostle, trying to give a hint of such beauty, said, *"Eye has not seen, nor ear heard,*
Nor have entered into the heart of man
The things which God has prepared for those who love
Him" (1 Cor. 2: 9).

It is the beauty of being with God, and the beauty of the heavenly Jerusalem *"prepared as a bride adorned for her husband"* (Rev. 21: 2). There is also the beauty of the angels, in addition to the beauty of hymns and songs, the beauty of spirituality and companionship of saints, the beauty of a life without sin, and the beauty of knowing God (Jn. 17: 3) and of seeing Him face to face (1 Cor. 13: 12). It is such a beauty as that which made the skin of Moses' face so shining that they put a veil on his face to be able to talk with him (Ex. 30: 29, 30)!

GOD'S HUMBLENESS

God alone is truly humble.

God, though alone the Highest whose greatness and glory are limitless, condescended to His creation out of His humbleness. The human beings are merely dust and ash, and were nothing before being created. So what humbleness can they claim, and what glory do they relinquish? Truly said one of the fathers when speaking about man's humbleness:

Man's humbleness is to know himself.

This happened with our father Abraham when he started to intercede for Sodom. He said to the Lord, "*I who am but dust and ashes have taken it upon myself to speak to the Lord*" (Gen. 18: 27). The father of fathers was aware of his own esteem; he did not condescend from a higher level, but just knew his actual level: that he was dust in spite of all his wealth and prestige.

God the King of Kings and Lord of lords (Rev. 19: 16), out of His humbleness, condescends and talks with this dust and these ashes.

He used to talk so much with Moses that they called Moses "God's spokesman". He gave Moses the opportunity to spend with Him forty days on the mountain through which God showed him the pattern of the Tent of Meeting (Heb. 8: 5), saying, "*According to all that I show you, that is, the pattern of the tabernacle and the pattern of all its furnishings, just so you shall make it*" (Ex. 25: 9). God talked with many other prophets and even started the talk.

God, out of His humbleness, used sometimes to tell His beloved about some of His dispensation before taking a decision on that.

Before burning Sodom, the Lord said, *"Shall I hide from Abraham what I am doing, since Abraham shall surely become a great and mighty nation, and all the nations of the earth shall be blessed in him?"* (Gen. 18: 17, 18). God even permitted Abraham to argue with Him and dare say, *"Far be it from You to do such a thing as this, to slay the righteous with the wicked, so that the righteous should be as the wicked; far be it from You! Shall not the Judge of all the earth do right?"* (Gen. 18: 25). Abraham continued arguing until the Lord said, *"I will not destroy it for the sake of ten".*

Likewise, when God wanted to consume the people of Israel because they worshipped the golden calf, He, out of His humbleness, told Moses first about that, saying, *"I have seen this people, and indeed it is a stiff-nicked people! Now therefore, let Me alone, that My wrath may burn hot against them. And I will make you a great nation"* (Ex. 32: 9, 10). Amazing indeed that the Lord asks Moses to let Him alone, and more amazing that Moses did not let Him do that! For Moses said to the Lord, *"Turn from Your fierce wrath, and relent from this harm to Your people. Remember Abraham, Isaac, and Israel Your servants"* (Ex. 32: 12, 13). And see what happened: the Lord responded to Moses' request as the Scripture says, *"So the Lord relented from the harm which He said He would do to His people"* (Ex. 32: 14)!

Not only did the Lord, out of His humbleness, talk to His servants the prophets, but He also talked with children.

The Lord talked with the child Samuel. He even entrusted Samuel with a message to old Eli the priest, though Samuel was yet so young that he could not discern God's voice!

God talked also with young Jeremiah. He said to Jeremiah, *"Before I formed you in the womb I knew you; before you were born I sanctified you; I ordained you a prophet to the nations"* (Jer. 1: 5). And when Jeremiah said to Him, *"Ah Lord God! Behold I cannot speak, for I am a youth"*, the Lord encouraged and strengthened him, saying, *"See, I have this day set you over the nations and over the kingdoms, to root out and to pull down, to destroy and to throw down, to build and to plant"*, *"For behold, I have made you this day a fortified city and an iron pillar, and bronze walls against the whole land ... They will fight against you, but they shall not prevail against you. For I am with you, to deliver you"* (Jer. 1: 10-19). How wonderful this humbleness with which the Lord speaks to a youth!

More wonderful indeed is the Lord's humbleness in His incarnation.

The Scripture says of that, *"He made Himself of no reputation, taking the form of a bondservant, and coming in the likeness of men. And being found in appearance as a man, He humbled Himself and became obedient to the point of death, even the death of the cross"* (Phil. 2: 7, 8).

In His humbleness He did not come to the world surrounded by the heavenly host and ranks of angels, but was rather born of a poor mother in a manger because there was no room for them in the inn (Lk. 2: 7). He lived humbly in His childhood, as it is written, *"Jesus increased in wisdom and stature and in favor with God and men"* (Lk. 2: 52). He was even subject to His mother and Joseph (Lk. 2: 51).

His humbleness made Him flee with His mother and Joseph to Egypt (Mt. 2: 13).

He could have struck Herod to death, but He did not do that. He went quietly to Egypt, not resisting the evil (Mt. 5: 39). In

Egypt He spent some years until Herod died, so He returned and dwelt in Nazareth.

In His humbleness, He spent thirty years without people knowing anything about Him.

He lived unknown till the age of thirty when He began His ministry subject to the Law. He could have done many great works all those years, but He did not because His hour had not yet come (Jn. 2: 4)!

He went humbly to be baptized the baptism of repentance.

He went to be baptized like all other people, *"to fulfill all righteousness"* (Mt. 3: 15). John the Baptist was even ashamed to do that, and said, *"I need to be baptized by You, and are You coming to me?"* (Mt. 3: 14). But He let John do that, though He was not in need of repentance because He is the Holy One (Lk. 1: 35).

He even humbly permitted Satan to tempt Him!

It was easy for Him to rebuke Satan as He did finally (Mt. 4: 10), but He gave Satan the opportunity even to choose the kind and place of temptation. He was so humble that Satan dared to say to Him, *"All these things I will give You if You will fall down and worship me"* (Mt. 4: 9)!!

The three temptations mentioned in the Gospel of Matthew and Luke were not the only temptations, for He was being tempted by Satan throughout the forty days He spent in the wilderness (Mk: 1: 13). His purpose, as mentioned in the Epistle to the Hebrews, was to be, *"in all points tempted as we are, yet without sin"*, that He might sympathize with our weaknesses (Heb. 4: 15); *"For in that He Himself has suffered being tempted, He is able to aid those who are tempted"* (Heb. 2: 18).

In His humbleness, He had nowhere to lay His head (Mt. 8: 20)

He had no home or dwelling place, but went about cities and villages preaching the gospel of the kingdom (Mt. 4: 23) (Lk. 13: 23). People used to host Him in their houses, but He had no house and sometimes used to spend the night on the Olive Mountain. He lived in poverty and need, as when they asked Him to pay the tax He had no money (Mt. 17: 24-27).

He was so humble that He accepted to argue with His opponents.

This often happened with the scribes, pharisees, sadducees, priests, and elders. All of those were seeking to catch Him in something He might say (Lk. 11: 54). Therefore they stood against Him whenever He worked a miracle on the Sabbath, but He humbly used to explain to them that it is lawful to do good on the Sabbath (Mt. 12: 12). And when they asked Him maliciously, *"Is it lawful to pay taxes to Caesar, or not?"* (Mk. 12: 17) He humbly explained to them what to do. The same happened when the Sadducees asked Him, *"in the resurrection, whose wife of the seven will she be? For they all had her"* (Mt. 22: 28). All their questions were malicious with an intent to put Him in a critical situation, but He answered them in spite of the evil intent or the attempt to trap Him!

He was so humble that He used to go to dinners at the houses of sinners.

He used to visit the sinners and eat with them to encourage them to repentance, but He was accused of being a glutton and a winebibber, a friend of tax collectors and sinners (Mt. 11: 19). However He kept saying to those accusers, *"Those who are well have no need of a physician, but those who are sick ... For I did not come to call the righteous, but sinners, to repentance"* (Mt. 9: 11-13). What great humbleness indeed to sit with the sinners and the sick! When He went to the house of Zacchaeus the chief tax-collector, the Jews complained that He went to the house of a sinner. But, with all humbleness, He answered them, *"Today salvation has come to this house, because he also is a son of Abraham; for the Son of Man has come to seek and to save that which was lost"* (Lk. 19: 5-10).

In His humbleness He kept Satan and did not consume him.

Though Satan persists to fight God's kingdom, and asked the Lord twice to tempt Job the righteous and complain against him (Job 1, 2), yet the Lord did not destroy Satan. He even permitted that Satan be released from his prison in the last days though He knows that Satan will go out to deceive the nations (Rev. 20: 7,8).

In His humbleness, the Lord accepted to be tried before the Senhedrin.

He permitted that the high priest, tearing his clothes, accuses Him of blasphemy, saying, *"He has spoken blasphemy! What further need do we have of witnesses?"* (Mt. 26: 65). He accepted also to be tried before Pontius Pilate, and to be sent to Herod and mocked at!

In His humbleness He accepted the pains of the cross and the insults.

His is humbleness mixed with love for our salvation; humbleness which accepted all kinds of challenge and mockery, *"for the joy that was set before Him, (He) endured the cross, despising the shame"* (Heb. 12: 2). His pleasure was to redeem us and to be a propitiation for the whole world (1 Jn. 2: 2). Therefore He accepted to be struck, whipped and spat at the face, as we say to Him in the Liturgy of St. Gregory [You let

Your back to the whips, and your cheeks to be struck]. This has been the fulfillment of the prophecy of Isaiah the prophet who said, *"I gave My back to those who struck me, and My cheeks to those who plucked out the beard; I did not hide My face from shame and spitting"* (Isa. 50: 6).

Is it not strange that the Lord let His crucifixion be publicly and His resurrection and ascension secretly?

In His humbleness, He let them crucify Him before all people and be hanged in their sight on the Golgotha mountain. But the glory of His resurrection He kept secret; no one saw it, but it was announced by the angels and the empty grave. His ascension also was only witnessed by His disciples (Acts 1: 9)

Let us give thanks to this humble Lord who is not ashamed to call us brethren.

He became the firstborn among many brethren (Heb. 2: 11-17). He even approved to make us share His kingdom and to dwell with Him in the heavenly Jerusalem which is the tabernacle of God with men (Rev. 21: 3). Then His promise will be fulfilled, when He said, *"Where I am there you may be also"* (Jn. 14: 3)

What are we, O Lord, that we may be with You? We are mere dust and ashes, things despised and nothing (1 Cor. 1: 28).

It is not that we are worth it, but it is Your humbleness.

You raise the poor from the dust, and lifts the beggar from the ash heaps to set them with princes (1 Sam. 2: 8)! You are our humble God who rejected the kingdom and accepted the cross on which You truly reigned. You gave us the image of God who is gentle and lowly in heart (Mt. 11: 29). Blessed be Your holy name for ever and ever.

SECTION III

GOD'S RELATIONSHIP WITH MAN

Contents of this Section:
* God's relationship with man is the story of love
* God's love is inexpressible
* God's relationship with man begins with giving
* The Covenant between God and the people
* God's blessing to the people
* God is the God of all
* God is the God of the weak
* God works quietly
* God the protector & God's wonderful protection
    * Our Good God
    * Kindness, compassion, and mercy are among
      God's attributes
    * God chastens and heals, wounds and bandages
      (Job 5: 18)
  * God's wisdom
  * God's wise dispensation
  * God's dispensation of the great Redemption and
    Salvation

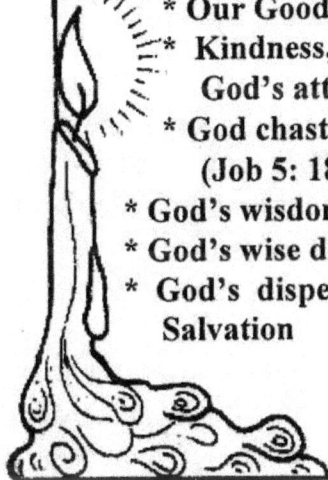

GOD'S RELATIONSHIP WITH MAN IS THE STORY OF LOVE

God's relationship with man is the story of love in which God took the initiative.

God loved man before his coming into existence, and that is why God brought him into existence. He loved man while still a thought in His mind and a pleasure in His heart

God was alone in the eternity. Long ages had passed before the existence of man or even of any other being. This would have continued had not God willed to create some beings and things. And God created the angels spirits (Ps. 104: 4), and created material. Then God willed to create a being having spirit and material, thus He made man. God first made dust, then breathed into it the breath of life (Gen. 2: 7). In this way we came into being, and God loved us.

Out of God's love, He made us in His own image, after His likeness (Gen. 1: 26, 27).

We had not done any good for which we deserve such love, but He had loved us for nothing before we existed. And after creating us He gave us blessing and power, and willed that we grow and multiply to fill the earth and have dominion as He said, *"Be fruitful and multiply; fill the earth and subdue it, have dominion over ... and over every living thing that moves on the earth"*(Gen. 1: 28)

It was indeed a story of love and giving from the very beginning. He gave man everything: intellect, spirit, and power. He made man lord and priest of the earth to manage it on behalf of God, as the psalmist said, "*You have him to have dominion over the works of Your hands; You have put all things under his feet*" (Ps. 8: 6). He wanted man to be lord of the whole earthly creation.

God put man in the garden, but man's will had to be tested to prove his love towards God.

God therefore gave man a command not to eat of the tree of knowledge of good and evil. By this command God wanted to test man's obedience and love; would he reject the temptation of the serpent and hold to God's command, or fail in the test and be separated from God?

God loved man, but did not want this love to be from one side only.

Such love should be from both sides: God and man. But would man prove himself worthy of God's love and respond to it? And man failed. Therefore it was impossible for him to eat – while in the condition of sin – of the tree of life. So God commanded cherubim to guard the way to the tree with flaming sword (Gen. 3: 24). God intended to cleanse man from his sin and save him to deserve to eat from that tree of life.

However God's love was not void of His justice. Therefore He punished man.

God sent man out of the garden because in his sin he was not worthy to dwell in it since his eyes opened and he lost his simplicity and chastity and became aware of his being naked. Thus God punished him by fatigue and pain while on the earth in order that he might always remember that he sinned against God. The man had to eat with toil and with the sweat of his face all the days of his life. And the woman with pain had to bring forth children (Gen. 3: 16, 19). Moreover, God, in His justice, punished man with death.

God's justice was not, however, void of His love. Though God punished man, He promised him of salvation.

God promised that the seed of the woman should bruise the head of the serpent (Gen. 3: 15). Probably Adam and Eve did not understand the significance of the promise, but at least they knew that the serpent who introduced sin to them should have its head bruised. So they became sure that they ought not listen to it again, and that of the woman's seed there would be someone to bruise its head. But who was He? Or when that was to happen? They probably did not know. Yet, all the human race lived and died having this hope.

God's love made Him take care of man after bringing him out of the garden. He gave him the commandment which would keep the purity of his heart.

If man had obeyed the commandment, he would have been pure and deserved reconciliation with God.

Therefore God sent him the prophets to guide him after providing him with conscience, which is the inner law by which he could discern between good and evil. By this law Joseph the righteous had refused to fall in the sin of adultery even before God gave the seventh commandment which says, "You shall not commit adultery". Yet, Joseph, before Moses the prophet by hundreds of years, had said, *"How then can I do this great wickedness and sin against God?"* (Gen. 39: 9).

When the people's conscience failed to be their guide, God's love sent them the written law.

Through Moses the prophet God sent the law written on tablets, *"The tablets were the work of God, and the writing was the writing of God engraved on the tablets"* (Ex. 32: 16). And many other commandments God ordered Moses to write, *"So Moses wrote this law and delivered it to the priests, the sons of Levi, who bore the ark of the covenant of the Lord"* (Deut. 31: 9)

But the people understood the law literally, caring for the letter rather than the spirit (2 Cor. 3: 6). So God summarized for them the whole law in one commandment, which is love. He said to them, *"You shall love the Lord your God with all your heart, with all your soul, and with all your strength"*(Deut. 6: 5).. God said this in the Old Testament, and the Lord Christ repeated it in the New Testament. When the Lord Christ was asked what was the great commandment in the law, He reminded them of those same words, *"You shall love the Lord..."*. Then He said to them, *"This is the first and great commandment. And the second is like it: you shall love your neighbor as yourself. On these two commandments hang all the Law and Prophets"* (Mt. 22: 36-40)

Why did the Lord Christ add the love of neighbor to the love of God? This is explained by our teacher St. John the beloved. He said,

"He who does not love his brother whom he has seen, how can he love God whom he has not seen?"(1 Jn. 4: 20)

Thus God wanted us to live according to the commandment of love. We should love Him because He loved us first (1 Jn. 4: 10), and love each other, *"for love is of God; and everyone who loves is born of God and knows God. He who does not love does not know God, for God is love"* (1 Jn. 4: 7, 8).

"God is love, and he who abides in love abides in God, and God in him"(1 Jn. 4: 16)

Such love which God wanted us to have, is not love in words or in tongue but *"in deed and in truth"* (1 Jn. 3: 18). Therefore God's love is connected with keeping His commandments, as He said, *"If you keep My commandments, you will abide in My love"* (Jn. 15: 10). The Lord God, in the Old Testament, said similar words:

"My son, give Me your heart, and let your eyes observe My ways" **(Prov. 23: 26)**

If we indeed give our hearts to the Lord, we certainly will observe His ways. But to observe His ways without giving the heart is completely rejected, for the Lord wants us to obey His commandments in love, not outwardly. For He loves us perfect love, *"Having loved His own who were in the world, He loved them to the end"* (Jn. 13: 1)

Out of His love He called us His children

St. John the apostle makes this point clear, saying, *"Behold what manner of love the Father has bestowed on us, that we should be called children of God"* (1 Jn. 3: 1). From the beginning He treats us as children caring for us in whatever we need. Thus He protected Joseph in the land of Egypt. He made him, *"a father to Pharaoh, and Lord of all his house, and a ruler throughout all the land of Egypt"* (Gen. 45: 8). God protected Daniel also in the lions' den. He sent His angel and shut the lions' mouths (Da. 6: 22). And He protected the three young men in the furnace of fire bringing them safe out of it, and promoting them in the province of Babylon (Da. 3: 25-30).

Out of His love He wanted us to be with Him where He is.

He said to His holy disciples, *"And if I go and prepare a place for you, I will come again and receive you to Myself; that where I am, there you may be also"* (Jn. 14: 3). He also promised that we be with Him in eternity in the heavenly Jerusalem which is said to be, *"the tabernacle of God (is) with men, and He will dwell with them, and they shall be His people. God Himself will be with them and be their God"* (Rev. 21: 3). Therefore the Lord said, *"Father, I desire that they also whom You gave Me may be with Me where I am"* (Jn. 17: 24)

We shall be with Him, and He likewise will be with us

He will be with us, for His name is "Immanuel", which is translated "God with us" (Mt. 1: 23). In the old He said to Jacob while flying from his brother Esau, *"Behold I am with you and will keep you wherever you go, and will bring you back to the land"* (Gen. 28: 15). God said also to Joshua the son of Nun, *"No man shall be able to stand before you all the days of your life; as I was with Moses, so I will be with you. I will not leave you nor forsake you"* (Josh. 1: 5)

It is the story of love that God chooses for Himself beloved people on the earth.

God walked with His beloved people and entrusted them with His secrets. He even listened to them and accepted their intercession. He esteemed them and gave them leadership to rule over the people and power to work with. See what beautiful words are said of Enoch, *"Enoch walked with God; and was not, for God took him"* (Gen. 5: 24). And of Moses the prophet hear the beautiful words, *"Not so with My servant Moses; He is faithful in all My house. I speak with him face to face, even plainly, and not in dark sayings; and he sees the form of the Lord"* (Num. 12: 7, 8)

It is also the story of love in shepherding.

The Lord called Himself "the Shepherd", and called us His flock and sheep. In the Old Testament He said, *"I will feed My flock, and I will make them lie down, says the Lord God. I will seek what was lost and bring back what was driven away, bind up the broken and strengthen what was sick"* (Ezek. 34: 15, 16). And in the New Testament He said, *"My sheep hear My voice, and I know them, and they follow Me. And I give them eternal life, and they shall never perish; neither shall anyone snatch them out of My hand"* (Jn. 10: 27, 28).

Thus sang David the prophet also of this shepherding; he said, *"The Lord is my shepherd; I shall not want;*
He makes me to lie down in green pastures,
He leads me beside the still waters.
He restores my soul;
He leads me in the paths of righteousness" (Ps. 23)

We have an example of God's love, care, and concern, His care for His people in the wilderness.

His care is represented in guiding them on their way by the pillar of cloud by day and the pillar of fire by night while He Himself going before them (Ex. 13: 21, 22). He divided the Red Sea and paved a way in it for them to walk on. He brought out water from the rock, and sent them quails and manna to eat. He preserved Elijah and the widow in Zarephath during the famine (1 Kgs. 17), and fed Egypt throughout the seven years of famine (Gen. 41). The history of God's care for His people and His love need a whole book to explain.

The greatest love of God to the human race is represented in the Redemption.

To make this clear the Lord said, *"I am the good shepherd. The good shepherd gives His life for the sheep"* (Jn. 10: 11). And He explained that this is due to great love; He said, *"Greater love has no one than this, than to lay down one's life for his friends"* (Jn. 15: 13); *"For God so loved the world that He gave His only begotten Son, that whoever believes in Him should not perish but have everlasting life."* (Jn. 3: 16). In his first epistle, St. John sang the praise of this love, saying, *"In this is love, not that we loved God, but that He loved us and sent His Son to be the propitiation for our sins"* (1 Jn. 4: 10).

The depth of this love is clear in the words of St. Paul the apostle, *"But God demonstrates His own love towards us, in that while we were still sinners, Christ died for us"* (Rom. 5: 8). The words *"while we were still sinners"*, *"died for the ungodly"*, *"For scarcely for a righteous man will one die"*, these words show how deep and wonderful His love is, the perfect, the holy, the righteous to die for the ungodly!

Therefore we love Him because He loved us first, and died for us. We feel ashamed because of this love, seeing that we sin against Him who loved us so much!

GOD'S LOVE IS INEXPRESSIBLE

God the Creator of heaven and earth, King of kings and Lord of lords, alone Unlimited, to whose greatness and awe there is no end, treats man who is made of dust with deep love and friendship.

When God created man, He treated him as a friend, and in love visited him in the garden, talked to him, and gave him dominion over all creation. David the prophet mentions this way of treatment, saying, *"You have crowned him with glory and honor. You have made him to have dominion over the works of Your hands; You have put all things under his feet"* (Ps. 8: 5, 6). And in the Liturgy of St. Gregory we say: [You have made me lacking nothing of your glorious works].

Out of God's love to man, He gave him freedom, will and discretion. Even when man sinned God came to him, asking, and giving him the opportunity to defend himself.

Wonderful indeed is that inexpressible love of God! See how He speaks with His creation, not only with the righteous but even with the sinners. God even spoke with Satan and gave him the opportunity to argue.

God talked to Cain the murderer. And when Cain said, *"Surely You have driven me out this day from the face of the ground ... anyone who finds me will kill me"* (Gen. 4: 14), the Lord God answered very tenderly defending that murderer, *"whoever kills Cain, vengeance shall be taken on him sevenfold"*. Then the Lord set a mark on Cain, lest anyone finding him should kill him. Can there be more gentle treatment than this to the first murderer on the earth, that cruel-hearted man who did not refrain from killing his own righteous brother!

God talked to Judas the betrayer as well.

The Lord warned Judas more than once and entrusted him with the money box. Furthermore, before that, the Lord had called him to be an apostle. And when that betrayer drew near and kissed Him, the Lord said to him, *"Friend, why have you come?"* (Mt. 16: 50). How amazing that the Lord address that betrayer by the term "Friend"!

God even spoke to Balaam, who led the people astray afterwards, and gave him true prophecies through inspiration.

Through inspiration Balaam said, *"I seem Him, but not now; I behold Him, but not near; a star shall come out of Jacob; a Scepter shall rise out of Israel"* (Num. 20: 17). Though God knew that Balaam would be treacherous, yet it is said of him, *"the Spirit of God came upon him"* (Num. 24: 2); *"the Lord met Balaam, and put a word in his mouth"* (Num. 23: 16)!

God gave prophecy to King Saul as well.

This made the people wonder at that, saying, *"Is Saul also among the prophets?"*(1 Sam. 10: 11).

The kind gentle God allowed even Satan to speak with Him concerning Job the righteous, and to work against Job. Moreover, God permitted Satan afterwards to tempt Him on the Mount. If this is God's way with Satan, treating him so gently, how much rather with the sinners! He was so kind when He said to the sinful woman, *"Neither do I condemn you; go and sin no more"* (Jn. 8: 11).

In God's love and gentleness, He considered some persons His friends.

He called Abraham out of his land and from his family to the land which God showed him. God also called Abraham "God's friend".

In this friendship, God spoke to Abraham about some of His dispensations.

When God wanted to burn Sodom, He told Abraham about that, listened to him, and granted him his wishes, saying, *"Shall I hide from Abraham what I am doing?"* (Gen. 18: 17)

The same happened with Moses, for the Lord God used to speak to him, befriend him, and defend him.

See what God said to Aaron and Miriam about Moses in His great love, *"If there is a prophet among you, I, the Lord, make Myself known to him in a vision; I speak to him in a dream. Not so with My servant Moses; He is faithful in all My house. I speak with him face to face, even plainly, and not in dark sayings; and he sees the form of the Lord"* (Num. 12: 6-8)

How deep was God's love, and how gentle His treatment to Jonah the prophet!

Though Jonah had disobeyed God and fled from Him, God did not forsake him until he left his obstinacy. When God asked Jonah, *"Is it right for you to be angry?"*, Jonah answered, *"It is right for me to be angry, even to death!"*. Yet, God's love did not forsake him, but delivered him of his anger!

More amazing still is God's behaviour towards Jacob who deceived his father, profited from his brother's hunger and took his birthright in exchange for red stew!

God did not even rebuke Jacob with a word, but appeared to him, blessed him, encouraged him, and gave him promises, saying to him, *"Behold, I am with you and will keep you wherever you go, and will bring you back to this land"* (Gen. 28: 15). God helped him also in meeting Rachel and Laban his uncle, and gave him many riches, many children, and venerable old age.

God's gentle treatment is inexpressible, but we should not misuse His love and gentleness, neglecting His commandments. We should rather awe Him as we love Him.

How beautiful is God's loving heart in His friendship with Enoch and in taking him up to Him (Gen. 5: 24), and His friendship with Abraham, Moses, and John whom He allowed to lean on His bosom!

How amazing also is God's love towards children and young men, speaking with them, entrusting them with messages and missions, and endowing them with gifts. Among those are Samuel, Jeremiah, and David.

God's love is clear also in His generous and kind promises to man, in His gifts, in His benevolence, in His forgiveness as in many other things. His love appears in that He likes always to dwell among people, whether here or in heaven, having His pleasure in them.

That is why He says, "*lo, I am with you always, even to the end of the age*" (Mt. 28: 20); "*I go to prepare a place for you. And if I go and prepare a place for you, I will come again and receive you to Myself; that where I am, there you may be also*" (Jn. 14: 2, 3). Therefore the heavenly Jerusalem is described as "*the tabernacle of God with men*" (Rev. 21: 3)

How beautiful it is to be in God's good company which He, in His love, grants us that we may be with Him here and there, now and forever.

On the Last Day, "*every eye will see Him, even they who pierced Him. And all the tribes of the earth will mourn because of Him*" (Rev. 1: 7). The most painful thing in the cross is that Christ was wounded in the house of His friends! (Zech. 13: 6)

God's wonderful love was given to all. He loved the sinners, so He saved them; and He loved the righteous, so He crowned them.

He loved the young and the old. He loved the young David and chose him as His own anointed and prophet. He taught him to play the flute and the harp, and trained his hands for war and his fingers for battle. Likewise, He loved the child Samuel, spoke to him and sent with him a message to the great priest.

God loved us and made us temples of His Holy Spirit and stewards of His divine mystries.

He is the gentle good God, who is loved by whoever has intimacy with Him. When David became His intimate, he said, "*Oh, taste and see that the Lord is good*". God's love is "*better than wine*" (Song 1: 2), by which those who loved Him became drunk.

The most amazing in God's love is that He ascribes His own works to His children!

Many many miracles are attributed to St. George, or to archangel Michael, or to the Virgin Mary. These miracles are worked by God Himself, but out of His love and humbleness He ascribes them to His saints. He calls His houses by the names of His saints. So we say the church of so-and-so, though it is the Church of God. Even His law, He sometimes called it the Law of Moses!

It is marvelous love indeed, that God introduces His children and distinguishes them.

In humble love the Lord says to His apostles, "*he who believes in Me, the works that I do he will do also, and greater works than these he will do*" (Jn. 14: 12)!!

Wonderful also is God's love, evident in His goodness towards His children. When Abraham asked to have a child in his old age and though his wife was barren, He gave them offspring like the stars of heaven and the sand of the sea in number!

In His love, He says, *"No longer do I call you servants ... but I have called you friends"* (Jn. 15: 15)

He does not only call us "friends", but He also calls us "children", not only in the New Testament, but He did so in the Old Testament as well. In the Song of Songs He called the Church His bride. And in the New Testament He called the Church a virgin betrothed by the apostle to Christ.

In His love, He says of our sins, *"I will forgive their iniquity, and their sin I will remember no more"* (Jer. 31: 34). With His love He washes us and we become whiter than snow (Ps. 51: 7)

God will not remember our sins, that is, He will not reproach us or remind us of them. He will not put them before Him in His dealing with us. He puts His love between Himself and our sins to hide them, or covers them with His blood and they no more appear.

When the lost son faced his father's love he could not say *"Make me like one of your hired servants"* (Lk. 15: 19)

The great love of the Father made him not remember also the divine love which made him a new creation, whiter than snow. The old things, that is the sins, vanished from His sight, and love alone remained.

It is that love which made Augustine feel ashamed and say: I delayed long in loving You.

GOD'S RELATIONSHIP WITH MAN BEGINS WITH GIVING

God has given, and always gives

He gives, and by this giving He gives us a lesson in giving.

He gives us without our request, and far beyond our request; He gives us with an openhand.

He gives us as a Father caring for His children, giving them good gifts.

Let us see then the story of giving in the relationship between God and man:

1. Our coming into existence is the first gift:

We remember this in the Liturgy of St. Gregory, for we say, [You have made me when I was not]. Had not God granted us this gift of existence, we would have been nothing. Therefore the first gift was that God created us.

God did not create us to glorify Him on the earth.

God is not in need of being glorified by us. Before creating us He had been glorified by the nature and by the angels. Even before creating the nature and the angels, He had been and still is glorified in His own divine attributes. He is glorified in His infinite majesty, in His omnipresence, in His omnipotence, and in His holiness. He needs not to be glorified by His creation.

Therefore we say also in the Holy Mass [You were not in need of my servitude, but it is I who am in need of Your Lordship]

God created us out of His goodness and righteousness. He was alone since eternity, but His excessive humbleness made Him create other beings to exist with Him. His kindness granted existence to the non existent.

2. God's wonderful gift is giving us His image and likeness:

God created man in His own image and likeness, in righteousness, in holiness, in reasoning, in utterance, in understanding, in immortality, and in free will, as well as in power as He gave man rule over the animals of the earth, the birds of the air, and the fish of the sea (Gen. 1).

3. God prepared everything for the comfort of man before creating him:

He created nature for man: He made light first, then water and plants, and finally created him. Therefore in the Liturgy of St. Gregory we address God, saying, [You have raised heaven for me as a ceiling, and paved the ground for me to walk on ... For me You have silenced the sea and tamed the animals. You left me in need of nothing of Your kindness]

For man, God created the sun to provide him with light by day and the moon and stars to provide light by night. God gave him food to eat, birds to sing for him, nature to enjoy its scenery, and all capabilities helping him to live.

4. God gave man health, power, and beauty:

When God created man, he was very beautiful with purity adding to his beauty. Man was physically strong and healthy, free from all physical and psychological diseases. He was perfect physically, psychologically, and spiritually

5. God gave man rule over everything:

God gave this same power (Gen. 1: 28) to Noah, and said to Noah the same words, *"Be fruitful and multiply, and fill the earth. And the fear of you and the dread of you shall be on every beast of the earth, on every bird of the air, on all that move on the earth, and on all the fish of the sea"* (Gen. 9: 1, 2). In the ark Noah had all the beasts with him and he had rule over them.

Man lost his rule over nature because of his sin. Man was not used to eat meat, or to hunt animals, or even to put them in cages to enjoy watching them. Therefore, there was no enmity between man and animals, and they would not kill or do him any harm. All creation was one family presided by Adam and God taking care of them.

6. The blessing is one of God's gifts to man:

God blessed Adam and Eve (Gen. 1: 28), and blessed Noah and his sons (Gen. 9: 1). He blessed Abram and said to him, *"I will bless you and make your name great; and you shall be a blessing ... in you all the families of the earth shall be blessed"* (Gen. 12: 2, 3). God gave the blessing also to the whole people on Mount Gerizim (Deut. 27: 12). Many details on the blessing are mentioned in (Deut. 28). However the blessings were given on condition that the people obey the Lord God, as it is said, *"And all the blessings shall come upon you and overtake you, because you obey the voice of the Lord your God"* (Deut. 28: 2-6)

Then God began to give the blessing to the people on the mouths of the prophets and clergy, as well as on the mouths of the elders and the parents. Our father Noah was a blessing to the whole world, and but for him the world would have perished at the time of the flood. God preserved him for us as a blessing and extension for the human race.

7. God gave man the grace of His friendship:

Our father Abraham was called by some "God's friend". And when God wanted to burn Sodom, He said, *"Shall I hide from Abraham what I am doing?"* (Gen. 18: 17). Thus God revealed to Abraham His intention and allowed him to argue the matter with Him. God even accepted Abraham's intercession for the condemned city because he is His friend!

The same happened when God wanted to destroy the whole people for worshipping the golden calf, He told Moses the prophet about that and allowed him to argue and to ask Him not to do. Moses was really God's friend as God said to Aaron and Miriam, *"If there is a prophet among you, I, the Lord, make Myself known to him in a vision; I speak to him in a dream. Not so with My servant Moses; He is faithful in all My house. I speak with him face to face, even plainly, and not in dark sayings; and he sees the form of the Lord. Why then were you not afraid to speak against My servant Moses?"* (Num. 12: 6-8). Then God inflicted a punishment on Miriam.

Among the wonderful examples of God's friendship is Enoch whose life is summarized in one amazing phrase, *"And Enoch walked with God; and he was not, for God took him"* (Gen. 5: 24). Enoch was God's friend, and God took him into heaven. That great father has not died up till now. Would that the great prophet Moses had wrote more about our father Enoch! However, Jude the apostle recorded a prophecy said by our father Enoch, which says, *"Now Enoch, the seventh from Adam, prophesied about these men also, saying: Behold, the Lord comes with ten thousands of His saints, to execute judgment on all ..."* (Jude 14, 15). This prophecy is not recorded in the Books of Moses, but the tradition kept it till Jude the apostle received it and wrote it. The subject of the prophecy, that is the second coming of the Lord at the end of the days, Enoch knew from God Himself who spoke to Enoch as a friend.

This friendship is mentioned also in the New Testament where St. John says, *"having loved His own who were in the world, He loved them to the end"* (Jn. 13: 1); "His own" here means His friends. In another place it is written, *"but I have called you friends"* (Jn. 15: 15). It is true friendship and companionship, but there is still more than that: that is tasting.

8. God gave His beloved to taste Him:

Thus says David the prophet, *"Oh, taste and see that the Lord is good"* (Ps. 34: 8). This tasting cannot be understood by the mind, but it is felt by the spirit. The mind stands astonished before that.

9. God gave humanity the grace of filiality:

He gave them the grace of becoming His children. For the first time the words *"sons of God"* were mentioned in (Gen. 6: 2). God used to address man as His son, saying, *"My son, give Me your heart"* (Prov. 23: 26). And Isaiah the prophet addressed God as Father; he said, *"But now, O Lord, You are our Father"* (Isa. 65: 8). God Himself said blaming His people for their sins, *"I have nourished and brought up children, and they have rebelled against Me"* (Isa. 1: 2).

In the New Testament, it is more clear that God is the Father of the human beings. The words *"the heavenly Father"* are repeated as in (Mt. 5-8). The Lord taught us to pray and say, *"Our Father in heaven"* (Lk. 11: 2) (Mt. 6: 9)

10. God gave also His elect honor and glory:

The Lord said, *"He who receives you receives Me"* (Mt. 10: 40); *"If anyone serves Me, him My Father will honor"* (Jn. 12: 26)

As for glory, it is said, *"For whom He foreknew, He also predestined to be conformed to the image of His Son ... these He also glorified"* (Rom. 8: 29, 30); *"if indeed we suffer with Him, that we may also be glorified together"* (Rom 8: 17). See also the wonderful words which the Son says to the Father, *"And the glory which You gave Me I have given them"* (Jn. 17: 22)!

11. God gave us the glory of the resurrection:

Through the resurrection, we rise in a glorified body. The apostle said of this, *"the Lord Jesus Christ, who will transform our lowly body that it may be conformed to His glorious body"* (Phil. 3: 21). The apostle explained also the glory of that body, that it will become a spiritual body and a heavenly body which will rise in glory (1 Cor. 15: 42-49).

12. God gave humanity the grace of continuity:

He gave humanity this grace through marriage; for He created them male and female, and said to them, *"Be fruitful and multiply"* (Gen. 1: 27, 28). He said the same words afterwards to Noah and his sons (Gen. 9: 1); for after the flood God kept us through Noah's family so that humanity might continue on the earth.

13. God gave humanity the grace of immortality:

He gave the human beings an immortal spirit, and granted them an eternal life. This eternal life is mentioned many times in the Scriptures as when speaking about the judgment of the wicked and the righteous, *"And these will go away into everlasting punishment, but the righteous into eternal life"* (Mt. 25: 46). And the Lord said to Martha, *"He who believes in Me, though he may die, he shall live. And whoever lives and believes in Me shall never die"* (Jn. 11: 25, 26). Thus we knew about *"the crown of life"* (Rev. 2: 10)

14. * God, because of His love, gave man good gifts:

For the apostle says, *"Every good gift and every perfect gift is from above, and comes down from the Father of lights"* (Jas. 1: 17). And St. Paul the apostle indicated these gifts in a full chapter (1 Cor. 12) where he said, *"There are diversities of gifts, but the same Spirit"*, *"But the manifestation of the Spirit is given to each one for the profit of all"*. He mentioned some of these gifts, then he said, *"But one and the same Spirit works all these things, distributing to each one individually as He wills"* (1 Cor. 12: 4-11)

* God gave some persons peculiar gifts:

God gave Solomon wisdom, dignity, and honor (1 Kgs. 3: 12, 13). To Samson God gave strength (Jud. 14: 5, 6), and to Balaam He gave revelation so Balaam became *"the man whose eyes are opened"* (Num. 24: 15). God gave also some persons the gift of working miracles and wonders, as He gave to the apostles.

15. God gave man the honor of working with Him:

God gave this grace to the prophets, to the apostles, and to all ranks of priesthood and ministers. Therefore St. Paul the apostle said about himself and Apollos, *"For we are God's fellow workers"* (1 Cor. 3: 9). He gave them the ministry of reconciliation to reconcile people to God (2 Cor. 5: 18, 20). He gave the priests the ministry of administering the divine mysteries, *"as servants of Christ and stewards of the mysteries of God"* (1 Cor. 4: 1). He gave them the power to speak His word and witness to Him (Acts 1: 8), and said to them, *"it is not you who speak, but the Spirit of your Father who speaks in you"* (Mt. 10: 20). He gave some to be workers or vinedressers in His vineyard (Mt. 21: 33). And as God allows us to work with Him or to do His work, He also works in us, with us, and through us.

16. He gave all those the grace of the divine call:

St. Paul the apostle said about himself, *"... God, who separated me from my mother's womb and called me through His grace ..."* (Gal. 1: 15). And the Holy Spirit said, *"Now separate to Me Barnabas and Saul for the work to which I have called them"* (Acts 13: 2). The Lord, in the New Testament, called His apostles and disciples (Mt. 10; Lk. 10) and, in the Old Testament, He called our father Abraham (Gen. 12). The call was extended to many people such as Jeremiah to whom the Lord said, *"Before I formed you in the womb I knew you; before you were born I sanctified you; I ordained you a prophet to the nations"* (Jer. 1: 5). And as the apostle said, *"For whom He foreknew, He also predestined ... these He also called"* (Rom. 8: 29, 30)

17. Among God's gifts to humanity are the angels whom God sent to assist them:

* God sent the angels to guide the people spiritually; for, *"Are they not all ministering spirits sent forth to minister for those who will inherit salvation"* (Heb. 1: 14). An example of their ministry is Angel Gabriel who God sent to interpret the vision to Daniel the prophet (Da. 8: 16).

* Another rank of the angels God sent to protect and save people, as the angel who freed Peter from prison (Acts 12), and the angel who opened the prison gates for Paul in Philippi (Acts 16). God sent an angel to save Daniel and shut the mouths of the lions (Da. 6: 22). As the Psalm says, *"The angel of the Lord encamps all around those who fear Him, and delivers them"* (Ps. 34: 7)

* God sent angels also to give people good news, as the angel sent to Zacharias the priest to say to him, *"your wife Elizabeth will bear you a son ... he will be great in the sight of the Lord ... He will also be filled with the Holy Spirit, even from his mother's womb"* (Lk. 1: 12-15). God sent angels also to announce the Lord's Resurrection (Mt. 28) (Lk. 24). Much can be said about the angels' ministry to mankind, but time is lacking in this book.

18. Sanctification is another gift from God to people:

God sent His Holy Spirit to dwell in people as the apostle says, *"Do you not know that you are the temple of God and that the Spirit of God dwells in you?"* (1 Cor. 3: 16). We get this gift through the holy anointing (1 Jn. 2: 20, 27) with the holy myron (chrismation). This gift was usually given previously by the laying on of hands, as the apostles had done for the Samaritans (Acts 8) and the Ephesians (Acts 19).

19. One of God's gifts for our salvation is repentance:

For, *"God has also granted to the Gentiles repentance to life"* (Acts 11: 18). God knows our weak nature and that we may fall and sin, therefore He gave us repentance by which our sins can be blotted out. And whoever turns from his wicked ways shall live and not die, for the Lord does not have any pleasure that the wicked should die, but that he turns from his ways and live (Ezek. 18: 23).

20. God gave us care and protection:

The psalmist says, *"If it had not been the Lord who was on our side when men rose up against us, then they would have swallowed us alive ... Our soul has escaped as a bird from the snare of the fowlers; the snare is broken, and we have escaped. Our help is in the name of the Lord, who made heaven and earth"* (Ps. 124: 2, 7, 8). And the Lord said to St. Paul the apostle, *"no one will attack you to hear you"* (Acts 18: 10), and to Jeremiah the prophet He said, *"They will fight against you, but they shall not prevail against you. For I am with you, says the Lord, to deliver you"* (Jer. 1: 19). To Joshua the son of Nun God said, *"as I was with Moses, so I will be with you. I will not leave you nor forsake you. Be strong and of good courage ... do not be afraid, nor be dismayed, for the Lord your God is with you wherever you go"* (Josh. 1: 5, 9). He said about the church, *"the gates of Hades shall not prevail against it"* (Mt. 16: 18)

21. The greatest gift given us by God is salvation by Redemption:

"For God so loved the world that He gave His only begotten Son, that whoever believes in Him should not perish but have everlasting life" (Jn. 3: 16). He gave us His holy blood on the altar for the forgiveness of sins, and gave us also baptism by which we get the deserts of His blood as He said, *"He who believes and is baptized will be saved"* (Mk. 16: 16)

22. God's gifts cannot actually be counted:

All that is mentioned on these pages are mere examples. Suffice the many promises for those who conquer, which God uttered to the angels of the seven churches in the Book of Revelation (Rev. 2, 3). Whoever denies God's gifts has eyes which do not see.

THE COVENANT BETWEEN GOD AND THE PEOPLE

The Covenant with man was initiated by God. God started a relationship with man

God wanted to have a relationship with man based on conditions. He, on His part, fulfilled His promises and was faithful to His word in spite of our unfaithfulness. As the apostle says, *"If we are faithless, He remains faithful; He cannot deny Himself"* (2 Tim. 2: 13). God's covenant with man is an everlasting covenant.

The first covenant between God and man was in the days of Noah, before and after their entry into the ark.

God put a condition that man comes out of the evil world, condemned to die and perish, and enter the ark in a covenant with God. God, on His part promised man life, safety, and peace under His care. Noah and his children entered into the covenant, and God blessed them.

And when the ark landed, and Noah offered an acceptable burnt offering, the Lord smelled a soothing aroma, and said, *"I set My rainbow in the cloud, and it shall be for the sign of the covenant between Me and the earth. It shall be, when I bring a cloud over the earth, that the rainbow shall be seen in the cloud; and I will remember My covenant which is between Me and you and every living creature ... the waters shall never again become a flood to destroy all flesh ... everlasting covenant"* (Gen. 9: 13-16)

The second covenant was that between God and Abram the father of fathers.

This second covenant was when God said to Abram, "*Get out of your country, from your family and from your father's house, to a land that I will show you. I will make you a great nation; I will bless you ... and in you all the families of the earth shall be blessed*" (Gen. 12: 1-3).

Another covenant with Abram was "the circumcision covenant"

God said to Abraham, "*This is My covenant which you shall keep, between Me and you and your descendants after you: Every male child among you shall be circumcised ... and it shall be a sign of the covenant between Me and you ... And the uncircumcised male child, who is not circumcised in the flesh of his foreskin, that person shall be cut off from his people*" (Gen. 17: 10-14)

Circumcision was a symbol of the death of the body to gain life.

Part of the body was to be cut, that is to die, as a symbol of the death of the body and material. Circumcision was thus a symbol of baptism in which we die with Christ in order to have life with Him. The circumcision covenant stipulated that the uncircumcised should be cut off from his people, and likewise the unbaptized.

It is noteworthy that the covenant embodied blessing as well as punishment

The blessing is such as that in the covenant which put an end to the flood and destruction to whoever entered the ark. The ark was a symbol of the life which whoever enters the church obtains (the church being also symbolized by the ark). Who enters the church obtains the blessing which was obtained by those who entered the ark through God's protection. The blessing is also clear in the covenant made with Abraham when he left the world for God's sake. However there was a punishment to whoever did not keep the promise, such as the punishment of the person who was not circumcised.

Both the blessing and the punishment were together in the written covenant: the Law covenant, as evident from (Deut. 28). This chapter contained blessings to whoever obeys the words of the Lord, and curses to whoever does not obey.

The covenant given Moses by the Lord was sprinkled with blood. It was for the first time a written covenant, to all the people, accompanied by a blessing and a curse.

"And Moses took ... the Book of the Covenant and read in the hearing of the people. And they said: All that the Lord has said we will do, and be obedient. And Moses took the blood, sprinkled it on the people, and said: This is the blood of the covenant which the Lord has made with you according to all these words" (Ex. 24: 6-8)

The Ten Commandments were likewise a covenant between God and the people.

The commandments we written on two tablets "The tablets of the covenant". They were placed in an ark "the ark of covenant". The ark of covenant was a symbol of God's presence with the people; God amidst His people. As long as the people kept God's commandment, God was their God and they His people. For this covenant God gave them the commandments; if they kept them God would keep and bless them.

God's commandments as a whole as well as His Scriptures were a covenant.

God's Scriptures in the old times were, and still are, called "The Old Testament", whereas His Scriptures after the coming of the Lord Christ are called "The New Testament". These Scriptures are a covenant between God and us. We became believers on this basis: that we keep the commandments included therein.

Whenever you look at the Scriptures, remember the covenant between you and God.

So long as we are God's children, and so long as we are in the faith, we are committed to keep the covenant and whatever is implied therein. We have to say as our fathers said, "*All that the Lord has spoken we will do*" (Ex. 19: 8). It is also a covenant sprinkled with blood.

Hence St. Paul the apostle described the Lord Christ as "*Mediator of a better covenant, which was established on better promises*" (Heb. 8: 6).

Indeed they are better promises. The land in the Old Testament was a symbol of the Land of the Living in the New Testament. Its being a land "*flowering with milk and honey*" was a symbol of the things which "*Eye has not seen, nor ear heard, nor have entered into the heart of man*". And the multitude of children refer to the spreading of faith and the multitude of believers. Likewise the long life is a symbol of eternity.

Another covenant we make with God is that of the baptism.

In baptism we reject the devil and all his evil doings, intrigues, thoughts, and forces. We declare it expressly "We reject you, O devil, we reject you, we reject you".

But do we still reject the devil and keep our promises? In baptism we promise to believe on the Lord and to follow His ways in the new life in which we have put on Christ.

Another covenant is that we make with the Lord in the holy communion and in repentance.

As for the covenant of the holy communion, the Lord says to us in the holy Mass [Every time you eat of this bread and drink of this cup, you proclaim my death, and confess my resurrection, and remember me till I come]. But do we – whenever we partake of the holy communion- proclaim the Lord's death for our sake and our death with Him? Do we proclaim His resurrection by which He raised us from the death of sin? Do we remember Him and continue to do so till He comes again? Or do we partake of the holy communion and make many promises, then after a day or two we forget as if we have promised nothing nor committed ourselves anything on the day of partaking!

All our vows are covenants between us and God

We are sometimes pressed by diseases, troubles, wishes, or needs, in these cases we give vows which may sometimes be beyond our ability to fulfill. Then we try to cancel, change, replace, or defer, but in all this we forget the words of the Scriptures,

"Better not to vow than to vow and not pay" **(Eccl. 5: 5)**

A covenant with God is worth seriousness and commitment. We should be aware with whom we enter into agreement or to whom we promise: it is with God, the Creator, the Unlimited, the Uncomprehensible, and Lord of lords.

We should know the punishment of the person who breaks the promise.

St. Paul the apostle mentioned this punishment in his Epistle to the Hebrews, where he said, *"Of how much worse punishment, do you suppose, will he be thought worthy who has trampled the Son of God underfoot, counted the blood of the covenant by which he was sanctified a common thing, and insulted the Spirit of grace? ... It is a fearful thing to fall into the hands of the living God."* (Heb. 10: 29-31)

Even God's covenants with the forefathers, they all are covenants with us ourselves.

Hence Moses the prophet said, *"The Lord our God made a covenant with us in Horeb. The Lord did not make this covenant with our fathers, but with us, those who are here today, all of us who are alive"* (Deut. 5: 2, 3). Yea, with us also the Lord made those covenants mentioned in the Scriptures, and we are committed to fulfill them all.

Our covenants with the Lord are sprinkled with blood, established on the blood of Christ.

All the grace we obtain in the Holy Sacraments are based on the deserts of the blood of Christ. Therefore, the apostle, speaking about the sanctification of the believers, mentions *"the blood of the covenant by which he was sanctified"*. In the Baptism Sacrament, our sins are abolished by the blood of Christ. The same happens through the Sacrament of repentance. And in the Eucharist Sacrament we partake of Christ's blood, which sanctifies everything.

Beautiful indeed are the words of David the prophet, *"Accept, I pray, the freewill offerings of my mouth, O Lord"* (Ps. 119: 108). Let us then ask the Lord to give us the power to fulfill our promises.

However I wonder that some people promise things beyond their ability and recognize this only at the time of fulfillment. Then seeing they are not able, they recognize that they promised unreasonably. Those perhaps make covenants without consulting their father confessors and obtaining their agreement.

Another thing I wonder at is that a person may impose punishment on himself before God when making the covenant! How awful it is for a person to say in the covenant: If I do not do such and such, strike me, O Lord, with blindness (or take the life of my son, or take my life ... etc)! And when such a person feels unable to fulfill what he had promised, he becomes afraid of the punishment.

Yet, though we make no new covenants, we are committed to fulfill the covenants we made in declaring our faith, in baptism, in repentance, and in the holy communion. Throughout our holy life with the Lord, we should not make new covenants but we renew the old covenants. Would that the Lord give us the power to be faithful to Him!

GOD'S BLESSING TO THE PEOPLE

Blessing is something felt rather than expressed in words.

The blessing may be whatever God's hand offers us of the work of His grace in our life. The blessing, as such, involves abundance, success, satisfaction, and expansion.

Blessed Persons:

The blessing is mentioned from the very beginning of the creation.

God blessed our forefathers and said to them, "*Be fruitful and multiply; fill the earth and subdue it; have dominion over ... ...*" (Gen. 1: 28). That blessing meant multiplicity and dominion. And the same blessing was given Noah and his children after the flood (Gen. 9: 1, 2).

Another blessing given by the Lord is that given to our father Abram, as the Lord said to him, "*I will make you a great nation; I will bless you and make your name great; I will bless those who bless you, and I will curse him who curses you; and in you all the families of the earth shall be blessed*" (Gen. 12: 2-3)

Examples of other blessings are:

The blessing Jacob asked the Lord to give him when the Lord wrestled with him, "*I will not let You go unless You bless me*" (Gen. 32: 26). The apostle also mentions such blessings of the Lord, saying, *"blessed us with every spiritual blessing"* (Eph. 1: 3). Suffice the words of the Lord Christ to those on His right hand, *"Come, you blessed of My Father, inherit the kingdom prepared for you from the foundation of the world"* (Mt. 25: 34). What a blessing from the Father to His children!

The blessing and keeping the commandments:

One may wonder: God does not speak to me directly like those, how then could I obtain God's blessing and be sure of that?

In fact, one can obtain God's blessing through keeping His commandments; it is the blessing of obedience.

The link between the blessing and keeping the commandments is asserted by God in the Book of Deuteronomy:

"If you diligently obey the voice of the Lord your God, to observe carefully all His commandments ... Blessed shall you be in the city, and blessed shall you be in the country. Blessed shall be the fruit of your body, the produce of your ground and the increase of your herds, the increase of your cattle and the offspring of your flocks. Blessed shall be your basket and your kneading bowl. Blessed shall you be when you come in, and blessed shall you be when you go out. The Lord will command the blessing on you in your storehouses and in all to which you set your hand" (Deut. 28: 1-8).

An example of this is the Lord's tithes commandment and the Lord's right to one's money.

Some may exclaim how one's income would suffice if the tithes were cut so long as the whole income is not sufficient! Truly the nine tenths with blessing is much more than the whole income without blessing. We often see some people with large income which is not sufficient for them because there is no blessing in their money.

Take for example "the land", the Lord God ordered that the seventh year be a sabbath, without sowing or gathering and God would bless the produce of the sixth year to suffice for both the sixth and the seventh years. That is why we pray in the Blessing Litany, saying "O God, who blessed the produce of the sixth year ...".

When God blesses a land, it gives plenty of fruit.

A good land can give a thirty, sixty, or hundredfold according to the Lord's blessing. On the contrary is the land that have no blessing, for God said hard words about such a land to Cain after his sinning, *"When you till the ground, it shall no longer yield its strength to you"* (Gen. 4: 12)

The same can be said about the Sabbath Commandment and time with the Lord's blessing.

One should not say time is not sufficient, even the seven days of the week are not sufficient, how much more if one day is lost! The same answer can be said here: six days with blessing are better than seven without blessing. God can bless even one hour to yield fruit more than numerous days without blessing. Seek then God's blessing.

Another example is the spirituality of ministry

The ministry blessed by the Lord yields fruit, even though very simply or short in time. God blessed the feeble effort to have deep effect. Therefore ask for the Lord's blessing for your ministry, for what avails is not the amount of ministry or the preparation for it, but the Lord's blessing which makes it successful.

Sources of blessing:

One may obtain the blessing directly from God.

This can be through putting one's work in God's hand. One stone in David's sling did what a whole army could not do. This is because David slung it in the name of the Lord of hosts (1 Sam. 17: 45, 46).

The stone was put in God's hand before being put in the sling.

The same can be said about the five loaves and two fish. When this small amount was put in the Lord's hand, five thousands ate and were filled, and moreover twelve baskets were left full.

Thus in order to obtain blessing, you should keep the commandments, and put all your work and your talents in God's hand.

One can also obtain God's blessing from the men of God who were bearers of His blessing.

When Elijah the prophet went into the house of the widow of Zarephath of Sidon, the blessing entered her house. Thus the Lord blessed the bin of flour and the jar of oil, so they kept full to the end of the famine. It was God's blessing received through His man.

The holy people were not merely bearing the blessing, but were themselves a blessing.

This is clear in the Lord's words to Abram, *"you shall be a blessing"* (Gen. 12: 2). Likewise, Elijah was a blessing in the widow's house, and Elisha was a blessing in the house of

Shunammite woman. Joseph also was a blessing in Potiphar's house, in the prison, in the land of Egypt, and wherever he went.

This makes us seek always the blessing of God's holy people, and we keep their relics for blessing in our churches and monasteries.

There is also the blessing of the priesthood and spiritual fathers.

God grants His blessing on the mouths of those fathers. An example of this is our father Abraham who received blessing from Melchizedek the priest of God Most High (Gen. 14: 18, 19). Another example is Hannah the mother of Samuel who received blessing from Eli the priest. These are only few examples from among countless cases.

God's blessing can also be obtained through one's own parents.

Isaac blessed his sons: *"By faith Isaac blessed Jacob and Esau"* (Heb. 11: 20).

Jacob asked Joseph his son to bring his sons Ephraim and Manasseh to have his blessing: *"Please bring them to me, and I will bless them"* (Gen. 48: 9).

Noah also: whom he blessed from among his sons became blessed, and whom he cursed (Canaan) became cursed (Gen. 9: 24-26). Therefore the Scriptures call upon us to obtain the blessing of the parents, *"Honor your father and your mother that it may be well with you and you may live long on the earth"* (Ex. 20: 12) (Deut. 5: 16) (Eph. 6: 2).

The blessing can also be obtained through serving the needy.

God gives you blessing when you have compassion on the needy; for the Lord said, *"inasmuch as you did it to one of the least of these My brethren, you did it to Me"* (Mt. 25: 40). By this you receive the blessing of the hungry whom you feed, the sick whom you visit, and every needy person you help. See what amazing words did Job the righteous say, *"The blessing of a perishing man came upon me"* (Job 29: 13). He meant that he gained the blessing of the person who was perishing and he saved!

Whenever you give something, you receive blessing

Whenever you give for building a church, you are not in fact giving, but rather receiving the blessing of participating in building a church. When you offer some vessels for the church altar, you are not actually giving, but receiving the blessing of these vessels.

We obtain blessing from the holy places which God has blessed.

It is true that God is present everywhere, but there are certain places that have a special blessing. See what David the prophet says, *"How lovely is Your tabernacle, O Lord of hosts! My soul longs, yes, even faints for the courts of the Lord"* (Ps. 84: 1); *"I was glad when they said to me: Let us go into the house of the Lord"* (Ps. 122: 1). But what is the reason? *"For there the Lord commanded the blessing, life forever"* (Ps. 133: 3)

The blessing can be given by a word of blessing, or by other means.

The blessing can be given by the laying on of hands for blessing, as when the Lord Christ blessed the children; it is said, *"He took them up in His arms, laid His hands on them, and blessed them"* (Mk. 10: 16).

It can also be given by making the sign of the cross, because the cross is the source of every blessing.

Another means for obtaining the blessing is through the sprinkling of water prayed on, for God said, *"Then I will sprinkle clear water on you, and you shall be clean"* (Ezek. 36: 25).

The holy Sacraments are also a means of obtaining blessing.

Faith likewise is another means of obtaining blessing, for it is said, *"So then those who are of faith are blessed with believing Abraham"* (Gal. 3: 9).

Numerous are the means of obtaining blessing, but we should seek it with all our power, not only material blessing of our income, but rather more spiritual blessing. For through the spiritual blessing we obtain gifts and fruit of the Spirit as well as the Lord's help in our spiritual life.

Would that your life be a blessing to you and to others!

Would that everyone who meets you feels that he has gained a blessing through such a meeting! Let your words and your behaviour flow over with blessing. The most effective people are those whose lives are a blessing to many generations even after their departure from the world.

122

GOD IS THE GOD OF ALL

"The earth is the Lord's, and all its fullness, the world and those who dwell therein" (Ps. 24: 1).

Everything is the Lord's, and He is the Lord of all.

He is the Lord of all and Creator of all. He cares for all, controls all and manages all.

He is the Lord of the angels, the human beings, the animals, the birds, and even of the inanimate nature.

"God created the heavens and the earth" (Gen. 1: 1). Hence God is the God of heaven with everything in it, and the God of earth with everything on it, beneath it and in between it and heaven.

He is the God of the fields; for He provides them with water and they live and grow. He is the God of the flowers in the fields, and the God of the bees that suck the nectar of the flowers and turn it into honey. He is the God of man who eats the honey made of the nectar.

He is the God of the birds that neither sow nor reap nor gather into barns and He feeds them (Mt. 6: 26). He is the God of the lilies of the field that neither toil nor spin, yet even Solomon in all his glory was not arrayed like one of them (Mt. 6: 28, 29). He is the God of the bird, saving it from the snare of the fowlers (Ps. 124: 7). He is also the God of the flowers that set the snare for the bird.

He gives to the beast its food and to the young ravens that cry (Ps. 147: 9). He even provides food to the worm that creeps beneath the stones!

He is the God of the spirits and the bodies, the God of those living on the earth and the dead who departed the present world.

He is the God of all, of all the peoples of the world.

He is the God of the Jews, the Gentiles, the Samaritans, and all the peoples all over the world. Some thought – wrongly - that the Lord Christ came for the Jews only! Nay, He came for the whole humanity, as He said to His disciples before His ascension, *"Go therefore and make disciples of all the nations ... teaching them to observe all things that I have commanded you"* (Mt. 28: 19, 20). He said also,

"Go into all the world and preach the gospel to every creature" (Mk. 16: 15)

And He said also, *"But you shall receive power when the Holy Spirit has come upon you; and you shall be witnesses to Me in Jerusalem, and in all Judea and Samaria, and to the end of the earth"* (Acts 1: 8). God is the God of all people, here and in the eternal life. This is clear in the words of St. John the apostle in the Revelation: *"After these things I looked, and behold, a great multitude which no one could number, of all nations, tribes, peoples, and tongues, standing before the throne and before the Lamb, clothed with white robes, with palm branches in their hands, and crying out with a loud voice, saying: Salvation belongs to our God who sits on the throne, and to the Lamb"* (Rev. 7: 9, 10)

Speaking further about faith, we remember that in our daily prayers we say, [O Christ ... who calls all men to salvation for the promised forthcoming rewards]. And the apostle says, *"God our Savior, who desires all men to be saved and to come to the knowledge of the truth" (1 Tim. 2: 3, 4).* For our sake He sent the prophets and the apostles, and appointed pastors and teachers as the apostle says to us: *"And He Himself gave some to be apostles, some prophets, some evangelists, and some pastors and teachers, for the equipping of the saints for the work of ministry, for the edifying of the body of Christ till we all come to the unity of the faith ... "* (Eph. 4: 11-13)

In this one body various members exist, and God is the God of all types of people. He is the God of the strong as well as the weak.

He is the God of the strong like Samson and Gideon (Heb. 11: 32, 33), *"who through faith subdued kingdoms ... stopped the mouths of lions, quenched the violence of fire"*, and like David the prophet who conquered Goliath and was described as *"a mighty man of valor, a man of war"* (1 Sam. 16: 18). He is the God of Zerubbabel to whom God said in the Book of Zechariah, *"Who are you, O great mountain? Before Zerubbabel you shall become a plain!"* (Zech. 4: 7). He is the God of strong persons like Nehemiah who built the walls of Jerusalem, and Ezra who cleansed the people of their sins.

However, God is the God of the weak also.

He is the God of Jacob who trembled from his brother Esau and prayed to the Lord, saying, *"Deliver me, I pray, from the hand of Esau; for I fear him, lest he come and attack me and the mother with the children"* (Gen. 32: 11). He is the God of Abel who was killed by his brother Cain, and the God of all those who were arrested, imprisoned, scourged and slain with the sword, becoming martyrs for His name. He is the God of John the Baptist whose head was cut off and offered on a platter to the daughter of Herodias (Mt. 14: 11), and the God of Stephen the first deacon who was stoned by the Jews, and while gazing into heaven he saw the glory of God and the heavens opened (Acts 7: 55, 56)

He is the God of the wise and the simple

He is the God of Solomon the wise, or rather the wisest person on the earth, and Paul the apostle, the educated man who was brought up at the feet of Gamaliel (Acts 22: 3). He is the God of Moses the prophet who was learned in all the wisdom of the Egyptians (Acts 7: 22), and Arsanius the teacher of the kings' sons, and Athanasius the greatest theologian whose brilliancy was revealed in the Nicaea Ecumenical Council.

He is also the God of the ignorant with whom He put to shame the wise (1 Cor. 1: 27), and the apostles who were mere fishers, as well as St. Paul who left the worldly wisdom and was given heavenly wisdom from high.

He is the God of the sick as well as of the healthy.

He is the God of that sick man at Bethesda who had an infirmity thirty-eight years and had no man to put him into the pool, but finally he found Him saying to him, *"Rise, take up your bed and walk"* (Jn. 5: 5-8). He is the God of all those suffering of various diseases and He laid His hands on everyone of them and healed them (Lk. 4: 40). Yet He is also the God of the healthy, giving them strength.

He is the God of the righteous whom He loved, and the sinners whom He led to repentance.

He is the God of the fathers and the prophets whom He foreknow, predestined, called, justified, and also glorified (Rom. 8: 29, 30). He is the God of the saints in the wilderness with all their holiness, and the God of Augustine, Moses the black, Pelagia, and Mary the Coptic. He turned all those from sin to repentance and even to high levels of holiness. He is the God of Saul of Tarsus when he was persecuting the church, and when he became the apostle of the gentiles preaching everywhere and suffering for His name. This apostle represents those who did not seek God, but it was God who took the initiative, visited them and called them. He is the God of Zacchaeus the tax-collector to whom He said, *"Today, salvation has come to this house*" (Lk. 19: 9), and the God of Matthew the tax-collector who became His disciple.

He is the God of all, and His grace works in all, but man should respond to the work of His grace.

Irianus the governor of Ensena under Emperor Diocletian, for instance, was the cruelest governor persecuting Christians, inventing means of tormenting them, but finally he responded to God's work in him, believed and was martyred. Cyprian the magician also responded to the work of grace in him and repented, then became a bishop. On the other hand those who rejected God's work perished. An example of those is Pharaoh who witnessed many wonders but his heart was hardened. Agrippa the king as well refused the Lord and said to Paul the apostle, "*You almost persuade me to become Christian*" (Acts 26: 28), but he did not become, as he lost the chance. Felix the governor also, though he trembled when Paul the apostle was speaking about righteousness, self-control, and the judgment to come (Acts 24: 25), yet he could not benefit from the work of grace in him. He rather said to Paul, "*Go away for now; when I have convenient time I will call for you*", but it is not written that the convenient time had ever come!!

God is likewise the God of the married and the celibate.

He is the God of all the monks, hermits, recluse, ascetics and other celibates, as well as of Abraham, Isaac, Jacob and the other married persons also.

On the Mount of Transfiguration the Lord was surrounded by Moses and Elijah. Elijah, who went up into heaven in chariot of fire (2 Kgs. 2: 11), was unmarried, whereas Moses was married more than once (Num. 12: 1). And at the cross there was the holy Virgin Mary and John the celibate, as well as Mary the wife of Cleopas who had many children.

God is also the God of those who lead a life of contemplation and those who lead a life of ministry.

He is the God of St. Anthony the ascetic and father of all monks, and the God of Athansius the twentieth Pope in his pastoral ministry and defence of faith. He is the God of those devoted to prayer as well as of busy persons like Joseph the righteous who worked as Minister of Supply, storing wheat and selling it reasonably to save the people from the famine.

God is the God of the clergy as well as of the laity.

He is the God of Pope Abram Ibn Zaraa and Simon the tanner. By the prayers of Pope Abram and the faith of Simon God willed that Mount Mokattam be moved. He is also the God of Pope Cyril the fourth, the hero of reform, and Ibrahim Al Gohari the Chief Clerk of Mohammed Ali (equals Minister of Finance), and his brother Guirgis Al Gohari his partner in righteousness and in government work. He is the God of Anba Abram bishop of Fayoum, Anba Sarabamon Abou Tarha bishop of Menoufia, Seidhom Beshay the saint and martyr, Pope Mattaeus the saintly Patriarch and his contemporary Anba Ruis who held no clerical or monastic rank yet God worked wonders and miracles through him.

He is the God of the chaste and who seek chastity with all their hearts.

He is the God of the saints and of those who seek a life of holiness and respond to God when led to it. He is the God of John His beloved disciple who stood at His cross, and Demas the thief who was crucified with Him and who said to Him, *"Lord, remember me when You come into Your kingdom"* (Lk. 23: 42), and also the God of those who crucified Him and for whom He asked, *"Father, forgive them, for they do not know what they do"* (Lk. 23: 34)

If God is the God of all people, are all of them equal? And what about those who refuse Him as a God?

He was their God, but they refused to belong to Him. Hence the Scriptures say, *"they shall be His people. God Himself will be with them and be their God"* (Rev. 21: 3)

Since God is the God of all people on the earth, **He is rather more the God of the weak**; those who have no one but Him. They cannot even save themselves.

GOD IS THE GOD
OF THE WEAK

Our compassionate God supports every weak person, as we describe Him in the church prayers:

[You, who are the hope of those who are hopeless and the help of those who have no helper, the comfort of the fainthearted, and the harbor of those in the storm]

Those who are fainthearted cannot bear the troubles of this world, nor the pains of sin or inconveniences caused by people. Such a person finds comfort in God as the ship in the tempest finds in God the safe harbor.

Our God is the God of the weak and the poor, always supporting them. When the storm arose against the ship of the disciples, they saw Christ walking on the water rebuking the wind and saving the ship from the waves (Mt. 14: 23-33).

God always takes the side of the weak against the powerful who take pride in their power.

He is against the hard-hearted, the arrogant, and the proud. Hence it is written, *"Pride goes before destruction"* (Prov. 16: 18). He was against the arrogant Pharaoh, and with Moses the modest and calm. He was with poor Jacob who was flying from his brother Esau; He comforted him with visions, promises, and good things, and turned from Esau the hard-hearted.

God was with poor Joseph who was cast in the well, sold as a slave, put in prison unjustly, and in all that he defended not himself.

God took the side even of the poor sinful woman who was caught in the very act, condemned harshly and exposed by the people who asked that she should be put to death. The Lord defended her though she did not ask Him to do nor asked for His help (Jn. 8: 3-11). God has said, *"But on this one will I look: On him who is poor and of a contrite spirit, and who trembles at My word"* (Isa. 66: 2). It is written also, *"The Spirit of the Lord God is upon Me, because the Lord has anointed Me to preach good tidings to the poor; He has sent Me to heal the brokenhearted, to proclaim liberty to the captives, and the opening of the prison to those who are bound"* (Isa. 61: 1). He went to save the poor sick person who had been sick for thirty eight years and found no one to put him into the pool (Jn. 5: 1-9). He sought the man born blind when the Jews cast him out of the synagogue (Jn. 9: 35)

These were examples of how the Lord supports the poor, the contrite, the brokenhearted, the captives, and the imprisoned. Truly He is the God of the weak.

God was with David who was weak before king Saul and the valiant Goliath.

He helped David who was fleeing in the wilderness, from the face of Saul with all his power, army, and cruelty. He helped David the child who stood against the Valiant Goliath.

The Lord defended also the woman who washed His feet with her tears, and He rebuked Simon the Pharisee for her sake (Lk. 7).

Likewise, He preferred the contrite tax-collector to the puffed up Pharisee (Lk. 18). He supported all the weak, defended the children, the woman, and the sinners, and accepted the lost son (Lk. 15)

Indeed, the Lord, *"executes justice for the oppressed"* (Ps. 146: 7). *"The Lord preserves the simple"* (Ps. 116: 6).

Therefore if you are weak, do not fear but say, *"For when I am weak, then I am strong"* (2 Cor. 12: 10). It is because the Lord says, *"My strength is made perfect in weakness"* (2 Cor. 12: 9). Had He not *"chosen the foolish things of the world to put to shame the wise, and ... the weak things of the world to put to shame the things which are mighty; and the base things of the world ... and the things which are not ... "* (1 Cor. 1: 27, 28)

Be then weak and the Lord with you, rather than strong and the Lord departing you.

The church was defenseless and weak before the power, the tyranny and the weapons of the Roman Empire. Yet the church conquered, because the Lord's power was with her.

If you find a church minister who has become arrogant, say to him: your end has come.

Say: In me, the weak, Your power, O Lord, will appear. You had mercy on Abraham, Isaac, and Jacob because they are holy men, but in me the sinner Your mercy appears. And the Lord said, *"I did not come to call the righteous, but sinners, to repentance"* (Mt. 9: 13)

Do not stand before God and give promises as if trusting your power to fulfill them, but stand as one who is weak and asking God's help.

Say to God: help me to stop this sin, for whenever I stop doing it I return to it again. Confess your weakness, and say to Him:

[You know, O Lord, the watchfullness of my enemies. My weak nature You know, O my Creator]. In your spiritual wars you conquer, not by your strength, but by your weakness. When you admit that you are weak, you will conquer with God's power in you.

In the prayers of "Agbia" (the hours prayers), we say, "*For strangers have risen up against me, and oppressors have sought after my life: they have not set God before them*" (Ps. 54) (The Sixth Hour Prayer). Those oppressors, "*In the way in which I walk they have secretly set a snare for me ... Refuge has failed me; No one cares for my soul*" (Ps. 142: 3, 4) (The Compline Prayer). Let us then stand before God as weak persons and say, "*How long shall I take counsel in my soul, having sorrow in my heart daily? How long will my enemy be exalted over me?*" (Ps. 13: 2)

A person who stands weak before God takes strength from Him, with which one can prevail over all.

St. Anthony said to the devils [I am too weak to fight the least of you], by this he could conquer the most powerful devils.

If you feel strong when standing before God, as if relying on your human arm, grace will forsake you so that you may feel your weakness and be humbled.

Speak with God plainly and reveal your weakness. Say to Him: I am weak before such a sin. But if only the strong do enter Your kingdom, will I, the weak, perish? If I am weak, who strengthens me but You, O Lord? Being weak I ask, O Lord, for Your strength, and being feeble I seek Your help. Being unsuccessful before the devils, I ask You to fight them for me, with Your weapons.

God always has compassion on the weak, the chained, and the feeble. How beautiful indeed are the words of St. Paul the apostle about having compassion on the weak; for he says,

"Remember the prisoners as if chained with them – those who are mistreated – since you yourselves are in the body also" (Heb. 13: 3)

The problem with the Pharisees was that they had over self-confidence in their own power, so they despised the sinners and the weak. Therefore the Lord reprimanded them.

If you despise a weak person who fell, be sure that you also will be subject to fall.

If God asks us to bear with the weakness of the weak, certainly He –blessed be His name– bears with them unlimitedly with His long-suffering. Wrestle with God, and stand before Him with your weakness to take power from Him. Stand before Him empty to take fullness from Him, and ignorant to take of His knowledge.

If you are sure that you are weak, you will learn to pray and will have humbleness.

For the strong rarely do pray and hardly can be humbled

If you stand before God in weakness, He will pour His gifts on you.

When Isaiah the prophet said, *"woe is me, for I am undone! because I am a man of unclean lips"* (Isa. 6: 5), he deserved that one of the seraphim touch his lips with a live coal from the altar and to be cleansed.

Do not trust yourself to be stronger than sin, for this trust may make you lose cautiousness and carefulness, lead you to self-conceit, and takes you afar from prayer.

In this way one falls, as the Scriptures have warned us against sin, *"For she (sin) has cast down many wounded, and all who were slain by her were strong men*" (Prov. 7: 26). Our holy fathers lived with the spirit of humbleness, not relying on their strength, for all those who relied on their strength perished.

Satan once said to God: Leave to me the strong for I can prevail over them, but I cannot prevail over the weak, for they, having no power, fight me with Your power!

The principle that God helps the weak does not mean that all Christians should be weak. On the contrary, Christianity is power, and the faithful is one who can do everything in Christ (Phil. 4: 13). So the rule is:

Feel that you are weak by yourself, but very strong by God who works in you. Keep the divine power working within you through your continuous humbleness.

The feeling that you enjoy the work of the divine power, not the human power, in you gives you more confidence. For the human power may fail, but God's power is always mighty and capable of everything.

Hence a Christian person is very strong, not with his own power or personality, but with God's power working in him.

If you are weak then, do not be afraid of your weakness. And if you are conquered from a certain sin, do not despair.

Augustine was weak and conquered by sin. Moses the black, Pelagia, Mary the Copt, and others were weak and conquered likewise. But God's power, which supports the weak, led those in triumph in Christ (2 Cor. 2: 14). The Scriptures say on the mouth of the prophet, "Let the weak say: I am strong." (Jl. 3: 10)

It is a big problem that a weak person thinks himself strong. Therefore lay your weakness before God and say to Him, *"to will is present with me; but how to perform what is good I do not find ... the evil I will not to do, that I practice"* (Rom. 7: 18, 19)

You, O Lord, give power to the weak, and give them wings like eagles (Isa. 40: 29, 31). You can make something of me.

Most of the sinners who continued in their sins were not frank with God, nor with their own selves. They did not lay there weakness before God, nor insisted on obtaining power from Him. They did not ask for new hearts, new spiritual weapons, and a new divine life to work in them.

Do not say to the Lord: I will no more do this sin; but say: give me power to stop doing it.

Unless You hold my hand, O Lord, I will not advance even one step; for without You I can do nothing. Be therefore like the patient who knows his disease and describes it to the physician so that he might be healed. If the patient denies his disease, he will continue sick.

The strongest are those who feel their weakness and take power from God. But those who think themselves strong, they will know that they are not stronger than Satan who is more cunning, more wise, more aware of the human soul, and more experienced in spiritual wars, and can only be overcome by God's power. For *"God will vanquish him, not man"* (Job 32: 13)

Put, therefore, God's power in your battles with the devils. However weak you are, the Holy Spirit in you is capable of conquering and overcoming.

GOD WORKS QUIETLY

Today I ask you to calm down. I suppose you are calm, but I wish you to continue so. Be sure that God works, but He works quietly. God works continually, and we as believers should put before us God's work.

God works for us, even if we do not ask.

God created the universe, but the universe had not asked God to bring it into existence. Non-existence had no ability to ask for something. Likewise, God created man, but dust had not asked Him to make it man! For us God made everything, He prepared the sun, the moon, the rivers and the seas. He provided the man with trees, fruits, and all means of comfort without being asked by the man to do that. He created Eve for Adam though Adam had not asked that, but God knew that Adam was in need for the woman to be a helper to him.

God made everything out of His love and care

God's care for the universe continued. He raises His sun on all, and gives the fruit of the land to all, even to the atheists who deny Him and to those who blaspheme Him. He gives even the sinners who disobey Him and break His commandments. He is the loving God, who works in the universe, goes about doing good, and gives blessing and grace to all. He is indeed the absolute love and the absolute goodness. He is everything to us, and the Father of all of us. As Father, He does not wait till His children ask Him for anything, for He knows what everyone needs and gives everyone what he needs.

"For your heavenly Father knows that you need all these things" (Mt. 6: 32)

Your heavenly Father knows what everyone needs, feels the beating of the hearts, reads the thoughts and feelings of everyone, and recognizes everyone's wishes. If He gives food to the birds who do not ask and gives beautiful colors to the lilies of field, how much rather would He give those whom He considered His children!

It is weak faith that makes us forget God's work for man!

Let us, therefore, put God before our eyes in all our personal needs, the needs of our country, and the needs of the whole world, this world that needs peace and love, the world that is worn down by wars and conflicts, where the brother stands against his own brother. God in His work is able to fill the hearts of all people with love and to implant within all people the noblest and most sublime emotions.

God gives people not only material things, but also good feelings and repentance

His Holy Spirit works in the human heart, and His grace full of love visits everyone to work in. The spirits of His holy people around us provides help, being entrusted by God to do so. God gives also inspiration, and gives an inner voice deep in our hearts. He gives all gifts.

"Every good gift and every perfect gift is from above, and comes down from the Father of lights" (Jas. 1: 17)

This is our belief, therefore we put God before our eyes continually, and we trust His work.

God worked in the past, still works, and will work all the time and for ever and ever.

The Lord Christ said the beautiful words, *"My Father has been working until now, and I have been working"* (Jn. 5: 17) Suffice then to sleep in God's bosom and take rest there, trusting

His heart full of love and compassion, and trusting that He knows what He is doing, and He does it perfectly.

When Joseph the righteous was in prison, God was working for him. And in due time God brought him out of the prison to the highest positions though Joseph had not asked for that.

Jonah the prophet also was saved by God from the sea though he had not dreamt of that. The Lord God prepared a great fish to swallow Jonah (Jon. 1: 17), and the fish brought him safely to the required place. Such means of deliverance had not occurred at all to Jonah's mind nor did he ask for it. But God was working of His own will for Jonah.

God says in Psalm, *"For the oppression of the poor, for the sighing of the needy, now I will arise, says the Lord, I will set him in the safety for which he yearns."* (Ps. 12: 5). He did not say for the prayers and requests, but for the oppression of the poor who had not asked anything, the Lord will rise and make salvation.

Not only prophets like Jonah or holy persons like Joseph the righteous have found care from God, but even the insects on the earth or under the dust find care from God who provides them with food and protection though they do not ask.

He is God who works for all, with His love, care, knowledge, and justice, thus keeping the whole universe in balance.

He is God Almighty, having control over the whole world. He is the Father of us all with all kindness, love, and care implied in the term "Father". He gives comfort to His children, therefore we call Him in our prayers "Our Father in heaven".

He is omnipotent as the Gospel says,

"With men it is impossible, but not with God; for with God all things are possible" (Mk. 10: 27)

Our main duty is to introduce God in every work.

If God interferes in our deeds, He will make them successful, and we, seeing His work, will bless the Lord for ever. We trust that our Loving Almighty God will work for Egypt our country, for He said, *"Blessed is Egypt, My people"* (Isa. 19: 25). As far as we believe, we will see God's blessings to Egypt.

God's work for us gives us faith, hope, and peace.

We, therefore, always ask God in the Holy Liturgy to take part with His servants in every good deed. And He responds to our request, saying, *"lo, I am with you always even to the end of the age"* (Mt. 28: 20). We feel God's presence in our life, and each of us says, *"I have set the Lord always before me; because He is at my right hand I shall not be moved"* (Ps. 16: 8). We see God standing between us and any problem. In our love we say,

"For if we live, we live to the Lord; and if we die, we die, to the Lord. Therefore, whether we live or die, we are the Lord's" **(Rom. 14: 8)**

God for us is everything. We live in God's heart, and He lives in our hearts. God, whom we worship, is always watchful, never slumbers nor sleeps. God's knowledge extends beyond whatever man or machines know.

God works continually, but quietly.

Quietly God created the world, and quietly He keeps and manages it. Look at the system of the celestial bodies, how they move calmly and how seasons succeed each other, as well as day and night, all in quietness. With the same quietness trees grow little by little in such a way that cannot be noticed. Quietly also all the body systems work and receive orders from their centers.

When God spoke to Elijah the prophet, he did not speak in the wind, nor in the earthquake, nor in the fire, but in "*a still small voice*" (1 Kgs. 19: 11-13). With the same quietness God saved Joseph, and saved the wise men of the east, and with the same quietness the Lord perfected the Incarnation and the Redemption. And when God was preparing His servants, He prepared them in the calmness of wilderness. He prepared Moses the prophet away from the clamor of Pharaoh's palace, and prepared David the prophet in calmness while feeding the flock, and playing the harp, the flute, and the lyre.

It is amazing indeed, my brethren, that all the planets are calm except this planet in which we live.

Our planet the earth loses its calmness every now and then and is shaken by strifes, divisions, and wars. The individuals themselves have often the mind clamorous, the senses and nerves in tumult, and the soul wavering with feelings and emotions. One wonders when will man calm down in mind, heart, and body.

In the coming life, the dream of quietness will be realized.

In eternity there will be no tumult, nor clamor, nor strife. Humanity will restore its calmness and live in that quietness which God willed for the people when He created man in His own image after His likeness. There, the people will be like the angels of God in heaven; quiet, without differences or strifes, but love and peace governing them. We pray that God may grant us this quietness which He willed for us, and that we may enjoy the taste of such quietness here on earth so that we might feel its beauty in the happy eternity. We pray that God may grant our country this quietness, and grant it also to the whole world so that the world may enjoy such quietness instead of merely looking at it as marvelous. For quietness gives chance to sound reasoning and sound solutions.

GOD THE PROTECTOR
&
GOD'S WONDERFUL PROTECTION

Among the most beautiful verses of the Scriptures about God's protection are those in (Ps. 121):

"The Lord shall preserve you from all evil;
He shall preserve your soul.
The lord shall preserve your going out and your coming in"

How beautiful and comforting are these words. They give comfort to the soul that one is in the protection of God the keeper and Protector. It is truly said about Him in (Ps. 91): *"He shall cover you with His feathers, and under His wings you shall take refuge ... You shall not be afraid of the terror by night, nor of the arrow that flies by day ... A thousand may fall at your side, and ten thousand at your right hand; but it shall not come near you"*. Therefore we thank God everyday for this protection, we say in the Thanksgiving Prayer *"Let us give thanks to the beneficent and merciful God ... for He has protected, aided, kept and accepted us"*. If we put this protection in our minds all the time, we will live comfortable in full peace of heart without fear.

This divine protection is clear in the story of Nativity.

King Herod was afraid of the birth of Christ who would be the king and would sit on the throne of His father David, and *"of His kingdom there will be no end"* (Lk. 1: 32, 33). Because of this fear, and to get rid of the born king, *"he sent forth and put to death all the male children who were in Bethlehem and in all its districts, from two years old and under"* (Mt. 2: 16). However, the only child that Herod wanted to kill was the only one who escaped this massacre, and with Him John who was to prepare the way before Him!! It is the divine protection.

If you are under God's protection, no power in the whole world will do you harm.

See the beautiful words St. Paul the apostle said, *"Do not be afraid, but speak, and do not keep silent; for I am with you, and no one will attack you to hurt you"* (Acts 18: 9, 10). With the same promise God comforted Jacob the father of fathers while fleeing in fear from his brother Esau. From above the ladder reaching from heaven to the earth God said to Jacob, *"Behold, I am with you and will keep you wherever you go, and will bring you back to the land"* (Gen. 28: 15).

Man's life is in the hands of God the keeper, not in the hands of the aggressors.

This made David the prophet sing in Psalm (118) *"The Lord is on my side; I will not fear. What can man do to me?"*, *"They surrounded me, yes they surrounded me ... They surrounded me like bees; they were quenched like a fire of thorns"*. But what did happen to you, O David, while you were under God's protection? David says, *"You pushed me violently, that I might fall, but the Lord helped me. The Lord is my strength and song, and He has become my salvation"*, *"The right hand of the Lord does valiantly. The right hand of the Lord is exalted. The right hand of the Lord does valiantly. I shall not die but live, and declare the works of the Lord"*.

St. Anthony experienced this protection in the wilderness.

The devils surrounded him in a terrible way and with the voices of wild beasts to terrify him, but, trusting God's power of protection, he said to them: If God has given you power over me, who am I to stand against God? But if God has not given you power over me, no one of you can hurt me! Yea, life is in the hand of God the keeper, not in the hand of anyone who wants to hurt. Could Saul the king with all his power and armies hurt young David who was fleeing from his face? Nay, for God kept David from all the intrigues of Saul.

God kept also Jonah the prophet from the sea and from the fish

God kept Jonah from the waves of the sea when he was cast in it, and kept him even in the belly of the fish when it swallowed him. God did not give the fish power to hurt him, so the fish did not eat or digest him, but it kept him inside till it cast him safe at the shore just at the place where God wanted him to go. Jonah was in the belly of the fish as if in a submarine!

God kept Daniel and the three young men.

God protected them by two wonderful miracles. For Daniel God sent His angel and shut the lions' mouths, so they did not hurt him when he was cast in their den (Da. 6: 22). Thus Daniel experienced God's protection. The three young men also in the fire furnace obtained God's protection, and the fire had no power on their bodies, and the hair of their head was not singed (Da. 3: 27)

Any danger, however serious it might be, will lose its danger if God wills to protect.

Pharaoh wanted to kill all the male children of the Hebrews (Ex. 1: 16), but God willed to protect the child Moses, and God kept him alive. They put him in an ark of burbushes and laid the ark in the seeds by the river's bank (Ex. 2: 3). But as the saying goes: Give me life and cast me in the sea. So it happened that Pharaoh's daughter took the child Moses and he was brought up in Pharaoh's house as the son of Pharaoh's daughter (Heb. 11: 24)

True indeed are the words of the psalm, *"The Lord preserves the simple"* (Ps. 116: 6).

As God kept Moses, He kept also the child Samuel and he was not affected by the corruption of the sons of Eli the priest (1 Sam. 2: 13, 22). He kept the child Jeremiah and said to him, *"They will fight against you, but they shall not prevail against you. For I am with you – says the Lord – to deliver you"* (Jer. 1: 19). He kept the young lad David when he stood against the valiant Goliath; He delivered Goliath into David's hand and made David conquer because *"The battle is the Lord's"* (1 Sam. 17: 46, 47)

With the same divine protection, God saved Isaac the son of Abraham

Isaac was bound on the altar upon the wood and the knife over him, but the Lord preserved him at the twenty fourth hour, or at the 1440 minute i.e. at the last moment. The human eye considered it was too late, but God saw that it was very suitable, just before the knife come down to slay him. The divine protection willed that the lad would live. Even if the knife had went into his body, it would have come out calmly and he would have lived!

God does not only keep the children and the young, but He also keeps the weak who need protection and who cannot protect themselves. He interferes, protects and keeps. Hence David the prophet said,

"Our soul has escaped as a bird from the snare of the fowlers" (Ps. 124: 7)

How weak was the bird before the snare of the fowlers! However, God willed to keep the bird as the psalmist said, *"The snare is broken, and we have escaped. Our help is the name of the Lord who made heaven and earth"*. David the prophet therefore sang, *"If it had not been the Lord who was on our side, when men rose up against us, then they would have swallowed us alive ... Blessed be the Lord who has not given us as prey to their teeth"* (Ps. 124)

Thus God was with the weak people who had the sea behind them and Pharaoh with his chariots in front of them.

God kept those weak people against Pharaoh with all his power, and kept them also from the waters of the sea. So water was like a wall on their right and on their left! True then were the words of Moses the prophet to them when he said, *"Stand still, and see the salvation of the Lord ... The Lord will fight for you, and you shall hold your peace"* (Ex. 14: 13, 14).

God, who keeps, sends also His angels to protect the people.

It is written, *"In all their affliction He was afflicted, and the Angel of His Presence saved them"* (Isa. 63: 9), and also, *"The angel of the Lord encamps all around those who fear Him, and delivers them"* (Ps. 34: 7). Our father Jacob also mentioned that

146

an angel had redeemed him from all evil (Gen. 48: 16). We cannot forget also the angel who saved St. Peter from the prison when king Herod was about to kill him after the Passover (Acts 12: 7, 4).

God kept the martyrs and confessors likewise.

He kept them through giving them the power to endure the pains and the torturing they underwent and which were beyond anyone's endurance. He kept them in the faith, for the purpose of torturing them was to make them deny faith. He kept them against all temptations and suspicions. He was with them in the trials before governors, kings and judges, and said to them, *"But when they deliver you up, do not worry about how or what you should speak. For it will be given to you in that hour what you should speak; for it is not you who speak, but the Spirit of your Father who speaks in you"* (Mt. 10: 19, 20)

God keeps His children from the wars of the devils.

God does not permit Satan to fight us with all his power, but He puts limits to him as in the temptation of Job. In the first temptation God said to Satan, *"Behold, all that he has is in your power; only do not lay a hand on his person"* (Job 1: 12). And in the second temptation God said to Satan, *"Behold, he is in your hand, but spare his life"* (Job 2: 6). To preserve the faith of the people God bound Satan (Rev. 20: 2). And on the last days Satan will be freed, God will shorten those days, otherwise no flesh would be saved (Mt. 24: 22).

Even when we are fought with sin, God keeps us.

As the apostle says, *"Where sin abounded, grace abounded much more"* (Rom. 5: 20). It is the protecting grace that stands on one's side when sin presses hard, and helps one so as not to fall. Not only in spiritual wars does grace keep and protect, but also in the case of danger.

God often keeps man from dangers.

God keeps us from various dangers, among which are the danger of earthquakes, floods, tempests, and journeys. St. Paul mentioned such dangers, saying, *"in perils of waters, in perils of robbers, in perils of my own countrymen, in perils of the Gentiles, in perils in the city, in perils in the wilderness, in perils in the sea, in perils among false brethren"* (2 Cor. 11: 26). The apostle had been exposed to all these perils, but God saved him from them all.

Likewise God kept the father anchorites and hermits who inhabited the deserts and mountains.

He kept them from cold and hot weather; from serpents, scorpions, and all reptiles; from diseases when there was no physician nor medicine, from boredom and worry; from the wars of fear and suspicion; and from the attacks of the devils.

This reminds us of the deep words of the Lord about His keeping us from dangers:

"Behold, I send you out as sheep in the midst of wolves" (Mt. 10. 16)

One wolf is capable of frightening all the sheep, how much more could many wolves surrounding the sheep! This was what happened to early Christianity. It was resisted by the Roman Empire with all its power and cruelty, by the Jews with all their intrigues and plots, by the heathen philosophy with its ideas and suspicions, as well as by the false brothers with their treachery, including the heretics who rose from within the church. However, God kept the church from all those. True indeed are the words of the psalmist, *"The floods lift up their waves. The Lord on high is mightier"* (Ps. 93). And thanking the Lord in his prayer, the psalmist said also, *"You rule the raging of the sea; when its waves rise, You still them"* (Ps. 89: 9).

In God's keeping of the church, when she was surrounded by wolves, God turned many of those wolves into sheep. Some of them believed, some were martyred, and others defended faith and spread it.

God preserves us whether we request it or not.

When our father Abraham said about Sarah that she was his sister, and Abimelech the king of Gerar took her to his house, God saved her from his hands though Abraham had not asked God for that. God even came to Abimelech in a dream and threatened him that he would die unless he left her. But Abimelech took her in the integrity of his heart not knowing that she was Abraham's wife. Therefore God said to him, "*I also withheld you from sinning against Me; therefore I did not let you touch her*" (Gen. 20: 2-7)

This requires us to have faith and trust, and to give thanks to God.

You need to trust that God keeps you. This will give you peace, because, "*He who dwells in the secret place of the Most High shall abide under the shadow of the Almighty*" (Ps. 91: 1). With this trust, you may sing with David the prophet, "*Yea, though I walk through the valley of the shadow of death, I will fear no evil; For You are with me*" (Ps. 23: 4). But he whose faith is weak, should pray God that He may give him such strong faith. Such a person can also remind himself of previous times when God preserved him or the others; for this may implant faith within him.

Faith and prayers precede God's keeping, and thanksgiving follows.

It is not proper that God keeps us and we do not give Him thanks! David the prophet used to sing, "*Bless the Lord, O my soul; and forget not all His benefits*" (Ps. 103: 2)

As thanksgiving is a result of God's keeping, faith also may be a result. The more we contemplate on God's keeping, the more our faith and trust increase.

We should thank God, not only for what we know that God kept us from, but for that which He kept us from and we do not know. He keeps us from certain hardships we are not aware of.

We should contemplate on Ps. 121 which says, "*The Lord shall preserve you from all evil; He shall preserve your soul. The Lord shall preserve your going out and your coming in*" Let it be the prayer of every father for his child, of every priest for his congregation, of every guide for his disciple, or it may rather be the prayer of the angels and saints for all of us. Let everyone pray this prayer for himself that God may preserve him from all evil, preserve his soul, and preserve his going out and his coming in. Say this psalm every time you go out from your home or return home, and every time you go to your work or leave it.

As God has preserved your coming into the world, may He preserve your going out of it! May He preserve your going into Paradise and into the eternal kingdom!

Who can keep himself? It is You, O Lord, who keeps us, who keeps my soul from all evil, from falling, and from temptation. It is You, O Lord, who taught us to pray, saying, "*deliver us from the evil one*". May You keep us always even if we do not keep ourselves! If you open our eyes to see all that You have kept us from, all our life will not suffice to thank You. Thanks to You, and glory to You for ever and ever. Amen.

OUR GOOD GOD

It is well said by Jeremiah the prophet in his Lamentations, *"The Lord is good to those who wait for Him, to the soul who seeks Him"* (Lm. 3: 25) What does goodness mean then?

Goodness is a mixture of love, meekness, gentleness, and gracefulness.

A good person is always loving, meek, gentle, and decent. All these attributes are perfect in God, blessed be His name. They are part of His nature.

Our Good God would not frighten us with His divinity, but He condescended to us in His goodness.

In this way we could talk to Him and discuss with Him as Father. In His meekness He appeared to man and spoke to him. Some people when they attain some power, haughtiness enter their heart and no one can speak to them!! But God who created such people, in His meekness and goodness spoke to man who is just dust and ash (Gen. 18: 27), and who is His creation!!

Out of His goodness, God removed fear which represented a barrier between Him and His creation.

This made St. Anthony once say to his disciples: I do not fear God. And when they exclaimed, saying: These words are hard, father; he answered them: It is because I love Him, and *"perfect love casts out fear"* (1 Jn. 4: 18). Thus God allowed us to speak to Him without any hindrance and without frightening us with His divinity.

God's goodness is clear in His benevolence.

In His goodness, He did not want to be alone, so He brought to existence some creation, among which are we, to exist with Him. He created man, and in His goodness, before creating man He prepared everything for him. He created the sun to give him light by day, and the moon and stars to give light by night. For him He created the earth, the plants and animals, food and shelter, and a beautiful nature to enjoy. Lastly God created man, so he lacked nothing, and put him in Paradise. How good God is!

In His goodness, God said, *"I will put My Spirit within you"* **(Ex. 36: 27)**

He made us His temple, and His Spirit dwells in us (1 Cor. 3: 16). In His incarnation He called us His brothers and is not ashamed to be the firstborn among many brethren, saying, *"I will declare Your name to My brethren"* (Heb. 2: 12). He said concerning the poor, *"inasmuch as you did it to one of the least of these My brethren, you did it to Me"* (Mt. 25: 40). And to the two Marys He said, after the Resurrection, about His disciples, *"Go and tell My brethren to go to Galilee, and there they will see Me"* (Mt. 28: 10).

Of His goodness, God made for Himself stewards and ambassadors from among mankind.

The apostle said, *"For a bishop must be blameless, as a steward of God"* (Tit. 1: 7). And the Lord spoke about those stewards, saying, *"Who then is that faithful and wise steward, whom his master will make ruler over his household, to give them their portion of food in due season?"* (Lk. 12: 42). Moses the prophet was called by God, *"He is faithful in all My house"* (Num. 12: 7). He made us also ambassadors, as the apostle said, *"We are ambassadors for Christ, as though God were pleading through us; we implore you on Christ's behalf, be reconciled to God"* (2 Cor. 5: 20)

In His goodness, He ascribed His Law to Moses the prophet, calling it Moses' Law.

The Lord said to the Jews, *"Moses, because of the hardness of your hearts, permitted you to divorce your wives"* (Mt. 19: 8). It was in fact God Himself who permitted them on the mouth of Moses. God even ascribed the Holy Scriptures to His children whether men or women. There are for example the Book of Samuel, the Book of Isaiah, the Book of Jeremiah, as well as the Book of Ruth and the Book of Esther. These Book are inspired by God, but He called them after the names of His children.

Out of His goodness He prepared for Aaron garments for glory and beauty.

He said to Moses the prophet, *"And you shall make holy garments for Aaron your brother, for glory and for beauty. So you shall speak to all who are gifted artisans, whom I have filled with the spirit of wisdom, that they may make Aaron's garments, to consecrate him, that he may minister to Me as priest"* (Ex. 28: 2, 3). What glory, O Lord, You give to one of Your creation! Glory is to You alone! We wonder at what the Lord Christ said to the Father concerning His disciples; for He said, *"And the glory which You gave Me I have given them"* (Jn. 17: 22). He is indeed the Good God who glorifies His children as the apostle says, *"For whom He foreknew ... He predestined ... these He also glorified"* (Rom. 8: 29, 30)

God's goodness is evident in all the good things He gave on the earth.

He sent rain from heaven; He brought out of the earth plants, fruit, and flowers. He brought good things from the subsurface such as water springs, gases, petroleum, innumerable metals both from the earth and the mountains including gold, silver, copper ... etc. How amazing are the generous gifts which His goodness gave us bountifully.

God's goodness even put ideal qualities in the irrational creatures.

He gave the ant unceasing energy, and the bee wonderful accuracy. He put amazing faithfulness in dogs, intelligence in foxes, simplicity in doves, and kindness in hens (Mt. 23: 37)!

He even gave the weak animals the means of escaping from the strong.

He gave the gazelle great speed to be able to run fast and escape from the lion which is much stronger and can kill it easily. He gave also the cat the power to climb trees or high places to escape from the dog which cannot climb such places. The mouse likewise, tiny as it is and can be a prey to animals or to man, is given the power to dig and hide, and so on.

God's goodness appears in His forbearance towards many sinners.

He could punish anyone who sins immediately, but in His longsuffering He gives a chance to the sinner to repent as He did with Augustine, Mary the Copt, Moses the black and many others. He did not punish them while in their sins, but patiently waited till they forsook their evil ways and even became saints! But the punishment will be great for the sinner who disdains God's forbearance, as the apostle says, *"And do you think this, O man ... that you will escape the judgment of God? Or do you despise the riches of His goodness, forbearance, and longsuffering, not knowing that the goodness of God leads you to repentance?"* (Rom. 2: 3, 4)

The most wonderful and deepest goodness of God appears in His dealing with Satan.

God did not create him a devil, but He created him an angel, a cherub. Ezekiel the prophet describes him as *"the anointed cherub who covers"* (Ezek. 28: 14), and as *"full of wisdom and perfect in beauty*" (Ezek. 28: 12). But this cherub fell and rebelled against God, and He led many other angels to fall with him. Moreover he led astray and deceived millions of human beings, and still defies God's kingdom. However, God did not destroy him though God could do that in a moment. How Good God is to defer his punishment to the end of ages!

Although Satan had lost his first holiness, God's goodness did not withdraw from him his angelic nature with its powers.

Satan still has the nature which enables his to move from one place to another in a glimpse of the eye. This same nature enables him to instill evil in the minds and the hearts and to appear as an angel of light (2 Cor. 11: 14). Satan is very cunning and intelligent like the serpent which tempted Eve, for it is described as more cunning than any beast of the field (Gen. 3: 1). Satan, however, continued to work and to exercise his power after his fall, as the Lord Christ said to those who rejected Him, *"this is your hour, and the power of darkness"* (Lk. 22: 53). God's goodness allowed Satan even to go to and fro on the earth and to walk back and forth on it (Job 1: 7; 2: 2). God allowed him to tempt Job the righteous, and to detain an angel from helping Daniel the prophet till archangel Michael saved him (Da. 10: 13)!! Amazing enough is the fact that the Lord permitted Satan to tempt Him on the mount. But when Satan became so daring, the Lord rebuked him, saying, *"Away with you, Satan!"*, and Satan thereupon left Him (Mt. 4: 10)

Strange indeed is God's goodness towards Judah who betrayed Him!

The Lord, though knowing what he was going to do, chose Judah among the twelve disciples, and with them He gave him the power to do signs and wonders (Mt. 10: 1, 4). The Lord even entrusted him with the money box to give the poor (Jn. 12: 4-6) though He knew that Judah was a thief! The Good Lord let

Judah sit beside Him at the supper, and dipped a piece of bread and gave him (Jn. 13: 26)!

Another example of God's goodness is His wonderful promises.

As it is written, *"Eye has not seen, nor ear heard, nor have entered into the heart of man the things which God has prepared for those who love Him"* (1 Cor. 2: 9). And the Lord said, *"where I am, there you may be also"* (Jn. 14: 3). Thus the heavenly Jerusalem will be distinguished in eternity for being the tabernacle of God with men *"He will dwell with them, and they shall be His people"* (Rev. 21: 3).

How beautiful it was at the time of transfiguration of our Good God on Mount Tabor that He did not appear alone, but with Him Moses and Elijah appeared talking with Him (Mk. 9: 2-5).

God's goodness is markedly evident in His forgiveness.

God is willing to forget all the wicked past of anyone in return of one's repentance. Human beings hardly forgive each other especially if the faults of some are serious. But God is wonderful in his forgiveness; He forgives every one; He forgives all the sins of all people. He says, *"I will forgive their iniquity, and their sin I will remember no more"* (Jer. 31: 34); *"reconciling the world to Himself, not imputing their trespasses to them"* (2 Cor. 5: 19). He blots out their sins and washes them so they become as white as snow (Isa. 1: 18) If a sinner repents, *"None of the transgressions which he has committed shall be remembered against him"* (Ezek. 18: 22)

Our Good God remembers every good work even though it be little.

He said about the good seed that it bears fruit and produces: some a hundredfold, some sixty, some thirty (Mt. 13: 23). He considered the seed that produces even thirty good as well. He even accepted those who came at the eleventh hour (Mt. 20: 9), and accepted the repentance of the thief on His right on the cross at the last hours of his life (Lk. 23: 43). He said also that whoever gives one of the little ones a cup of cold water, shall by no means lose his reward (Mt. 10: 42). His goodness made Him say about the tree that gave no fruit for three years, *"let it alone this year also ... if it bears fruit, well. But if not, after that you can cut it down"* (Lk. 13: 8, 9).

God's forbearance is indeed a sign of His goodness.

He tolerated all the dissolute, the corrupt, the sinners, as well as the atheists and the blaspheming persons. He tolerated the scientists and philosophers who implanted doubts concerning His existence in the hearts of the people, and who mocked His name and denied His miracles!! Who of the human beings can bear even a little of all this?!

KINDNESS, COMPASSION, AND MERCY ARE AMONG GOD'S ATTRIBUTES

God is indeed kind, compassionate, and merciful as the Scriptures tell us through revealing God's relationships with the human beings and the whole creation. Various examples can be traced such as:

The words of David the prophet in the psalms, *"The Lord is merciful and gracious, slow to anger, and abounding in mercy"* (Ps. 103: 8); *"The Lord is gracious and full of compassion"* (Ps. 111: 4) (Ps. 145: 8); *"Gracious is the Lord, and righteous"* (Ps. 116: 5) (Ps. 112: 4)

Man may be cruel, but God is all kindness. Therefore David said,

"Let us fall into the hand of the Lord, for His mercies are great; but do not let me fall into the hand of man" (2 Sam. 24: 14) (1 Chr. 21: 13).

God's kindness is evident in His dealings with the sinners, even with the stiff-necked people. Therefore Nehemia said to the Lord in his prayers, *"Nevertheless in Your great mercy You did not utterly consume them nor forsake them; for You are God, gracious and merciful"* (Neh. 9: 31). And king Hezekiah said to the people, *"The Lord your God is gracious and merciful, and will not turn His face from you if you return to Him"* (2 Chr. 30: 9). Hence the Psalmist sang in the psalm, saying,

"He has not dealt with us according to our sins,
Nor punished us according to our iniquities
For as the heavens are high above the earth,

158

So great is His mercy toward those who fear Him;
As far as the east is from the west'
So far has He removed our transgressions from us.
As a father pities his children,
So the Lord pities those who fear Him" (Ps. 103: 10-13)

God is also compassionate in His commandments and judgments

Saint John the beloved, says, *"His commandments are not burdensome"* (1 Jn. 5: 3). And we read in the Bible that the Lord rebuked the scribes and Pharisees because *"they bind heavy burdens, hard to bear, and lay them on men's shoulders; but they themselves will not move them with one of their fingers"* (Mt. 23: 4). The Lord, therefore rebuked them, saying, *"Woe to you, scribes and Pharisees, hypocrites! For you shut up the kingdom of heaven against men; for you neither go in yourselves, nor do you allow those who are entering to go in"* (Mt. 23: 13). In His compassion towards His disciples, the Lord said to them, *"I still have many things to say to you, but you cannot bear them now"* (Jn. 16: 12). And His disciples, having learnt the lesson, upon accepting the Gentiles, said, *"It seemed good to the Holy Spirit, and to us, to lay upon you no greater burden than these necessary things; that you abstain from things offered to idols, from blood, from things strangled, and from sexual immortality"* (Acts 15: 28, 29). Furthermore, St. James the apostle, described the wisdom that is from above as, *"first pure, then peaceable, gentle, willing to yield, full of mercy and good fruits ..."* (Jas. 3: 17)

God the compassionate gives with the commandment the power and grace to perform it.

He even gives His Holy Spirit to work within us as the beautiful words of St. Paul tell us, *"for it is God who works in you both to will and to do for His good pleasure"* (Phil. 2: 13). He explained his experience in this respect, saying, *"But by the grace of God I am what I am, and His grace toward me was not in vain, but I labored more abundantly than they all, yet not I, but the grace of God which was with me"* (1 Cor. 15: 10)

It is indeed the compassion of God that made His Holy Spirit dwell in us.

As the Scriptures say, *"Do you not know that you are the temple of God and that the Spirit of God dwells in you?"* (1 Cor. 3: 16). He dwells in us, and works in us, as St. Paul, speaking about himself and his companion Apollos, said, *"For we are God's fellow workers"* (1 Cor. 3: 9). It is God's compassion that made us partners in communion with the Holy Spirit (2 Cor. 13: 14), and *"partakers of the divine nature"* in work and holiness (2 Pet. 1: 4). Since the far past He promised to let His Holy Spirit dwell in us; for He said in the prophecy of Ezekiel, *"I will put My Spirit within you and cause you to walk in My statutes, and you will keep My judgments and do them."* (Ezek. 36: 27). He promised to let His Spirit abide with us forever, and teach us all things, and bring to our remembrance all things the Lord has said to us (Jn. 14: 16, 26). His Holy Spirit will also guide us into all truth (Jn. 16: 12), and it is not we who speak, but the Spirit of our Father who speaks in us (Mt. 10: 20). What compassion and what kindness is this towards our weak nature to find such support from God's Spirit!

God's care for us is an aspect of His compassion.

Did He not say, *"I am the good shepherd. The good shepherd gives His life for the sheep"* (Jn. 10: 11); *"My sheep hear My voice, and I know them, and they follow Me, And I give them eternal life, and they shall never perish; neither shall anyone snatch them out of My hand"* (Jn. 10: 27, 28). He said also in the Old Testament, *"I will feed My flock, and I will make them lie down —says the Lord God- I will seek what was lost and bring back what was driven away, bind up the broken and strengthen what was sick"* (Ezek. 34: 15, 16); *"I Myself will search for My sheep and seek them out ... so will I seek out My sheep and deliver them from the places where they were scattered ...* " (Ezek. 34: 11, 12). Therefore David sang in the psalm, *"The Lord is my shepherd; I shall not want. He makes me to lie down in green pastures; He leads me beside the still waters. He restores my soul, He leads me in the paths of righteousness ...*" (Ps. 23). God's care is full of love and kindness, therefore it is said, *"When He saw the multitudes, He was moved with compassion for them, because they were weary and scattered like sheep having no shepherd"* (Mt. 9: 36) (Mk. 6: 34)

Out of His kindness, God sends His angels to His people.

He sends His angels who are described in the Scriptures as *"ministering spirits sent forth to minister for those who will inherit salvation"* (Heb. 1: 14). Among those angels is the guarding angel, *"The angel of the Lord encamps all around those who fear Him, and delivers them"* (Ps. 34: 7); *"In all their affliction he was afflicted, and the Angel of His Presence saved them"* (Isa. 63: 9); *"For He shall give His angels charge over you, to keep you in all your ways. In their hands they shall bear you up, lest you dash your foot against a stone."* (Ps. 91: 11)

It is He, our merciful God who cares for us and leads us in triumph (2 Cor. 2: 14)

He is the merciful compassionate Lord, *"Delivering the poor from him who is too strong for him ... and the needy from him who plunders him"* (Ps. 35: 10). Many also are the commandments given by the Lord for the poor, for the strangers, for the slaves, and for the disabled. His commandments are full of mercy and compassion.

Even in the temptations we face, His kindness appears clearly.

As the apostle says, *"God is faithful, who will not allow you to be tempted beyond what you are able, but with the temptation will also make the way of escape, that you may be able to bear it"* (1 Cor. 10: 13). The Lord Himself said, *"But the very hairs of your head are all numbered"* (Mt. 10: 30); *"But not a hair of your head shall be lost"* (Lk. 21: 18). The Lord underwent the temptation in His incarnation to help us, *"For in that He Himself has suffered, being tempted, He is able to aid those who are tempted"* (Heb. 2: 18)

See how God aided Job the righteous in his temptation!

God even gave Job twice as much as he had before, and blessed his latter days more than his beginning, and Job saw his children and grandchildren for four generations (Job 42: 10-16). How beautiful also what He said to the angel of the church of Philadelphia:

"I also will keep you from the hour of trial which shall come upon the whole world" (**Rev. 3: 10**)

It is evident therefore that God the merciful and compassionate supports His children at the time of temptations, aids them, and delivers them. However, God's mercy does not cover His children only, but extends further.

His mercy and compassion extend even to the animals and to the nature.

As God gave man rest on the Sabbath, He commanded also that even the ox, the donkey, and the cattle should take rest as well as man (Deut. 5: 14)! In His kindness He commanded, *"You shall not plow with an ox and a donkey together"* (Deut. 22: 10). It is because the ox is stronger and faster in movement than the donkey, thus if they plow together, the donkey will be weakened and injured. He commanded also, *"You shall not see your brother's ox or his sheep going astray, and hide yourself from them; you shall certainly bring them back"* (Deut. 22: 4).

162

He commanded that if one's sheep falls into a pit on the Sabbath, one should lay hold of it and lift it out (Mt. 12: 11). In His kindness He said, *"You shall not muzzle an ox while it treads out the grain"* (Deut. 25: 4). He wanted them to leave its mouth free to eat –whenever tired or hungry- from the grains. He gives every mouth food, and kindly satisfies the desire of every living thing (Ps. 145: 16). *"He gives to the beast its food, and to the young ravens that cry"* (Ps. 147: 9). And even the birds of the air, *"your heavenly Father feed them"* (Mt. 6: 26)

God's mercy extends even to the sinners.

"Even when we were dead in trespasses, (God) made us alive together with Christ ... and raised us up together, and made us sit together in the heavenly places in Christ Jesus" (Eph. 2: 5, 6). Therefore Paul the apostle sang praising God's kindness, *"But God demonstrates His own love towards us, in that while we were still sinners, Christ died for us"* (Rom. 5: 8). This kindness, mercy, and compassion towards the sinful world appeared evidently in the Redemption, *"He was wounded for our transgressions, He was bruised for our iniquities"* (Isa. 53: 5)

In His kindness He did not hurt the feelings of the sinners, and compassionately accepted their repentance.

He did not hurt the feelings of the Samaritan woman, but rather led her very gently to confession (Jn. 4). He did the same for the woman that was caught in the very act; He delivered her very kindly from the hands of those who wanted to stone her, and said to her, *"Neither do I condemn you; go and sin no more"* (Jn. 8: 11).

Neither did the Lord blame Zacchaeus the tax-collector for his past life full of cruelty and oppression, but rather accepted him very kindly and went into his house in spite of the disapproval of the Jews. He addressed them, saying, *"Today salvation has come to this house, because he also is a son of Abraham; for the Son of Man has come to seek and to save that which was lost"* (Lk. 19: 9, 10)

The story of the lost son reveals to us the extent of God's compassion towards the repenting sinners, as it is said, *"But when he was still a great way off, his father saw him and had compassion, and ran and fell on his neck and kissed him"* (Lk. 15: 20). And in the story of the indebted servant, when the servant prayed his master to have patience with him, *"the master of that servant was moved with compassion, released him, and forgave him the debt"* (Mt. 18: 27). Another example of God's compassion is what the Lord told Simon the Pharisee about himself and the weeping sinner, *"There was a certain creditor who had two debtors. One owed five hundred denarii, and the other fifty. And when they had nothing with which to repay, he freely forgave them both"* (Lk. 7: 41, 42). And to the woman He said, *"Your sins are forgiven ... Your faith has saved you. Go in peace"* (Lk. 7: 48, 50).

It is God's compassion towards the sinners who cannot pay off their debts; He forgives them all!

This compassion of God is most evident in forgiving His crucifiers, and in forgiving the thief crucified with Him

For His crucifiers, the Lord said, *"Father, forgive them, for they do not know what they do"* (Lk. 23: 34), thus in His deep kindness, He even gave them excuse! And to the repenting thief He said, *"today you will be with Me in Paradise"* (Lk. 23: 43), thus blotting out all their sins as if they had not been! We remember also His kindness when He accepted the repentance of Peter who wept bitterly after he had denied Him (Mt. 26: 75). The Lord furthermore comforted Peter concerning his apostolic rank, when He said to him thrice after the Resurrection, "Tend My sheep" (Jn. 21: 17)

His compassion is clear in the wars of sin against us.

He shortens the days of tribulations, saying in His compassion, *"unless those days were shortened, no flesh would be saved"* (Mt. 24: 22). And His grace supports us in these wars, as the apostle says, *"when sin abounded, grace abounded much more"* (Rom. 5: 20)

God's compassion extends even to the enemies.

"He makes His sun rise on the evil and on the good, and sends rain on the just and on the unjust" (Mt. 5: 45). He did so for the atheist countries which denied His existence, and for the heathens who worshipped idols. In His mercy, He endured the communist countries till they returned to faith and did not stop to give them, all the time, knowledge, progress, and prosperity.

He taught us to do like Him, saying, *"love your enemies, bless those who curse you, do good to those who hate you, and pray for those who spitefully use you and persecute you"* (Mt. 5: 44). It is written also, *"If your enemy is hungry, feed him; if he is thirsty, give him a drink"* (Rom. 12: 20). More amazing still is that He permitted the demons to enter the herd of swine when the demons begged Him to do (Lk. 8: 32)!! What gentle treatment it was, even with a legion of demons!!

The miracles worked by the Lord Christ was combined with mercy and compassion.

In healing the sick, we read, *"He saw a great multitude; and He was moved with compassion for them, and healed their sick"* (Mt. 14: 14). And when the leper implored Him saying, *"If You are willing, You can make me clean"* (Mk. 1: 40, 41), *"Jesus, moved with compassion, stretched out His hand and touched him, and said to him; I am willing; be cleansed."* Likewise, when the two blind men outside Jericho cried out, saying, *"Have mercy on us, O Lord, Son of David"*, *"Jesus had compassion and touched their eyes. And immediately their eyes received sight, and they followed Him"* (Mt. 20: 34). The same happened in the miracle of raising the son of the widow in Nain. The widow was weeping behind the coffin of her dead son, so *"When the Lord saw her, he had compassion on her and said to her: Do not weep"* (Lk. 7: 13). Then He came and touched the coffin, raised her son, and presented him to his mother. The deepest sign of His compassion and kindness was clear in raising Lazarus from the dead; for the Gospel says, *"Jesus wept"* (Jn. 11: 35)!

But does this compassion, kindness, or mercy of God prevent Him from Chastening? The answer comes in the following chapter.

166

GOD CHASTENS AND HEALS, WOUNDS AND BANDAGES
(Job 5: 18)

God loves His creation, and treats His children with all love, *"He loved them to the end"* (Jn. 13: 1). He shows mercy and compassion towards them, but without fondling which may lead them astray, for the Scriptures say,

"For whom the Lord loves He chastens" (Heb. 12: 6)

It is said also, *"Behold, happy is the man whom God corrects; therefore do not despise the chastening of the Almighty. For He bruises, but He binds up; He wounds, but His hands make whole"* (Job 5: 17, 18). The chastening is for our benefit and for our healing. We benefit from it as we benefit from all God's gifts and talents. St. Paul the apostle says about this chastening, *"If you endure chastening, God deals with you as with sons; for what son is there whom a father does not chasten? But if you are without chastening, then you are illegitimate and not sons"* (Heb. 12: 7, 8)

This chastening is not with cruelty, but is combined with mercy.

That is why it is said, *"He bruises, but He binds up; He wounds, but His hands make whole"*

Since the beginning, God dealt with humanity in this way as we know from the story of our forefathers Adam and Eve. He created the first man in the best image, *"in the image of God He created him"*. And God blessed them and gave them dominion over the whole earth (Gen. 1: 27, 28). But when this man fell, God punished him, and said to him, *"In the sweat of your face you shall eat bread*", "*Cursed is the ground for your sake; in toil you shall eat of it all the days of your life. Both thorns and thistles it shall bring forth for you*" (Gen. 3: 17, 18). And to the woman He said, "*I will greatly multiply your sorrow and your conception; in pain you shall bring forth children*" (Gen. 3: 16)

However, while punishing Adam and Eve, God announced to them His salvation.

He announced to them that the woman's seed would bruise the serpent's head (Gen. 3: 15). And it thus happened that the Lord Christ, the seed of the woman, came to bruise the head of the serpent (that is Satan) (Rev. 20: 2). Hence the promise of salvation came at the same time of the punishment. Truly God wounds but makes whole! He drove Adam and Eve out of the garden, but He promised salvation to them and to the whole humanity!

The same happened in the story of Jonah the prophet.

Jonah sinned, disobeyed God's command, and fled from Him in a ship to Tarshish. So God inflicted punishment on him: a mighty tempest on the sea so that the ship was about to be broken up. Then Jonah was thrown into the sea, but God had prepared a great fish to swallow him (Jon. 1: 17), and did not allow it to hurt Jonah, so Jonah was in the belly of the fish three days and three nights. After that Jonah came out safe to perform his mission. Truly indeed God bruises but He binds up; He wounds, but His hands make whole! How beautiful also are the words of David the prophet:

"The Lord has chastened me severely, but He has not given me over to death" (Ps. 118: 18)

Indeed, so many were the punishments with which God chastened His servant David. God rebuked him on the mouth of Nathan the prophet, saying, "*Why have you despised the commandment of the Lord, to do evil in His sight? ... Now therefore, the sword shall never depart from your house"* (2 Sam. 12: 9, 10). The Lord permitted also Abshalom, David's son, to resist David and humiliate him to the extent that David went up the Mount of Olives barefoot and weeping (2 Sam. 15: 30). God permitted also Shimei the son Gera to insult him with hard words (2 Sam. 16: 5-8), and Ahithophel to betray him (2 Sam. 20). God even prevented David from building the Temple and let him suffer many other tribulations. However, God was with him, blessed him, and saved him. Therefore, David sang praise to the Lord, saying, *"The Lord is my strength and song, and He has become my salvation"* (Ps. 118: 14)

The Lord God dealt also with Solomon the son of David in the same way, and said,

"If he commits iniquity, I will chasten him with the rod of men and with the blows of the sons of men. But My mercy shall not depart from him" (2 Sam. 7: 14, 15).

Both chastening and mercy are combined together. And though God appeared twice to Solomon: once in Gibeon, and the other in Jerusalem, yet He punished him when he sinned. His punishment was kind and He did not remove His mercy from him as He did with Saul. He said addressing Solomon, *"Because you have done this, and have not kept My covenants and My statutes, which I have commanded you, I will surely tear the kingdom away from you and give it to your servant. Nevertheless I will not do it in your days, for the sake of your father David; I will tear it out of the hand of your son. However I will not tear away the whole kingdom; I will give one tribe to your son for the sake of My servant David, and for the sake of Jerusalem which I have chosen"* (1 Kgs. 11: 11-13). Truly He wounds, but His hands make whole (Job 5: 18)!

Thus the Lord said to the church in the past,

"For a mere moment I have forsaken you,

but with great mercies I will gather you"(Isa. 54: 7)

He left her humiliated in the hands of the Gentiles, but gathered her together again, delivered her to captivity in Babylon and Assyria, and let Nebuchadnezzar attack her; and left her wall broken down, and her gates burned with fire (Neh. 1: 3), but He stirred up the spirit of Cyrus king of Persia (Ez. 1: 1) to bring out and restore the articles of the house of the Lord which Nebuchadnezzar had taken from Jerusalem and put in the temple of his gods (Ez. 1: 7, 8). God gave Nehemiah also favor in the sight of king Artaxerxes to send him to Judah to rebuild Jerusalem (Neh. 2: 4-9)

Although God let His holy children fall captive, He gave them favor in the land of captivity.

An example of this is the story of Daniel and the three holy young men.

Captivity was considered as chastening for the whole people, but it was to Daniel and the three young men a deep spiritual experience. They saw in it God's hand binding up and making whole. God permitted that His beloved Daniel be persecuted by all the governors of the kingdom, the administrators and the satraps, the counselors and the advisors. They all consulted together and made a plot by which Daniel was cast in the lions' den. But *"God sent His angel and shut the lions' mouths"* (Da. 6: 22). The result was a decree from the king that all the people worship the God of Daniel (Da. 6: 25-28), a success for Daniel!

Although God permitted that the three young men be cast into the furnace of fire, He was walking with them in the midst of the fire (Da. 3: 25), and the fire did not hurt them. This made Nebuchadnezzar order that their God be worshipped, and he promoted them in position. Indeed God wounds, then makes whole

This reminds us of what happened to Mordecai at the hands of Haman.

God permitted Haman to make gallows fifty cubits high and hang Mordecai on it unjustly (Esth 5: 14). But that night king Ahasuerus could not sleep and he commanded that the records of the Chronicles be read before him. And there was found written that Mordecai had saved the king from two persons who had sought to lay hands on the king. The king was very delighted and honored Mordecai greatly (Esth 6). God gave Esther also favor in the sight of the king, so she could expose Haman and reveal his conspiracy. Finally Haman was hung on the gallows that he had prepared for Mordecai (Esth 7: 10).

God permitted that Joseph the righteous be tempted, but He brought him out of the temptation in honor

God permitted his brothers to persecute him, to cast him into a pit, and to sell him as a slave (Gen. 37). He permitted Potephar's wife to accuse him unjustly, and be cast in prison for some years. However, God was with him and made him successful in everything, and gave him the gift of interpreting dreams. Then God sent the chief butler and the baker of Pharaoh two dreams, and made Joseph interpret them well. Thus Joseph had favor in the eyes of Pharaoh, and he made Joseph second in the kingdom. His brothers also came to him in Egypt asking for grain and bowed down before him! But Joseph comforted them, saying, *"it was not you who sent me here, but God"* (Gen. 45: 8). And after the death of his father, Joseph said to them, *"you meant evil against me; but God meant it for good ... to save many people alive"* (Gen. 50: 20). How You wound, O God, and make whole again!

God permitted that some holy woman be barren and bear no children.

He closed the womb of Rachel and she bore no children while her sister bore many sons. Rachel envied her sister, and said to Jacob, "*Give me children, or else I die*" (Gen. 30: 1). But God remembered Rachel, and He listened to her and opened her womb. And Rachel conceived and bore a son, "*God has taken away my reproach*" (Gen. 30: 22, 23). God gave her Joseph before whom all his brothers bowed down.

God permitted also that Hannah be barren and that her rival Peninnah provoke her. Hanna wept and did not eat (1 Sam. 1: 6, 7). But God who wounds but always makes whole, had prepared for her a son; Samuel, who anointed David as king (1 Sam. 16).

God closed also the womb of Sarah, then gave her afterwards Isaac the father of the fathers. Elizabeth also was made barren, but God afterwards gave her John than whom "*among those born of women there has not risen one greater*" (Mt. 11: 11). It is indeed God who wounds then makes whole.

Remember how He permitted that Ruth becomes a widow and a stranger, and gleans behind the reapers, but He had arranged for her to marry Boaz and to become a grandmother for Christ (Ruth 4: 13, 21, 22)

Many also are the tribulations God permitted His apostles and martyrs to suffer.

He said, "*In the world you will have tribulation*" (Jn. 16: 33); "*They will put you out of the synagogues; yes, the time is coming that whoever kills you will think that he offers God service*" (Jn. 16: 2); "*they will lay their hands on you and persecute you, delivering you up to synagogues and prisons. You will be brought before kings and rulers for My name's sake*" "*And you will be hated by all for My name's sake*" (Lk. 21: 12, 17). However, God who said this, said also, "*I will give you a mouth and wisdom which all your adversaries will not be able to*

contradict or resist" "But not a hair of your head shall be lost"
(Lk. 21: 15, 18). Truly God wounds and makes whole.

God permitted that His beloved saint John be exiled to the island called Patmos where He gave him the marvelous Revelation. God made him see the heaven open and God's throne and the heavenly hosts (Rev. 4), and revealed to him what will happen at the end of the ages.

He let Paul the apostle suffer many pains, so he was, *"in labors more abundant, in stripes above measure, in prisons more frequently, in deaths often" "in perils of waters, in perils of robbers, in perils of (his) own countrymen, ... in perils among false brethren"* (2 Cor. 11: 23-26). But at the same time God caught him up to the third heaven, into Paradise where he heard inexpressible words (2 Cor. 12: 2-4).

God even prevented Moses the prophet from entering the promised land though Moses was faithful in all God's house (Num. 12: 7). However, God let Moses enter that land on the Mount of Transfiguration with Him and with Elijah the prophet (Mk. 9: 4). Indeed God bruises but His hands bind up!

Therefore, brother, experience God in whatever wounds or chastening He gives you.

Experience the Lord, not only when He brings you up to the third heaven, but also when He gives you a thorn in the flesh (2 Cor. 12: 7). Experience his temptations and rejoice in them as the apostle said, *"My brethren, count it all joy when you fall into various trials"* (Jas. 1: 2). Remember that St. Paul and St. Silas were put in the inner prison with their feet fastened in the stocks, yet they were praying and singing hymns to God and the prisoners were listening to them (Acts 16: 24, 25).

If you get wounded in your love towards God, do not be troubled, but say,

"Faithful are the wounds of a friend" (**Prov. 27: 6**)

Say also; The bitter which the Lord chooses for me is better than the honey I choose for myself. O Lord, I never doubt Your love in spite of any wounds I experience or chastening I suffer from. I know that everything is for good and for a blessing. Your rod and Your staff comfort me. They lead and guide me, and I feel no pain from them. You chastens but heals, wounds but binds up. You did not mean pain to Job the righteous, but You wanted to give him blessing through suffering, and You delivered him in a better condition. You gave Job twice as much as he had before, and blessed the latter days of his life more than his beginning (Job 42: 10, 12). Blessed be the name of the Lord all the time. This Job said, not when God healed him, but while he was in the midst of the temptation and suffering (Job 1: 21)

174

GOD'S WISDOM

Introduction:

Wisdom is one of God's well-known attributes. People often marvel at God's judgments and say: Oh for Your wisdom, O Lord! As the Scriptures say:

"Oh, the depth of the riches both of the wisdom and knowledge of God! How unsearchable are His judgments and His ways past finding out!" (Rom. 11: 33)

Job the righteous was not aware of the mystery of the temptation, and he was arguing. But finally, after talking with God, he said to Him, *"I know that You can do everything, and that no purpose of Yours can be withheld from You ... Therefore I have uttered what I did not understand, things too wonderful for me, which I did not know ... I have heard of You by the hearing of the ear, but now my eye sees You"* (Job 42: 2-5)

Yea, sometimes we do not understand God's wisdom, but we have to trust it even if we never understand.

Wisdom is indeed very important, since the second Person of the Holy Trinity is called the Wisdom. The Lord Christ is therefore described as *"the power of God and the wisdom of God"* (1 Cor. 1: 24); *"in whom are hidden all the treasures of wisdom and knowledge"* (Col. 2: 3)

God, Himself the wisdom, grants wisdom as a gift

St. Paul the apostle mentioned wisdom among the gifts of the Holy Spirit of God, He said, *"to one is given the word of wisdom through the Spirit"* (1 Cor. 12: 8). Likewise, St James the apostle said, "*But the wisdom that is from above is first pure, then peaceable, gentle, willing to yield, full of mercy and good fruits*" (Jas. 3: 17). We know also that our God is the source of all wisdom, and that He gave Solomon wisdom, saying to him, "*See, I have given you a wise and understanding heart, so that there has not been anyone like you before you, not shall any like you arise after you*" (1 Kgs. 3: 12)

The Scriptures say that God is wisdom, and with Him is wisdom.

He said about Himself, "*I, wisdom, ...* " (Prov. 8: 12). And it is said of Him, "*With Him are wisdom and strength, He has counsel and understanding*" (Job 12: 13). God's Spirit is also described as, "*The Spirit of wisdom and understanding, the Spirit of counsel and might, the Spirit of knowledge*" (Isa. 11: 2). It is also said, "*... the mystery, which from the beginning of the ages has been hidden in God ... that now the manifold wisdom of God might be made known by the church to the principalities and powers in the heavenly places*" (Eph. 3: 10).

God's wisdom apparent in His creation:

Sea what the Psalmist says:
"O Lord, how manifold are Your works!
In wisdom You have made them all" (Ps. 104: 24)

And the Scriptures say also, "*The Lord by wisdom founded the earth; by understanding He established the heavens*" (Prov. 3: 19).

Take for example the timing of creation; it was all chosen with wisdom. He created water before plants and herbs to irrigate them, and created these before creating animals so that animals might have herbs for food. Finally He created man to have plants for food and have animals to serve him (Gen. 1)!

God's wonderful wisdom appears also in the functions of the body systems and members.

God's wisdom gave certain functions for each of the brain centers, and gave a certain function to the heart and a relationship between the heart and the brain. In the functions of all body systems His wisdom is evident, as we see in the function of the liver, the kidneys, the digestive system, the circulatory system, the blood, the bones, and also the role of the mind, the conscience, and the nerves.

See also God's wisdom in the heredity laws.

The embryo inherits the qualities of his parents and some of the qualities of his grandfathers and the qualities which descended to his uncles. Observe the role of the genetics, the hormones, and the chromosomes ... See God's wisdom in the heredity related with the person's shape, stature, color of the eyes and hair, features, the blood group ... etc.

God's wisdom appears in the various peculiarities in His creation.

He created the angels spirits far from material, "*Who makes His angels spirits, His ministers a flame of fire*" (Ps. 104: 4). He created also things which are all material, such as mountains, rivers, and stones. Some other creation He made of flesh and soul, such as animals, birds, fish, and insects. Then He made man of a material body, a soul, and a spirit (1 Thess. 5: 23)

All creation in a wonderful variety:

All creation vary in color, shape, understanding, temper, attitude, and thinking, and vary even in the ability to talk, and in the voice. This variation makes creation not feel bored when seeing each other.

Imagine this variation did not exist, what would be the result?

If all people had one mentality, one frame of mind, and one shape, one would look to the other as if looking in a mirror! Therefore variation exists even within the same creation. Among the angels there are principalities, dominions, powers, cherubs, seraphims, and thrones. Even those are not one level or one type; there are angels for singing praise to God and standing before the divine throne (Isa. 6). Other angels are designated for ministry, "*Are they not all ministering spirits sent forth to minister for those who will inherit salvation*" (Heb. 1: 14)

In nature also there is variety.

God made pressure, temperature, air, clouds, and rain. There is heavy pressure and light pressure, and air changes from heavy to light pressure. High temperature decreases pressure, and the high speed of air turns it to wind and tempest, then carries water vapor upwards turning it into clouds which condense and fall as rain, and so on.

Imagine what would happen if the water of the clouds felt proud for being high while the sea water is lower down! Therefore the water of the clouds fall in the form of rain, and the sea water goes up in the form of vapor. It is God's inapproachable wisdom!

See also God's wisdom in the laws He set for the celestial bodies!

What a fixed, wise, and wonderful order is that with which the celestial bodies work. Observe the relationship among the suns, the planets, the stars and the rest of the celestial bodies. Observe the seasons depending on these bodies, the resulting atmosphere temperature, light and darkness, and the link between all this and man's life.

God's wisdom is apparent also in forming societies and caring for them from all aspects.

Society Management:

God's wisdom made every good thing in the society sufficient for it. He made a wonderful balance between equality and disparity. All people are equal in free will and in the inclination towards good or evil. However there is an amazing disparity in income, in character, and in mentality. God in His exceeding wisdom permitted all this to exist; there are leaders as well as workers and servers. If all were leaders, who would obey and who would lead? And if all were rich to the same extent, who would take the blessing of giving, and who would rejoice and give thanks on receiving? There is, of course, desparity with regard to the kind of activity, the giving, the attitude, as well as with regard to the use of freedom.

God, in His wisdom, gave freedom to all His creation:

All the creation has the choice to do good or not. This is reasonable; for who does good voluntarily, with love and satisfaction shall be rewarded. Likewise, who does evil voluntarily shall be punished.

God, in His wisdom, did not destroy Satan, but He kept him to the end of the world to be cast into the lake of fire (Rev. 20: 10). Thus God observes who accepts the temptation of Satan, and who refuses it. Satan is also given -justly- an equal opportunity to work, and thereupon be justly rewarded. Moreover, Satan will be a witness to the righteous who refused him.

See also God's great wisdom apparent in the plan of the Tabernacle of Meeting!

He designed the court, the holy place, and the most holy. For each part He set an order, and with His wisdom He perfected its beauty. He chose for this Bezalel, and filled him with the Spirit of God, in wisdom, in understanding, in knowledge, and in all manner of workmanship (Ex. 31: 2-3)

With His wisdom, God appointed certain kinds of sacrifices; the passover lamb (Ex. 12), the burnt sacrifice (Lev. 1), sin offering, and peace offering.

With His wisdom He set the ranks and kinds of priesthood, fathers and prophets, then the Aaronic priesthood, and the priesthood of Melchizedek.

Everything in the universe is wisely managed.

God's wisdom clear in the course of occurences:

God's hand is wonderful in the course of occurences. A clear example is the life of Joseph the righteous. We are amazed how God raised Joseph to power in all Egypt, and how all events were managed by God's will. God with His wonderful dispensation arranged everything: the plot and the cruelty of the brothers, the corruption of Potipahr's wife and her false accusation, the companions in prison and the revealing of their thoughts to him, his interpretation of theirs and Pharaoh's dreams, the plentiful years and the years of famine ... God turned evil to good and harm to benefit.

See also how God interfered in the story of king Ahasuerus, Haman, and Mordecai: on a certain night the king could not sleep, so he commanded that the book of the records of the chronicles be brought and read before him (Esther 6). The result was that Mordecai was honored instead of being killed and Haman's plot was worked against him.

So many times God interfered in the course of events, as when He defeated the counsel of Ahithopehl (2 Sam. 15: 34), and when He saved the church from Arius. God also led St. Anthony to the angelic monastic system, for since the beginning God made him feel impressed by his father's death, then with the readings he heard in the church, and even with the advice (or rather reproach) of that shameless woman.

God's wisdom in temptations and pain:

An example of this is the plots of king Saul against David the prophet, which refined his personality, gave him strength and firmness, gave him depth in prayers and psalms, and made him suitable for the kingdom. The other temptations he underwent, whether with Joab the son of Zeruiah, Shimei the son of Gera, or Absalom his son, all these were for his spiritual benefit.

God's wisdom also allowed pain to exist!

Some serious diseases spread in the body silently and cannot be discovered except very late when there is no hope for healing, such as some kinds of cancer. Hence God's wisdom allowed some pain to help discovering the disease and curing it. Some diseases also that attack children cannot be discovered except when the child feels pain somewhere in the body because little children cannot speak or describe what they feel.

Pain is also useful for leading a person to repentance.

One hour of severe pain may restore a person to God more than dozens of sermons. Pain makes one feel near the end of life and get prepared for entering, or feels a dire need for God and seeks Him.

Pain also creates a feeling of kindness and sympathy

It makes one sympathize with those in pain, and try to relieve them of their suffering. This may also deepen the relations between them. Some people may also give out of their blood or give some members of their bodies to those in need. Physicians and scientists usually exert every effort to find a remedy for the people's pains and sufferings, and this realizes promotion in the fields of science and medicine.

Even psychological pains have their benefits, as Shawki, Egypt's poet laureate, said:

I was endowed with the genius pain to enjoy;
for the extremest genius in life is pain.

God's wisdom and death:

God permitted death to exist in order to transfer man from a material mortal life to a spiritual eternal life. Death will also be the first step towards transferring our bodies to glorified incorruptible bodies (1 Cor. 15: 42-49)

God's wisdom permitted that all people undergo death so that weak unable old people will not continue for successive generations, but rather to give way to new generations of lively, active, and productive youth.

Death also makes people prepare themselves for eternity, since they know that they will not continue for ever on the earth. Therefore the Twelfth Hour Prayer reminds us of death, eternity, and repentance to be ready for the eternal life.

God's wisdom and the Redemption:

As we have indicated several times: God with all wisdom arranged the Redemption for our salvation. He chose the right time when the holy Virgin will come who could bear the glories of the holy conception and the glorious maternity. He chose the time when John the Baptist will come to prepare the way before the Lord, and the holy apostles who will spread the Redemption Dogma all over the world. It was also the time when the whole people will have maturity enough in mind to accept the idea of Redemption or Salvation through propitiation throughout a long past full of symbols and prophecies.

God's dispensation arranged for the birth of the Redeemer, the Holy One without sin, who was to carry the sins of all people in all generations and die for them, and whose propitiation is limitless because of His unity with the Godhead.

God who solved the problem of salvation with such wisdom through the Redemption, is capable with His wisdom to solve all problems of the people.

Faith in God's wisdom:

Our faith in God's wisdom has many benefits in our life

Through this faith we trust God, and trust His good dispensation and we submit our whole life to Him. We grow in faith whenever we see various examples of God's wisdom in the incidents of the Scriptures as well as in our life and in the life of the others around us.

Our hearts are humbled before God's wisdom, and this makes us not rely on our own intelligence and planning but rather comply with the words of the Scriptures, *"lean not on your own understanding"* (Prov. 3: 5)

If we trust God's wisdom we will stop grumbling and complaining, and stop blasphemy, feeling that whatever God does is all wisdom and love whether we understand it or not.

God's wisdom may also be a subject for contemplation which would implant within us the glorification of God for His wisdom and thanks to Him for the good His wisdom bears for us.

184

GOD'S WISE DISPENSATION

God provided every creature with what is suitable and comfortable.

The polar bear, for instance, is provided by God with fur which gives it warmth because it lives in cold areas. The horse, on the other hand, is not in need of that. The camel is provided with hoof to be able to walk on sand, whereas the monkey is created with flexible spins that enable it to climb trees. Likewise, God gave wings to the birds, fins to the fish, and means of escape to the weak animals.

Once I passed by a vine; there I saw God's amazing dispensation!

In winter the vine shakes off its leaves, so the sun ray enters to give warmth to whoever sits by the vine. Then, in summer, the leaves return and fill the vine to be a shade from heat to whoever sits by it. The same happens with all leafy trees; an amazing wisdom for the benefit of the people and the tree itself.

See also the wonderful divine dispensation evident in man's physiological functions.

God provided everything, an amazing eye-lens, a wonderful pump in the heart, strange centers in the brain, wondrous sensitivity in all senses: touch, smelling, taste, ... etc. There are also the wonderful joints in the limbs, the amazing flexibility in the spines, and the excellent work done by all the body systems.

When a person eats a piece of candy, the teeth and tongue do their work. The tongue chews it, the teeth crush it and prepare it to be swallowed, then various kinds of secretions handle it, each kind is for a certain substance (fats, starch, sugar …). Afterwards, the substance is digested, assimilated, and turned into tissues and blood of the same kind of one's blood!!

God, not only did make His creation and end His work of creation, but He also continued to manage the life of His creation, even the nature and celestial bodies, caring for the whole creation in general, and for each separately.

See God's wonderful planning for the bee. How very amazing is His planning for such an insect! How does He make it collect the nectar from the flowers and turn it into honey as if it were a chemist! And how does it extract the queen's food as if it were a skilful pharmacist preparing the strongest medicine! Moreover, God enabled the bee to make the cells in such a wonderful way as if it were an efficient engineer! This besides the very wise management capability given it, and the relationship among the laborers, and between them and the queen so that Shawki the poet laureate said about this:

A kingdom managed by a powerful woman;

Having authority and control over laborers & artisans;

Amazed am I at laborers subjects to an empress.

God gave also wonderful capabilities to birds in their journeys and in leading such journeys. The animals are also given orderly management with regard to reproduction. Similarily, plants are endowed with orderly action by which a tree yields fruit, whose seed is in itself according to its kind (Gen. 1: 11, 12)

As to human beings God manages their life collectively and individually.

Each person's life is managed very wisely as if such a person were a particular action done by God leading to the divine dispensation provided that the person submits himself to God's work and dispensation.

Take Joseph the righteous for example: God intended to make him king over all Egypt. But to attain such a position he should be near to Pharaoh and gain his trust. In order to reach Pharaoh God gave Pharaoh certain dreams that need interpretation, and made all magicians and fortunetellers unable to interpret those dreams. Then God made the chief butler tell Pharaoh about Joseph and his ability to interpret dreams.

This also was arranged by God; for God sent dreams to Pharaoh's chief butler and chief baker in the prison, and they needed an interpretation. That all this might happen, God arranged the means by which Joseph would enter the prison. That means was the plot of Potiphar's wife against Joseph; for which Joseph was to be a servant in Potiphar's house. This happened when the Ismaelites bought Joseph and sold him to Potiphar after being cast in the pit by his brothers. In order that they might do this, God permitted that Joseph's brothers envy him because of the colored tunic and because of two dreams God gave Joseph which meant that he would preside over his brothers. How amazing is all this! Joseph summarized it all to his brothers in one phrase, *"you meant evil against me; but God meant it for good, in order to bring it about as it is this day"* (Gen. 50: 20), He said also on another occasion, *"it was not you who sent me here, but God"* (Gen. 45: 8)

Indeed most amazing and wonderful are God's arrangements and dispensation! Could Joseph say to God: Why, O Lord, have You done all this to me? It was the intention of God the loving to make Joseph king, father to Pharaoh, Lord of all his house and a ruler throughout all the land of Egypt (Gen. 45: 8)

Another example is David, whom God wanted to make a king.

For this purpose, David had to be strong, experienced and tempted, so that he might be able to manage a broad kingdom and various battles. However, David was just a young man, ruddy, with bright eyes, and good looking (1 Sam. 16: 11, 12). Therefore God arranged that David be exposed to Saul's wars and plots against him. This provided him with experience, endurance, and nobility, besides skill in war. So he sang in the psalm, *"Blessed be the Lord my rock, who trains my hands for war, and my fingers for battle"* (Ps. 144: 1). Temptations refined David's personality, and made of him a powerful ruler. More beautiful still is that temptations made of him a man of prayers, who submits all thoughts of his heart to God, confessing, asking, thanking, and praising. Thus he left us in his psalms a treasure of prayers and meditations used by all churches.

God used the same wise dispensation with His prophet Samuel.

God wanted him to be a prophet, to minister to Him in the temple, to anoint kings with the holy anointing oil. Therefore God made his mother barren and longing to have a son, and when her rival provoked her, she went to the temple, wept in anguish, and vowed in a deep prayer that if God gave her a son she would give him to the Lord all the days of his life (1 Sam. 1). Thus it came to happen, and Samuel was brought up in the temple and deserved what the Lord arranged for him.

God, smilarily, arranged a way by which Jonah would submit and Nineveh repent.

He ordered Jonah to go to Nineveh and cry out against it. God, with His divine foreknowledge knew that Jonah would disobey, and it happened actually that God Himself arranged for him the ship in which he fled from the presence of the Lord! God also arranged for a great wind and a mighty tempest on the sea so that the ship was about to be broken and the mariners were afraid. Thereupon the passengers prayed and believed, offered a sacrifice and made vows (Jon. 1: 16). So, by the disobedience of Jonah God saved the passengers on the ship.

Furthermore, God prepared a great fish (a whale) to swallow Jonah. Thus Jonah came to himself, prayed, and God saved him. This time Jonah cried out that Nineveh would be overthrown, and the people of Nineveh fasted, prayed, repented, and turned from their evil way. God, seeing all this, forgave and saved them, but Jonah was displeased and angry because his word had not come true, and he wished to die.

God did not leave Jonah, but He prepared for Jonah a plant and made it come up over him. Then God prepared a worm and it so damaged the plant that it withered. Immediately God made the sun beat on Jonah's head, so that he wished death for himself. At this point God argued with Jonah convincing him so that he might be saved.

How wonderful is God's dispensation by which He saved the passengers on the ship, the people of Nineveh, and Jonah himself! How amazingly did God use the wind, the sea, the fish, the plant, the worm, and the sun with His wise divine dispensation!

So many are the cases in which God used similar arrangements with holy people, and even with sinners.

God arranged for St. Paul to see a funeral of some dead person, and the hear a talk among some people in that procession, from which he felt how life is worthless and how trivial are the judgements of the people. God further arranged for him to be taken by an angel to the wilderness, and there a raven to bring him food. Finally, God arranged that St. Anthony visit St. Paul at the last days of his life to know his story, to relate it to us, and to bury him!

God arranged also for St. Anthony to be affected by the death of his father, and by a verse of the Bible he heard in the church, and afterwards by the word of a shameless woman who said to him: If you are a monk, go and dwell in the mount, for this place is not for the dwelling of monks. So he did and became the father of all monks!

Even the sinners were led to repentance by God's dispensation. Mary the Copt, Pelagia, Baeisa, Sarah, Augustine, and Moses the Black, each of them experienced God's dispensation. God's hand was behind the repentance of each of them. He did not only lead them to repentance, but He also turned them to saints by whose conduct and prayers all the world benefitted.

God arranged solutions that have never occurred to one's mind for many problems.

He divided the Red Sea –for the first time in history- in order to save Moses and God's people. Moreover, He fed all those in the wilderness with manna and quails, and gave them water from the rock to drink (Ex. 17: 6), and guided them on their way with a pillar of fire by night and a cloud by day (Ex. 13: 21)

People often failed when they sought human solutions, but God's solutions interfered in time.

Many stories can be mentioned but for the limited space.

More important yet than all this is God's dispensation for the salvation of humanity and the wonderful Redemption He arranged and completed. This is the topic of the following chapter.

GOD'S DISPENSATION OF THE GREAT REDEMPTION & SALVATION

We have spoken about God's wise dispensation for everything: for nature, and for the life of the people, and now let us speak about His wise dispensation of Incarnation and Redemption.

After Adam and Eve had sinned, God promised to save them. He said that the woman's seed would bruise the head of the serpent (Gen. 3: 15). By this God meant that the Lord Christ would come of the seed of the woman and bruise the head of the serpent, that is Satan (Rev. 20: 2). This was to be realized through the Redemption he was to offer for the salvation of all mankind.

However, the serpent continued bearing its head high, and conquering mankind, leading them to destruction through idol worship and many evils. Where was the divine promise then?

Salvation would only be achieved through the Redemption. Had it been given at that time, no one would have understood it. Therefore God had to prepare their minds to understand the Redemption.

They had to understand the idea of redemption, and the redemption through blood. God therefore arranged for the suitable time, the characters, the language, and the means of conveying the work of salvation and redemption.

Preparing the minds to understand:

This preparation took place in many stages, each of which God willed to take enough time so that it might be implanted in the mind. These stages are as follows:

1. When our forefathers sinned, they felt they were naked and they covered themselves with fig leaves. The Lord God, knowing that the fig leaves were not fit, He made tunics of skin and clothed them (Gen. 3: 21). The skin was of course the skin of an animal slaughtered. Thus man learnt this principle:

Sin causes nakedness, and sacrifice covers sin.

2. Afterwards people learnt that they should offer sacrifices. The first sacrifice mentioned in the Scriptures is that offered by Abel the righteous who offered of the firstborn of his flock and of their fat (Gen. 4: 4). As God accepted the offering of Abel, people learnt the second lesson:

The sacrifice to be offered should be the firstborn and the best.

3. When God ordered Abraham to offer Isaac as a burnt offering, God said, *"Take now your son, your only son Isaac, whom you love ... and offer him there as a burnt offering on one of the mountains of which I shall tell you"* (Gen. 22: 2). Here humanity learnt a third principle:

Offering the only beloved son.

4. It is observed that all the sacrifices offered in the Book of Genesis were burnt offerings which were usually consumed by fire and turned into ashes (Lev. 6: 10). No one was allowed to eat from them.

The burnt offerings were all for God, consumed by God's fire to please His heart.

The fire that consumed the offerings was holy fire, the same first fire that descended from heaven to consume the burnt offering. They kept this fire because God did not allow any profane fire to be offered before Him (Lev. 10: 1, 2).

5. Then God gave them the law of the Passover: The Lord's Angel was to pass through the land of Egypt and strike all the firstborn. But the firstborn of the Hebrews would be saved – according to the Lord's command- by sprinkling the blood of the passover lamb on their doors. As the Lord said to them, "*When I see the blood, I shall pass over you*" (Ex. 12: 13).

This was the origin of the word Passover, and the Hebrews learnt another lesson:

Blood is the means of salvation from death; for the lamb's blood was shed to redeem them.

The concept of "Redemption":

St. Paul afterwards said, "*For indeed Christ, our Passover, was sacrificed for us*" (1 Cor. 5: 7). Through the Passover they began to know the concept of the redemption: The blood of an innocent sacrifice is shed and it died for them.

Hence, redemption meant that an innocent dies for the guilty.

6. God then gave them the law of the sacrifices: each sacrifice signifies a certain aspect of the redemption. They were commanded that the person who offers the sacrifice lays his hand on the sacrifice and confesses his sins before slaughtering it. Thus the sacrifice carries the sins instead of the person who sinned. Therefore the lamb offered as a sacrifice represented the fact that:

An innocent, without sin, carries the sin of the others; an innocent, who does not deserve to die, dies on behalf of a guilty person condemned to death.

After many generations, Isaiah the prophet utters a prophecy concerning the sacrifice of the Lord Christ; he says, *"All we like sheep have gone astray; we have turned, every one to his own way; and the Lord has laid on Him the iniquity of us all"* (Isa. 53: 6)

This is then the Redeemer, who put on Himself the sins of us all.

7. Another meaning of the Redemption is introduced in the Scriptures concerning the Great Day of Atonement (Lev. 16)

Aaron was to lay both his hands on the scapegoat, and confess over it all the iniquities of the people, and all their transgressions and sins, then send the goat away into the wilderness bearing all their iniquities (Lev. 16: 20-22), and is never seen again. The meaning is explained by David the prophet referring to the Lord, *"As far the east is from the west, so far has He removed our transgressions from us"* (Ps. 103: 12)

8. There had to be a long span before people could understand the significance of the redemption and the characteristics of the ransom that was to be offered in the person of Christ.

So many generations have passed and the people used to connect between the forgiveness by blood and the death of an innocent on behalf of a guilty person bearing the sins of the guilty instead of him. But who was that innocent sacrifice? They knew for certain that he would be of the seed of the man who had been condemned to die, that is "The Son of Man". Therefore, every woman longed to bear a son, for perhaps he would be the Savior. Accordingly, being barren was a shame to

194

any woman. Then this shame ended when the prophecy announced that the Savior will be born of a virgin,

"Behold, the virgin shall conceive and bear a Son, and shall call His name Immanuel" (Isa. 7: 74)

Prophet Isaiah said also, *"For unto us a Child is born, unto us a Son is given; and the government will be upon His shoulders. And His name will be called Wonderful, Counselor, Mighty God, Everlasting Father, Prince of Peace. Of the increase of His government and peace there will be no end, upon the throne of David and over His kingdom ... "* (Isa. 9: 6, 7)

Before that, there had been a prophecy that the Savior would be from the tribe of Judah. For our father Jacob said, *"The scepter shall not depart from Judah, nor a lawgiver from between his feet, until Shiloh comes; and to Him shall be the obedience of the people."* (Gen. 49: 10)

Hence the description of the woman's seed who was to bruise the head of the serpent can be summarized as follows:

He is the Son of Man, born of a virgin, the offspring of David, from the tribe of Judah. At the same time He is a Mighty God, through whose blood salvation is attained; for He bears on Himself the sins of all and dies on their behalf, and removes away their sins so that they might be seen no more.

Many prophecies and symbols were given to prepare the minds of the people to understand.

Preparing the Characters :

9. **The virgin who was to give birth to the Redeemer had to be prepared.**

She should be a holy person that deserves to give birth to Christ the Redeemer. At the same time she should be humble so that she might endure such sublime glory. All this was found in the Virgin Mary who is called blessed by all generations because *"He has regarded the lowly state of His maidservant"* (Lk. 1: 48).

It was necessary that the Virgin be prepared who can accept the idea of conceiving while still virgin and who can submit to the divine will, who says, *"Let it be according to your words"* (Lk. 1: 28).

10. The righteous old man, Joseph the carpenter, had also to be prepared first to protect Mary and take care of her, and also to keep her virginity trusting what the angel told him, *"that which is conceived in her is of the Holy Spirit"* (Mt. 1: 20).

11. Even the angel who was to prepare the way before the Savior had to be prepared.

It is the angel who was to prepare the people by the baptism for repentance, and ascribe no glory to himself but rather say, *"It is He who, coming after me, is preferred before me, whose sandal strap I am not worthy to loose"* (Jn. 1: 27). And when asked, *"Who are you?"*, he said, *"I am not the Christ"* (Jn. 1: 20)

12. The apostles, who were to carry Christ's message to the far ends of the earth and spread the Christian faith powerfully enduring all types of persecution, had likewise to be prepared.

13. The fullness of time was waiting till the wicked come who were to crucify the Redeemer, and also the priests and the elders who envy Him and seek to kill Him. Judah the betrayer who sell His master for thirty pieces of silver was to be born, and in him realized the words of the psalm, *"Who ate my bread, has lifted up his heel against me"* (Ps. 41: 9). Even the coward governor Pilate who, afraid of the Jews, judged that Christ be

crucified, though he was certain that Christ is blameless (Acts 3: 13) (Jn. 17: 38), had to come first.

14. For the fullness of time to come when the Redeemer was to be born, there should be realized many things:

The prophecies perfected, all symbols realized in Him and people understand their significance, and all the characters - whether righteous or wicked - who will have a role in the event will have existed. There was also a preparation for the birth of Christ and for His carrying out the message.

Preparing the language and the roads:

There had to be an international language in which evangelizing takes place

For this purpose, the Greeks entered the Middle East countries by means of Alexander the Great in 323 B.C. Through them the Greek tongue spread and became an international language in which the gospels were afterwards written, and which the holy fathers spoke.

Furthermore, during the reign of Ptolemy II, the Old Testament was translated in Alexandria into Greek (the Septuagint text). This prepared the Greeks to accept the introduction to the birth of Christ as included in the Old Testament. Moreover, God gave the gift of speaking tongues to cover any other languages required.

Then the Romans –according to their custom- paved the roads.

This was useful for the movement of the evangelists and preachers from one place to the other carrying the good tidings of salvation to the far ends of the empire.

When all this had taken place, the fullness of the time came when, *"God sent forth His Son, born of a woman, born under the law, to redeem those who were under the law, that we might receive the adoption as sons"* (Gal. 4: 4, 5)

As we have seen, God, with wonderful wisdom, prepared all things pertaining to the Redemption. He did everything in the proper time when all things assembled together, and this was the fullness of the time in which all things participated in an organized way to effect the good divine dispensation.

So, do not think, brother, that God delayed, nor ask Him to make haste; for everything is arranged to take place in the proper time.

As God arranged everything for the divine Incarnation in the fullness of time, He makes arrangements also for everything.

The Dispensation of Salvation:

God who arranged the order of creation, arranged also for Salvation.

God had arranged for man's salvation before man sinned, and even before being created. He arranged for the amazing Incarnation and the divine Redemption. Moreover, God arranged for man to understand such theological matters through long teaching on sacrifices and burnt offerings, then through practice. By many prophecies God made humanity accept the steps of salvation. He gave prophecies on the Lord's birth from a virgin, His crucifixion and death, His love for mankind and His condescension to save them, His resurrection, and His ascension.

As God arranged for the redemption to save man, He likewise set the order of the church sacraments.

With a very wise dispensation God set for us all the means by which we can gain the great salvation through the work of His Holy Spirit in the church sacraments. How beautiful are the words of the Liturgy of St. Gregory [You tied me up with all medicines causing life] He set for us Baptism, Chrism, Repentance, Eucharist, and Priesthood that administers all sacraments. He arranged for us the divine channels through which we receive the wonderful salvation. He stayed with His disciples forty days to explain to them the divine doctrine, the rituals, the practices, the worship, and the sacraments necessary for God's kingdom (Acts 1)

With His wise dispensation the Lord did not leave us orphans, but He sent us the Holy Spirit, gave us various gifts of the Spirit, ordained shepherds and teachers, and organized all things in His church according to His blessed good will. He left us not in need of anything of the work of His glory.

True indeed are the words of David the prophet:

"Who in the heavens can be compared to the Lord? Who among the sons of the mighty can be likened to the Lord?" **(Ps. 89)**

His wisdom is evident in the arrangements He makes, and in the proper time He chooses for His dispensation. Everything has its suitable time which He knows, as the Lord said, *"It is not for you to know times or seasons which the Father has put in His own authority"* (Acts 1: 7)

Our human mind may choose unsuitable time for anything, whereas the Lord arranges for everything to take place in the most suitable time. Though we may protest against the time chosen by God, yet His choice is certainly the best.

God's dispensation for the people:

In the history of salvation we read the words *"the fullness of the time"* (Gal. 4: 4)

The words *"the fullness of the time"* refers to the divine wisdom in arranging the time.

Man often is confused with regard to his spiritual life, and often exclaims: When, O Lord, may I attain? But the Lord chooses the time which He knows to be the best time for the life of that person.

God chose for Augustine a certain time for repentance, which was at the age of thirty. He chose for him also a certain means of repentance as He did for Moses the black. God chose different circumstances for the repentance of Mary the Copt and Pelagia.

So there is not one way God arranges for all people, but for each one He sets a suitable way and a suitable time.

However different the arrangements or the times are, but the common factor in all is the wisdom, the love, and the goodness which characterize God's dispensation. When we read the Scriptures or the biography of the saints, we notice that God used a different dispensation for each saint.

Sea how God arranged the life of Moses the prophet since his childhood!

God sent him Pharaoh's daughter to take him as son. Then Moses was learned in all the wisdom of the Egyptians, and God taught him calmness and forbearance in the wilderness. God afterwards chose him to take the leadership, and gave him power over Pharaoh, supporting him with miracles and talking to him directly. All this was a dispensation from God which Moses almost had no hand in.

Joseph the righteous, likewise, had everything arranged for him by God through dreams, tribulations and evils which turned to good for him. And David the prophet was chosen by God from among his brothers, and God's Spirit descended on him, and he was trained by hardships and pains which turned into tunes in his psalms. The psalms were also God's dispensation for our spiritual benefit.

The life of all those persons were hymns in God's harp.

The life of each of those was a string giving a certain tune when the divine dispensation played it, composing a wonderful symphony for the whole mankind to listen to. How amazing God dispensation is for each person!

Let us submit our life to His dispensation:

It will be marvelous indeed if we submit our life to God to manage it Himself.

The life of God's people in the past was under God's management in everything, whether in worship, in leadership, or in movement. He was king over the people managing them by His dispensation. Therefore when the people wanted to have a king to rule over them, God said to Samuel, *"they have not rejected you, but they have rejected Me"* (1 Sam. 8: 7)

Their request to have a king was a request to be independent and separate from God and His management. But as they departed from Him they failed!

Abraham the patriarch did not benefit from his own human arrangement when he chose Hagar and Keturah; for only by God's dispensation he was given Isaac in whom Abraham's seed was to be called (Gen. 21: 12).

It is good for man to be united with God in intention and in work, submitting himself completely to the divine dispensation.

Such submission requires complete trust in the wisdom and benefit of God's dispensation, confidence in the goodness of the divine action, and certainty that the time appointed by God is the best time.

Trust in the divine dispensation and the satisfaction with it give a person peace and comfort, and moreover grant him a life of joy and thanksgiving.

Would that we pray all the time that God may manage our life!

Would that God manage our life and not leave us to our own thoughts or wisdom! Would that He lead us in every step as He led the people in the wilderness! But we should not doubt in spite of any circumstances, nor grumble against God's dispensation. We should only say *"Let Your will be done"*

See how amazingly God arranges and manages our life, not only when we come into this world but also before we are born or even conceived of! He said so on the mouth of Jeremiah, *"Before I formed you in the womb I knew you; Before you were born I sanctified you; I ordained you a prophet to the nations"* (Jer. 1: 4, 5)

In the same way God arranged the life, the work, and the mission of John the Baptist even before being conceived of in Elizabeth. And Paul the apostle said, *"when it pleased God, who separated me from my mother's womb and called me through His grace ... that I might preach Him among the Gentiles ..."* (Gal. 1: 15, 16).

If it is so, let us rejoice and be pleased in God's dispensation.

SECTION

MAN'S RELATIONSHIP WITH GOD

Contents of this Section:

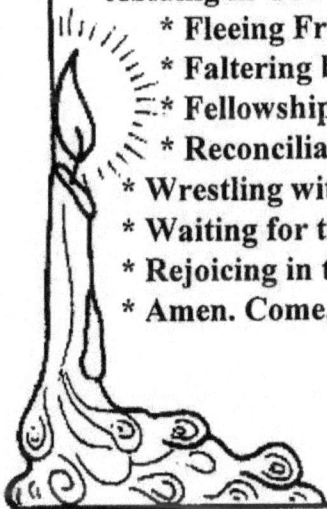

GOD'S PLACE
IN OUR LIFE

To have a spiritual life means to have God solely filling all your life. If one puts anything besides Him, one's spiritualities get confused and the ego may become first in one's life.

When Satan fought our forefathers Adam and Eve, seeing that God was everything in their life, He made them think of becoming equal to God. He said to them, *"you will be like God, knowing good and evil"* (Gen. 3: 5). So when the ego began to grow, God began to disappear from their life.

When a person concentrates on himself, he cannot concentrate on God. Therefore it is good for him that God deprives him of the things that made him deviate.

This was what happened to Job the righteous when the ego began to appear and grow and he began to concentrate on himself, saying, *"When I went out to the gate by the city, when I took my seat in the open square, the young men saw me and hid, and the aged arose and stood; the princes refrained from talking, and put their hand on their mouth; the voice of nobles was hushed, and their tongue stuck to the roof of their mouth. When the ear heard, then it blessed me, and when the eye saw, then it approved me ... "* (Job 29: 7-11)

So, God deprived this saint of everything, whether money, property, children, or health. Thus he lost everything, but God alone remained with him, and this was very good for him. Then Job could say, *"I have heard of You by the hearing of the ear, but now my eye sees You"* (Job 42: 5)

Jonah the prophet also the ego stood between him and God. This was when God sent him to Nineveh to cry out against it. But Jonah knew that Nineveh would repent by his call and would not be destroyed, and his word would fall, so he fled from the presence of the Lord. Again when the city repented and was saved, Jonah was very angry even unto death, and but for God's care for him and dialogue with him he would have perished (Jon. 4)!

Lot is another example; for when he put before him the wealth and the good land and did not have God as his only goal, he accepted to dwell in Sodom. There, *"that righteous man, dwelling among them, tormented his righteous soul from day to day by seeing and hearing their lawless deeds"* (2 Pet. 2: 8). Furthermore Lot lost everything and was himself about to perish but for God who sent two angels to save him.

A righteous person does not put other goals in his heart besides God, but God is always his only aim, and he rejects everything else.

The rich young man went sorrowful because the love of money was within his heart besides God, although he had kept the commandments from his youth! The Lord therefore said, *"No one can serve two masters"*

A holy man like our father Abraham did not allow any other love to separate him from the love of God, not even his natural love towards his only son, whom he loved, Isaac. So, when God's command came to him that he should give this son as burnt offering, he rose very early, took his son, and took the wood and the knife without any hesitation (Gen. 22: 3)

Regrettably even some holy things may separate men from God when they turn into a goal instead of God, and when God's commandments are broken because of them.

Our father Jacob had a good desire: to take the rights and the blessing of the firstborn. But this holy desire turned into a goal in his heart whereas God should have been his actual goal. This made Jacob realize his desire through lying and delusion, and through deceiving his father who had lost his sight. In all this he did not put God before him.

Another example is those who lose God under the pretext of defending the faith!

Those may use insults, cruelty, and severe wrestling, falling in wrong words, wrong sentiments, and wrong means. They are filled with malice and hatred towards anyone who refuses their dogmas. In all this they do not have God before them, for God is Love and is not pleased with all this. An example of those is the Arians who accused St. Athanasius unjustly and caused his exile many times!

Faith itself may turn into a goal to some people and cause them to be separated from God!

They may even break all God's commandments to attain such a goal. This does not mean that defending the faith is something wrong. Nay, it is rather a virtue, but the wrong thing is to lose God as a goal and to accept a substitute for Him by defending the faith through wrong means that make you lose God.

This type of people includes those who minister to God, but the ministry becomes their goal and forget God for its sake!

Here the ministry becomes a field for quarrels, where the ministers accuse each other and dispute against each other. Thus the ministry becomes a field of enmity and the ministers lose the purity and cleanliness of their hearts because they put the ministry as a goal separate from God, from His commandments, and from His communion! That is why many religious spheres are impure, full of controversy, anger, insults, and lack of spirituality. In brief they are not in the image God wanted them to be.

Religion may also turn into sectarianism, and sects or denominations wrestle!

In all this we search for God but cannot find Him; we search for God's image in man and do not find it. God has disappeared as a goal.

Do not think that Satan works in the places of entertainment only.

Satan can enter into the places of worship and works. He even can learn verses from the Holy Bible, can argue in theology, can put on the garments of theologians, and can introduce a variety of heresies and heterodoxies! By this Satan can turn the religious field to a flame of fire .. for his service! Thus when the ministry becomes a goal instead of God, the minister falls.

The ministry may also become a field for selfassertion!

Questions may rise like: who will be first? Who will be head? Who will manage and control? Who is the best? And the ministry may become a room for growing famous, gaining popularity, or for ostentation. This means that the goal has deviated, and instead of having God as a goal, the ego has become the real goal.

Hence one should examine oneself continuously.

See whether the goal has deviated or not. Is God still your aim? What is God's place in your life?

See if God fills your life or there is still some space within you that needs to be filled with other desires. Consider whether God satisfies you and with Him you need nothing or not? Is God for you all in all, or there are various goals and desires within you? What actually, pleases you, is it God's gifts that please you or God Himself?

Be wary for your life; for Satan can easily leave you on your spiritual way, and let you pray, minister, read the Bible, and even pray, then he lets the ego appear. In this way all the holy practices turn into goals or into means for satisfying oneself! God then will have no real presence in your life! All your concern will be about yourself: what are you? What will you become, and when? How will you grow, and who may stand against you? How could you prevail over such persons? You will find the ego occupying all your time, all your mind, and all your heart. Would that you stop and ask yourself what God's place is in your life, and whether the ego still hides Him.

Some person may also serve in the church out of love towards God, but many preoccupations may so distract him that he finds no time for God. Ministry becomes to such a person his whole life, but he forgets God and soon will wither losing the aim!

You should therefore hold to the Lord and return to your first love.

Let God be beloved always on your mouth. Sing to Him everyday a new song, and let Him be the cause of your heart throbbing. Let Him be your dream by night and your hope by day, and even be your whole life.

Sit to yourself, argue with yourself and correct your way.

See whether God is your aim, or a means to realize your aims!

Consider why you pray to Him. Do you want Him to grant you what you desire, or He is all your desire? Do you seek Him to help you in your life, or because He is your whole life as Paul the apostle said, *"For me, to live is Christ"* (Phil. 1: 21); *"It is no longer I who live, but Christ lives in me"* (Gal. 2: 20)

Who is God for you? And who was He for the saints?

Ask David the prophet -who was a man of war and battles- about the cause of His power in the wars, he will says *"I will praise You, for You have answered me, and have become my salvation"* (Ps. 118: 21)

Ask the saints who the Lord is for them, they will answer He is the teacher, the shepherd, the physician, the companion, the friend and the beloved, He is the goal and the means, and He is everything.

Know that He will fight for you, and you shall hold your peace (Ex. 14: 14); He will speak on your mouths (Mt. 10: 20); He intercedes for you, and He feeds you; He is the vine and you the branches (Jn. 15: 1-3); He is the groom and you the bride (Mt. 15: 1, 2); He is the living bread descending from heaven (Jn. 6); He is everything to everyone. This will be the place of God in your life if only you taste and see how good He is (Ps. 34), for He has no similar among the gods.

We believe not only in the God of the Scriptures or the God of heaven, but we rather believe in God who lives with us day and night, or rather who lives in us (Gal. 2: 20).

We believe in this God who we have seen, heard, and touched with our hands (1 Jn. 1: 1). We worship Him not that He might bring us to eternal happiness, for He is our eternal happiness, He is the One who *"Eye has not seen, nor ear heard, nor have entered into the heart of man"* (1 Cor. 2: 9). The happiness with Him in the eternal life no eye has ever seen.

But let me ask: Is God within you, or outside you?

Do you seek Him in books or in certain places? Then see what the prophecy says, *"Therefore if they say to you: 'Look, He is in the desert!' Do not go out; or 'Look, He is in the inner rooms!' do not believe it"* (Mt. 24: 26)

He is within you, in your heart. Augustine sought Him in philosophy, in knowledge, and in books, but he did not find Him. But, at last, he found Him within his heart, and he sorrowfully said: O Lord, You were with me all the time, but, for my great misery, I was not with You.

NOTHING BESIDES GOD

Everyone seeks happiness, and can find it in one or more sources. But a spiritual person finds his happiness solely in God who is the source of this happiness. And the higher one's spirituality is, the more one becomes satisfied with God and the more one's life is filled with God who becomes to such a person all in all.

One of the sins in which Adam and Eve fell was seeking happiness outside God. They thought they can find happiness in knowledge, particularly in the knowledge of good and evil, or in arrogance and pride. So they were satisfied with God.

It is Satan's way to attempt spoiling the heart's purity by introducing into it an aim or a desire other than God.

To Adam and Eve Satan introduced the fruit and the knowledge. And to Christ, he introduced other desires: all the kingdoms of the earth and their power, the greatness of being carried by the angels, and the bread. But Christ refused them all, being satisfied with the Father.

The desires is the game which Satan often plays in his fighting man.

What then makes you happy and pleased, God or other desires? Can you feel satisfied with God, or you want to add something besides Him?

The saints who lived in deserts, mountains, and caves of the earth, in complete unity with God feeling all happiness with God, and having no need for any thing besides Him. Truly a heart rising above the desires is an unattainable fortress.

When Satan introduces to man a certain desire separate from God, he starts also to disturb his mind and heart attempting to make such a desire occupy the heart which is consecrated to God.

What about you? Is God your aim, or you have another aim? Or has He become to you a means to achieve other aims?

Many people see God as a means leading to achieving their desires. They present to God many desires and ask Him to realize these desires for them. They do not have God as their only desire.

When will the time come in which one prays to God, saying: I want You, O Lord, You alone? David said, *"Your face, Lord, I will seek. Do not hide Your face from me"* (Ps. 27: 8, 9). Examine yourself then if there is another aim in your heart besides God which love made it replace God. See if anything new has entered your heart.

What was the problem of the Jews with respect to Christ?

The problem was that Christ was not their goal, but only a means leading them to rule, independence and restoration of the empire of David and Solomon. He was to them the means that would enable them to get rid of the foreign ruler. Therefore when Christ refused to be king they were disappointed and began to plot against Him. Judas also lived with Christ, but Christ was not his aim; he had other desires than Christ with whom he lived.

On the other hand, the saints who had the Lord as their only aim, those could leave everything for His sake. Paul the apostle for example said, *"I have suffered the loss of all things, and count them as rubbish, that I may gain Christ"* (Phil. 3: 8). And Peter the apostle said to the Lord, *"See, we have left all and followed You"* (Mt. 19: 27)

Because Abraham the patriarch had God as his only aim, he found no difficulty in complying with the Lord's command when the Lord said to him, "*Get out of your country, from your family and from your father's house, to a land that I will show you*" (Gen. 12: 1). But when Abraham let the desire to have offspring enter into his heart, he sought human ways; he married Hagar (Gen. 16: 3, 4), then Keturah (Gen. 25: 1). When God saw his great desire to have children, God said to him, "*Take now your son, your only son Isaac, whom you love ... and offer him there as a burnt offering*" (Gen. 22: 2). But when Abraham succeeded in the trial, God granted him offspring as numerous as the stars of the heaven and the sand of the sea.

Would that everyone examines himself to find out what exists in his heart besides, or instead of, God, and whether such things are desires or goals, and whether they prevail over him or he prevails over them.

Lot led with Abraham a life of strangement and worship, in tents and in the altars, but when the desire for the good land found a place in his heart that he might have a lot of sheep, he chose the land of Sodom. There he began to lose his spirituality, and finally he went out of Sodom with nothing, having lost all he had. When the good watered land became the first aim and God the second, Lot lost everything: the plants, the sheep, his wife and his sons in law.

Solomon the wise let desires into his heart; whatever his eyes desired he did not keep from them (Eccl. 2: 10). Thus he was about to perish but for the Lord's care which made him feel that all is vanity (Eccl. 1)

Contemplation on death is actually a lesson given by God everyday.

Whenever a person dies, people know that he left the world with nothing of his property and none of his beloved. He left the whole world to stand before God. Anthony the rich young man took his lesson from the death of his father. Would that we also learn the lesson whenever we hear of the death of someone.

Would that we learn that the world is passing away, and the lust of it as the Scriptures say (1 Jn. 2: 17)

Moses the prophet relinquished all the desires, hopes, and lures of the world when he left the palace of Pharaoh, *"esteeming the reproach of Christ greater riches than the treasures in Egypt"* (Heb. 11. 26). God was his only aim rather than riches and rule, and this made it easy for him to relinquish all such worldly matters.

Satan endeavours always to put another aim than God before man, even in the field of ministry and prayers.

When you start the ministry, Satan may allow you to do, but he will take part with you introducing his advices. Therefore, in the name of faithfulness, he may make you so involved in the ministry that you find no time for prayer, contemplation, or spiritual readings. Afterwards, in the name of holy zeal, he urges you to criticize and condemn others, to get angry, uprage and dispute with other, and even to fight them. In this way, Satan will have attained his goal when he allowed you at the beginning to take part in the ministry. Finally, he could make you have something besides God in your life.

Here the ministry started as a means leading to God, then it turned into an aim in itself!

The same applies also to prayers. The prayers of some people are so fervent that their mind may swim in beautiful spiritual meditations. Here Satan cannot prevent such a person from praying, but he praises such deep meditations, then convinces him of their benefit to the ministry and that they should be recorded before being forgotten. At this point that person stops praying and starts to record his meditations! He leaves God and focuses on the ministry and on knowledge. Hence the ministry becomes an aim, whereas God comes next!

It is Satan's plan to introduce to you replacements for God, endeavoring as far as possible that such replacements be acceptable to you.

To a sinner, Satan introduces worldly lusts. And to the righteous, he introduces ministry involvements and church work requirements, so that a person in any case may forget God and forget even himself.

Satan introduced to the lost son the love of freedom, money, inheritance, and enjoyment of his possessions with his friends with prodigal living. Whereas to the elder son who served his father so many years, Satan made him so involved in serving his father that he lost communion with his father and lost his love.

A wise person therefore should examine himself now and then to see how he is proceeding and where is God's place in his life; whether he is all in all or is forgotten amidst the many preoccupations. St. Arsanius used to do this and to examine himself continually.

Happy is the person who holds to God as the only aim in his life, and finds his pleasure in God, not taking Him merely as a means to realize his desires.

The verse says, "*My son, give Me your heart*" (Prov. 23: 26), but it is completed with the verse which says, "*You shall love the Lord your God with all your heart*" (Deut. 6: 5). But many people, though they admit that the heart should be given to God, do not give it all. They put many things in it besides God, such as certain types of love rivalling God's love in their hearts. Sometimes some sinful love enters their hearts disguised in the clothing of virtue. Such people may also be fought in a gradual way which they cannot be aware of or on guard against.

Beware side goals in your spiritual life.

Give everything its proper estimation, for this will determine your behavior.

If you give prayers a higher estimation than work or ministry, you will put it in the proper place, and will give time for it instead of giving yourself execuse for lack of time or preoccupations. For such execuses mean that you give preference to such preoccupations. The ego may sometimes occupy the first place in one's life and lead every behavior the wrong way.

Try therefore to modify or change your view to the various aspects of life.

If you say that you have no time for prayer, or that you say your prayers on your way to work or to any other place, this means that the awe due to prayers has no place in your life. More serious the case will be if the opponent himself gives such estimation; this will make your life confused.

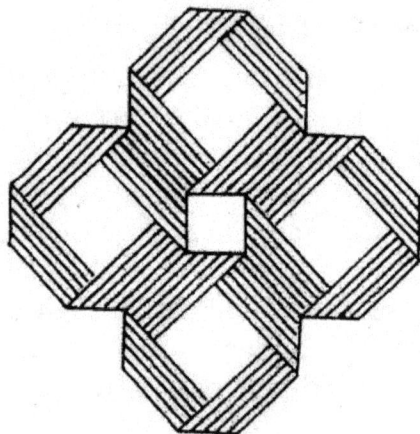

GOD IS THE FIRST AND THE LAST

The Lord said in the Book of Revelation, *"I am the Alpha and the Omega, the First and the Last"* (Rev. 1: 11, 8, 17) ; *"I am the Alpha and the Omega, the Beginning and the End, the First and the Last"* (Rev. 22: 13). And in the Book of Isaiah the prophet He said, *"I am the First and I am the Last; besides Me there is no God"* (Isa. 44: 6). To interpret this He said also, *"Before Me there was no God formed, nor shall there be after Me"* (Isa. 43: 10).

Truly He is the First; the cause of all existing beings, for He is the Creator who brought everything into existence. No being had existed before Him, because, *"All things were made through Him, and without Him nothing was made that was made"* **(Jn. 1: 3)**

Every created thing had a creator who existed before it. So no one or created thing can claim to be the First, for the Creator is the First and the Eternal. This is true from the theological point of view, for God is the Creator existing alone since eternity and before anyone and anything.

But spiritually speaking we would like to know:

How would God be the First in our life?

How can we give Him priority with regard to time and importance? It is His request or rather command as evident from many examples we will present to you. He is the First and should continue so. Suffice to know that the cause of any sin we commit is that we did not make God the First in all our behavior.

In the Ten commandments, God is the First.

The commandments pertaining to God come first; these are the first four commandments written on the first board. They speak about the worship of God, not to take His name in vain, and keeping the Sabbath (Ex. 20) (Deut. 5).

Then come the six remaining commandments written on the second board. These pertain to the human relationship. They start with: Honor your father and your mother, then: You shall not murder; you shall not commit adultery; you shall not steal; you shall not bear false witness; you shall not covet anything that is your neighbor's.

In the Lord's Prayer as well, God is the First.

The first requests are all for God: Hallowed be Your name; Your kingdom come; Your will be done. Then came the requests for ourselves (Mt. 6: 9-13) (Lk. 11)

The same applies to love: God's love is first.

The first and great commandment is *"You shall love the Lord your God with all your heart, with all your soul, and with all your mind"*. The second commandment is like it, *"You shall love your neighbor as yourself"* (Mt. 22: 37-39). The Lord expounded the reason for that; He said, *"He who love father or mother ... son or daughter more than Me is not worthy of Me"* (Mt. 10: 37). Not even life itself should one love more than God, for He is the First, and He said, *"He who finds his life will lose it, and he who loses his life for My sake will find it"* (Mt. 10: 39)

Even with respect to obedience, the Scriptures say, *"We ought to obey God rather than men"* (Acts 5: 29)

Since God is the First, any command from any person which contradicts God's commandments should not be complied with. God is to be obeyed even more than the natural human emotions. That is why when God ordered our father Abraham to give his only son, whom he loves, as burnt offering, Abraham did not hesitate a moment, but he proceeded to carry out the order. God to him was First, whereas his own feelings and his son came last.

We have in the Scriptures other examples of saints who gave God the first place in their life:

Moses was a prince and the son of Pharaoh's daughter. He lived in the royal court, but he refused to be called the son of Pharaoh's daughter *"choosing rather to suffer affliction with the people of God ... esteeming the reproach of Christ greater than the treasures in Egypt"* (Heb. 11: 24, 25). He gave God the first place, and money and greatness the last, or rather esteemed them as nothing.

The Baptist: He refused to be praised in any way and directed all focus on Christ, saying his immortal words, *"He must increase, but I must decrease"* (Jn. 3: 30). He said about Christ, *"He who is coming after me is mightier than I, whose sandals I am not worthy to carry"* (Mt. 3: 11) (Jn. 1: 30)

Hannah, Samuel's mother: God gave her a son after her being barren for long years, and after many prayers with tears and humiliation. But when she had that son, she lent him to the Lord to serve in the Temple, preferring by this the Lord to herself (1 Sam. 1: 27, 28). Hannah is an example for interest in consecration. Her conduct reprimands every mother who withholds her son, or wife who withholds her husband, from becoming consecrated to the Lord.

Among the examples that require that God be First are the following:

- The commandment of giving the firstlings:

The Lord God said in the past, *"Consecrate to Me all the firstborn, whatever opens the womb ... both of man and beast; it is Mine"* (Ex. 13: 2). This commandment included all the firstfruit of the plants and the land, to be consecrated to God. These days the commandment may be applied to the first salary one receives or the first rise in the salary.

- The commandment of giving the tithes:

When giving the tithes, a spiritual person should put God's portion at the head of the list not at the end after one's other obligations. One should first subtract the tithes, give it to God, then satisfy the other needs, even if such a person is needy. The Lord blessed and praised the widow who gave out of her poverty. He said that she paid more than all the others (Mk. 12: 44). This is because she made God first in her life.

Among those who gave preference to God are the martyrs.

Those offered God their lives, and endured all kinds of pains and torments, putting in mind that faith in God comes first before life itself and before their comfort.

The faithful ministers also gave preference to God in their lives.

St. Paul the apostle, for instance, said, "*I have suffered the loss of all things, and count them as rubbish, that I may gain Christ and be found in Him*" (Phil. 3: 8, 9). Therefore he was in labors more abundant, in stripes above measure, in prisons more frequently, and in deaths often (2 Cor. 11: 23). He was bent only on having the Lord First, and the testimony to His name first. His ego, his comfort, and his own name were nothing to him.

Priority should be given to God also with regard to time.

Hence we offer God the first day of the week (Sunday) as the Lord's Day, as well as the first hour of every day. God is the first to whom we speak and to whom we give the firstling of the time. David the prophet said addressing Him in the psalm, "*O God, You are my God; early will I seek You; my soul thirsts for*

You" (Ps. 63: 1); "*I will awoken the dawn. I will praise You, O Lord*" (Ps. 108: 2, 3). And we pray to Him every morning, saying with David, "*My eyes awake before the watches of the night, that I may muse on all Your works*".

Would that we start every work with prayer and with talk to God!

We should pray before eating and after we finish eating; for God is the First and the Last. We should pray before we go out of home and when we go in. before we talk with anyone we should pray that God may give us a word when we open our mouths, and at the end of our talk we should also pray and give thanks. We should pray when we meet people, or when we go to our work because God is the First. And we should end our day with a prayer before we go to sleep, for He is also the Last.

Even when we fast, God should be the First.

One should not give priority to one's health and to the needs of the body, concentrating on delicious and tasty foods. On the contrary, one should think of God first, and think of how to be more deeply attached to Him during the fast, and how to control oneself to realize a proper relationship with God. A righteous person gives priority to God first, then to the people second, and lastly to himself.

In contrast, whoever gives priority to other than God is mistaken.

Lot: Lot preferred the watered land to God and to the company of Abraham and the altar. He lived in Sodom, amidst a bad community that did not glorify God. But as the apostle told us, "*that righteous man, dwelling among them, tormented his righteous soul from day to day by seeing and hearing their lawless deeds*" (2 Pet. 2: 8). Thus he lost everything and came out, with nothing, only through the intercession of our father Abraham.

The rich fool, and the rich man, and Lazarus, as well as many others were mistaken in giving priority to other things than God. They gave priority to money, so they lost eternal life and deserved to be rebuked. The Lord rebuked the rich fool who cared only for his barns and possessions, saying to him, *"Fool! ... whose will those things be which you have provided?"* (Lk. 12: 20). And our father Abraham rebuked the rich man who oppressed Lazarus, saying to him, *"remember that in your lifetime you received your good things"* (Lk. 16: 25)

Jonah also erred when he cared only for his dignity and for his word and did not rejoice for God's kingdom nor for the repentance of Nineveh even if his word fell (Jon. 4).

Whoever submits to his own desires and lusts is certainly mistaken as well.

Mistaken are those who prefer their lusts to God and to enjoying life with him, as Adam and Eve did when they ate from the tree, breaking God's commandment.

Solomon also did the same when he took foreign wives who made him turn from God (1 Kgs. 11), and when he plunged himself in an easy luxurious life, as he said, *"Whatever my eyes desired I did not keep from them"* (Eccl. 2: 10). The result was that wisdom and God's knowledge quit him till he finally repented and knew that all is vanity and grasping for the wind.

In the same error fell those who desired to be first.

The disciples once thought who will be the first! The Lord reprimanded them for that, and the psalmist also reprimands them, *"Not unto us, O Lord, not unto us, but to Your name give glory"* (Ps. 115: 1). Let us not focus on ourselves or on the love of leadership; who will manage? Who will control? Who will lead? Let us rather focus on God's kingdom. The Lord Himself taught us self-denial when following Him. He said, *"If anyone desires to come after Me, let him deny himself, and take up his cross, and follow Me"* (Mt. 16: 24)

Never make God a means for realizing your desires.

Never let your prayers be for this purpose, as if your desires are first, and God the means to attain them! Nay, this is not the spirituality of prayers, for the Lord said, *"seek first the kingdom of God and His righteousness, and all these things shall be added to you"* (Mt. 6: 33)

Who makes God first in his life can make Him all in all.

Such a person does not want except God alone, as the psalmist said, *"There is none upon earth that I desire besides You"* (Ps. 73: 25), *"God is the strength of my heart and my portion forever"* (Ps. 73: 26)

God is indeed the First and the Last.

Life with Him is the first thing we should seek and the aim with which we end. God is the beginning of our spiritual life; for in baptism we believe in Him and are born of Him. He is also the end which we seek, for we aspire to be with Him in the happy eternity (Jn. 14: 3) (Rev. 21: 3). In every day of our life He is the First and the Last. We start our day with Him, and talk first to Him, and we end our day with Him and He is the Last One we talk to. Blessed be the Lord's name now and forever. Amen.

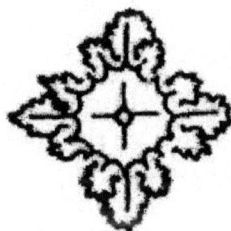

GOD'S WORD TO YOU

God's word reaches everyone, a special word for each one.

God, in various ways, spoke to the fathers (Heb. 1: 1)

God spoke to Moses from the bush (Ex. 3), at a time he never expected to have a word from God and in such a way. God spoke to Moses sometimes also from the tabernacle of meeting or from over the mountain He spoke also to Saul of Tarsus while on the way at an unexpected time (Acts 9).

God even spoke to unworthy sinners.

He spoke to Cain after he had killed Abel his brother (Gen. 4: 9-15), and spoke to Balaam who led astray all the people of Israel (Num. 22: 9, 12)

The word of God came directly to some persons, and indirectly to others.

He spoke to Ahab the evil king through Elijah the prophet (1 Kgs. 21: 17-19), and to Eli the priest through Samuel (1 Sam. 3: 10-14), and to Herod through the wise men from the East (Mt. 2). But God spoke directly to others.

God spoke also to various people, even to children.

He spoke to Samuel the child who could not discern that it was the Lord speaking to him, and God repeated the word to Samuel thrice. He spoke also to young Jeremiah who was not able to speak because he was yet a youth (Jer. 1: 4-19)

God's word was also for various purposes and aims.

He spoke to Jeremiah and to Saul of Tarsus to call them to ministry, and spoke to Moses the prophet to entrust him with the Law to convey it to the people. He spoke to Abraham, once to try him, and another time to tell him of His intention to destroy Sodom, and spoke to him many other times. He spoke to Cain to inflict punishment on him, and to the wise men from the East to warn them against Herod.

Whatever was the purpose, there is certainly a word from God to each one; a word carrying a message. See then what God's message to you is.

God goes about doing good, sending His word to the people, sowing His seeds on all lands, even on stony places and thorny ground (Mt. 13). He sows His word and leaves the choice to the hearer to accept or refuse it.

Many persons received God's word but refused it.

The rich young man heard the word of Christ, but he went away sorrowful for he had great possessions (Mt. 19: 22). Others heard the word but they gave excuses, someone because he had bought a five yoke of oxen, the other because he had bought a piece of ground, and the third because he had married (Lk. 14: 18-20).

God's word is sent to all and is received by all. No one is deprived of it, even Judas the betrayer, for he received God's word more than once.

How beautiful is the phrase, *"The word of the Lord came to Elijah"* (1 Kgs. 18: 1). The word came to him in particular not to all the people; a special word. Beautiful also are the words said by the Lord to Simon the Pharisee, *"I have something to say to you"* (Lk. 7: 40)

The words of the Lord may be given in a miraculous way or in a normal way:

St. Anthony entered into the church, listened to the same chapter of the Gospel all the people heard, but a certain verse had its impact on him; he felt it was addressed to him in

226

particular: *"Go, sell what you have and give to the poor ... and come, follow Me"* (Mt. 19: 21). As soon as he heard these words; he considered them addressed to him, and he went and sold all his possessions. When he was fought with regard to his sister, how she would do alone, he went to the church expecting to hear something in this concern and he heard the message, *"Do not worry about tomorrow"* (Mt. 6: 34).

Some people have sensitive ears to the words of God, *"have their senses exercised"* (Heb. 5: 14). Such senses can discern the word sent them from God.

Those people do not take the word of God from the Holy Scriptures only.

St. Anthony —at the beginning of his monasticism- lived by the river. There he saw an Arabian woman putting off her clothes and descending naked into the river. He was astonished and said to her: O woman, are you not ashamed to appear naked in front of me while I am a monk? But the woman laughed and answered him: If you were truly a monk you would go into the far wilderness, but this place is not a dwelling place for monks. St. Anthony, hearing these words, understood that they were a message from God to him on the mouth of the woman. Thereupon he arose immediately and went far into the wilderness according to "God's word" to him.

Do not think then that the word of God comes to you only on the mouth of a prophet or an angel, for it may come on the mouth of such a naked woman.

The same happened to Mar Ephram the Syrian. While he was walking, a woman kept gazing at his face, for it seems that he was very good-looking. He felt ashamed and asked her why she was looking so long to him though she was a woman. The woman replied: It is not strange for a woman to look to the man from where she was taken (from one of his ribs), but the man should look down to the ground from which he was made (from its dust). St. Ephram felt that these words were a message from God to him on the mouth of that woman. He went his way benefitting from these words.

Many saints received the word of God in the same way.

St. Macarius the great received God's word to him from the mouth of the youth Zacharia. When the boy said to the saint: You, the pillar and light of the wilderness, ask for a word from me! But St. Macarius said: I am sure by the Spirit of God within you that you have something I need to hear!

St. Moses the Black did the same. And St. Paul also experienced the same when he became an anchorite. St. Paul disputed with his brother and went to the court. But on the way to the court he saw a funeral and heard some words from which he took the word of God to him. Immediately, he left the dispute, the funeral, and the whole world, and became an anchorite.

Likewise, those who used to come from the farthest ends of the earth to hear "a word of benefit" from the mouth of some saint, they took it as the work of God not of the saint.

It is the word of God He put on the mouth of the saint for the benefit of the people. He sent it to them through that saint; for God [spoke in the prophets], and He said, *"it is not you who speak, but the Spirit of your Father who speaks in you"* (Mt. 10: 20)

The exercised senses can receive God's words, and perhaps words of reproach sent by God through some people.

David the prophet, while fleeing from his son Absalom, met Shemi son of Gera who insulted him bitterly, and when David's companions wanted to take revenge because the man insulted the Lord's anointed, David prevented them. David said to them, *"let him curse, because the Lord has said to him 'Curse David'"* (2 Sam. 16: 10). David actually benefitted from the insults as if from God.

On the other hand, pitiable is the person to whom God sends a word but he either does not benefit from it, or refuses it as if not from God.

God sent the wise men from the East to Herod with a message, but he did not benefit from it. And Pilate received the word of God but did not benefit. King Agrippa also received words from God through Paul the apostle; he was impressed, and he said, *"You almost persuade me to become a Christian"* (Acts 26: 28), yet he did not become.

God's word was sent likewise to Felix the governor.

Felix was impressed like Agrippa. He was even afraid when Paul the apostle was speaking about righteousness, self-control, and the judgment to come (Acts 24: 25). However, Felix did not let God's word work within him. This was exactly what Agrippa did.

God's word came to Martha as well as to Mary.

Martha, receiving the word of God, engaged in other things and was distracted. While Mary benefitted from the Lord's word, Martha was worried and troubled (Lk. 10: 39-41)

A spiritual person not only discerns God's word but also hids it in his heart, meditates on it, and benefits from it. See the beautiful words said about our mother the holy virgin Mary;

"His mother kept all these things in her heart"(Lk. 2: 51)

Because God's word is useful, the church reads a chapter of the Gospel in each hour of the Agbia Prayers, a chapter when raising the Sunset Incense and the Morning Incense, and a chapter in the holy Mass, in addition to some chapters of the

Epistles and the Acts of the Apostles. But we hear them as if not hearing, or as if the word is not addressed to us! We do not have the exercised senses that can pick up a message from God in what we hear!

In the past days, there was more interest in God's word than in the present days!

The Scriptures, speaking of God's word in the Book of Deuteronomy, say, *"And these words which I command you today shall be in your heart. You shall teach them diligently to your children, and shall talk of them when you sit in your house, when you walk by the way, when you lie down, and when you rise up. You shall bind them as a sign on your hand, and they shall be as frontlets between your eyes. You shall write them on the doorposts of your house and on your gates"* (Deut. 6: 6-9)

God's word may reach you through a certain event.

It may come to you through your, or others', illness, or through the departure of some acquaintance, or through a certain event. It may be a clear message or a special word, but do not let such events pass without benefitting from them.

You need only some cleverness or little attention to understand such messages.

Many indeed are the messages sent us by God, and they are clear and legible to all people, but we lack the exercised senses.

I like the words in the Book of Acts about the Jews on the Day of Pentecost;

"Now when they heard this, they were cut to the heart, and said ... what shall we do?" (Acts 2: 37)

Indeed the word of the Lord is a spur, strong and effective, like a two-edged sword. It had its impact on Zacchaeus the chief tax-collector, so he repented truly, and salvation came to that house. The word of the Lord had its effect also on the keeper of the prison in Philippi and he with all his family were baptized (Acts 16: 30-33)

However, some people may feel cut to the heart –like Agrippa and Felix- but they let the matter pass without taking a decision or acting in any way!

Do not then let the word of the Lord pass without taking strength from it.

If you read the Bible and stop at a certain verse which you feel different from other verses or having a certain impression or a certain message to you, do not let it pass. Think rather that the verses of the Holy Bible are sent to millions of people, but this particular verse is sent especially to you.

IF YOU HEAR HIS VOICE HARDEN NOT YOUR HEARTS (Heb. 3)

God speaks to us in various ways as He spoke in times past to the fathers (Heb. 1: 1). What are these ways?

St. Anthony heard God's voice through a verse of the Gospel he heard in the church. He felt that those words were addressed to him. Through some events he heard God's voice again. He felt that the death of his father is another message from God to him. Afterward, God's voice was heard by him through a woman who was bathing in the river in front of him.

Through various means God's voice reached St. Anthony; whether through the church and the Gospel, through certain events or through certain people. So, let us look for such sources and find out God's voice therein.

God's voice has been heard by many people on the mouths of God's holy people or from inside themselves, or on some occasion.

If only we have the exercised senses, we would easily discern God's voice!

When God spoke to young Samuel, he thought it was the voice of Eli the priest. Samuel could not discern God's voice because he was young and not experienced (1 Sam. 3: 4-7).

St. Paul, likewise, talking about the men who were with him at the time of the vision on the way to Damascus, said, "*And those who were with me indeed saw the light ... but they did not hear the voice of Him who spoke to me*" (Acts 22: 9). The reason perhaps is their undeservedness or not being called.

One, therefore, should be aware whenever God's voice reaches him so that one might discern it and respond to it.

A sermon or a spiritual reading many be the means by which God's voice is conveyed.

You may read or hear a certain verse of the Gospel and feel that it is addressed to you personally as if God addresses you, and you alone, with it. You may feel that such a verse implies a certain meaning or significance to you, and it is God's voice to you. You may have read or heard so many verses, but this one in particular has its impact on your mind, your heart, your feelings, and your conviction. You hear God's voice in it. The same may also happen to you while hearing a sermon, in which you feel that you are addressed by it. In such cases remember the words of the Scriptures, *"Today, if you will hear His voice, do not harden your hearts"* (Heb. 3: 15). Do not let the voice pass without leaving an impression.

The Lord's voice is present, and it reaches everyone. But, besides, there are the words of the Gospel, *"He who has ears to hear, let him hear!"* (Mt. 13: 9)

God's words reached every creature (Mk. 16: 15), and went out through all the earth to the end of the world (Ps. 19). The problem however is, *"He who has ears to hear, let him hear"*. Therefore the Lord said to His disciples, *"Blessed are your eyes for they see, and your ears for they hear"* (Mt. 13: 16)

Though Pharaoh had ears, he could not hear. The same applies to the people of Sodom who drowned in the flood.

All of them heard the Lord's voice: Pharaoh heard it through Moses, and the people of Sodom through Lot, and others through Noah. But, though they heard, their hearts hardened, perhaps because their ears were not for hearing. In other words, perhaps their ears were not able, or were not willing, to convey the words to the heart or to the will.

The rich young man heard the voice from the Lord Christ Himself, but he had no ears to hear. This made him go sorrowful after hearing the Lord's voice because ne had many possessions! How regretful it is if the Lord's voice comes but one does not hear, or is hardened and gives no response!

The virgin in the Song once heard the Lord's voice calling her very gently, but she apologized, and He turned away and was gone (Song. 5: 6)

When the virgin in the Song refused to receive the Lord, she had no ears to hear, so her heart hardened. She returned to herself and repented, and began to seek Him but found Him not. So she said, *"My heart leaped up when he spoke. I sought Him, but I could not find Him. I called Him, but He gave me no answer"* (Song 5: 6)

Sometimes God's voice comes through tribulations.

One may undergo some tribulation which seems to have no solution, and hears God's voice within warning that the trouble is because of some sins. Sometimes one may hear the voice advising from within: Repent and the trouble will end. Then God will have compassion because of one's repentance.

God's voice may come in one's illness or the illness of one's beloved. In this case one may hear a voice within calling one to pray or to make a vow; it is God's voice.

When Joseph's brothers were in trouble in Egypt as they came to buy wheat, they said to one another, *"We are truly guilty concerning our brother, for we saw the anguish of his soul when he pleaded with us, and we would not hear; therefore this distress has come upon us"* (Gen. 42: 21). Afterwards they said to Joseph, *"What shall we speak? Or how shall we clear ourselves? God has found out the iniquity of your servants"* (Gen. 44: 16). It is God's voice within them that reminded them of their sin and reprimanded them.

234

David likewise, when he was insulted by Shemi the son of Gera, he heard God's voice within him rebuking him for his past sin. Therefore he said to those around, *"the Lord has said to him: Curse David"* (2 Sam. 16: 10)

God's voice can be heard by the whole world in times of famine and earthquakes. At such times, God wants to say, *"Return to Me, and I will return to you"* (Mal. 3: 7). The voice may also be a call to some to support the stricken countries, and to others to take a lesson and repent or to be prepared to meet God.

Listen then in every affliction to God's voice within you to know what He wants to say to you.

God's voice may reach you through the Holy Spirit.

The Holy Spirit may put within you certain spiritual yearning, and you find yourself at a certain time longing for repentance, or for prayer. You may find within you a longing for God, a feeling of renouncing of worldly pleasures, or a feeling of disgust against sin. You may not know the reason for all that, because it is God's voice within you through the Holy Spirit.

This case is known by some saints as "visits of the grace"

God's grace may push one to His way, rebuke for a sin, or give a longing for the spiritual life. God stands knocking at the door (Rev. 3: 20), asking you to open. Would that you respond!

God's voice was clear in the days of martyrdom, so, many people accepted faith.

Through the endurance of the martyrs, through God's grace with them, and through the miracles worked by them or to them, God's voice was there calling the people to accept faith, but the closed hearts did not believe!

God's voice was often heard accompanying the miracles.

For who called the thief at the right hand of the Lord to believe? No one! But the darkened sun, the torn temple, the quaking earth, and the opened tombs, all this was the voice that called him to faith, so he cried out, *"Lord, remember me when You come into Your kingdom"* (Lk. 23: 42). The same happened to the soldier who pierced Christ's side with a spear, he did not hear any preaching, but God's voice from the blood and water that came out of the Lord's side was clearly heard.

The miracles that accompanied the apparition of the holy Virgin in Zeitoun had a voice stronger than that of many preachers; for it was God's voice. However, many see the miracles but do not hear the voice, because they have ears that do not hear, and hearts that are hardened.

God's voice came even to the most wicked sinner.

To Judas the betrayer God's voice came rebuking him for his sin. Judas immediately took the money and returned it to the chief priest confessing, *"I have sinned by betraying innocent blood"* (Mt. 27: 3, 4). He was remorseful, yet he despaired and hanged himself.

Even Pilate heard God's voice that spoke the truth in his heart, and he said that he found no fault with that righteous Man. He even sought to release Him, but he finally surrendered and gave Him to the people to crucify Him!

Let us then listen to God's voice on every occasion, and from all sources that our heart might not be hardened.

God's voice calls, in various ways, but it is our role to discern it, and to open our ears to hear, and when we hear we should not harden our hearts.

OUR KNOWLEDGE OF GOD

Many do say that they know God, but in fact they do not, or rather do not know Him the true knowledge. For to know God properly is a long deep matter relating to the spirit and the life more than to the mind and tongue.

The True Knowledge:

To worship God, we should first know Him. But, regretfully, many people worship Him without truly knowing Him!

Hence the question, 'Do you know God?' is not addressed to the atheists or unbelievers, but rather to many of those who repeat the Creed [Truly we believe in One God ...], and who pray and fast, yet to them are addressed the words of John Baptist:

"There stands One among you whom you do not know" (Jn. 1: 26)

Many of us do not know the Lord, though He said, *"Lo, I am with you always, even to the end of the age"* (Mt. 28: 20); *"For where two or three are gathered together in My name, I am there in the midst of them"* (Mt. 18: 20). This reminds us of the words of St. Augustine speaking about the period when he was still young. He said, addressing God, [You were with me, but, for my wretchedness, I was not with You]. We remember also the words in the Gospel of John:

"He was in the world, and the world was made through Him, and the world did not know Him" (Jn. 1: 10).

Indeed, He is the true Light, the Light that shines in the darkness, but the darkness does not comprehend it (Jn. 1: 5)!

The intellectual knowledge:

Those who lift their hands and pray "*Our Father in heaven*", if asked what they know about this heavenly Father, the most learned of them will say: He is God the Creator, filling the sheavens and the earth, alone Eternal, Unlimited, Almighty, Unbound. All this is right, one might have read in some books without knowing their deep significance.

By this is described God as mentioned in the books, in theological seminaries, or in theoretical theology, but without personal knowledge.

Actually, books, lectures, or information alone are not sufficient. Those only fill the mind with ideas but the heart remains empty, with no feelings, no love, no sentiments, nor emotions. It is the case of a person who reads about God, but does not know Him! Truly said one of the fathers: What will you benefit if you know everything about the Holy Trinity without having the Holy Trinity abiding in you or you in Him?

It is mere intellectual knowledge, in the mind not in the heart.

It is the knowledge of a scholar not a worshipper nor a lover. Such knowledge may turn into theological arguments and strifes, or to a philosophy that is comprehended only by the most learned. Who then knows? As the apostle says, "*knowledge puffs up*" (1 Cor. 8: 1). This is true; for many theologians may be puffed up or boast of their knowledge, while some simple people are more learned about God, and more near to God's heart than them.

Our father Adam, in his simplicity and innocence, knew God, but ...

When, Adam ate of the tree of knowledge, he became ignorant!

Adam's ignorance appears in the words He addressed to God, *"I heard Your voice in the garden, and I was afraid because I was naked; and I hid myself"* (Gen. 3: 10). The fact that he hid himself is an evidence of his ignorance, because if he had truly known God, he would have known that his hiding behind the trees would not make him invisible to God. He should have known that God can see him wherever he was, and can see even the inside of his heart and mind. Adam did not also know God in His love and in His forgiveness.

The people's ignorance of God and their straying from Him continued. Therefore the Lord Christ, in His long soliloquy with the Father, said,

"O righteous Father! The world has not known You, but I have known You." (Jn. 17: 25)

The world has not known God, even the Jews who worshipped Him, offered Him the sacrifices and burnt offerings, prayed and fasted to Him, and who received the right faith. Their faith was mere intellectual faith; a kind of intellectual knowledge which could not make them attain God's love. As St. James the apostle says, *"Even the demons believe-and tremble"* (Jas. 2: 20). But it is only intellectual faith based on intellectual knowledge, of no avail because of the lack of love. That is why the Lord Christ said in His soliloquy with the Father,

"I have declared to them Your name, and will declare it, that the love with which You loved Me be in them, and I in them" (Jn. 17: 26)

The knowledge implying communion and love:

Such is the true love; which leads to God's love. And the Lord puts before us a clear fact: any knowledge that leads not to God's love is futile knowledge. For religion is not mere information or doctrines that feed the mind, but the essence of religion is to know God and to love Him.

Religion without God is nothing; for God is the core, the aim, and the means of religion. Even if we attain all righteousness and virtue, but do not attain God, we will be nothing. Such virtue or righteousness will not be true virtue or righteousness. They will be mere practices or works of the Law. The only virtue from which all virtues branch is God's knowledge and love.

If one truly knows God, one will love Him. And if one loves God, one will know Him more and more.

Indeed, if one knows God, and knows His beautiful attributes; if one knows His love, wisdom, and goodness; if one knows His meekness, kindness, and forgiveness; and if one knows that He is fairer than the sons of men (Ps. 45: 2), one will certainly love Him.

Consequently, if one loves God, God will reveal to him Himself that he may know God more and more. This knowledge will not be through any human or any books, but through God Himself.

But what is meant by knowing God and His attributes? By this is meant experiencing Him in one's life; experiencing His love when feeling it; experiencing His wisdom in seeing His dispensation; experiencing His forgiveness in the peace He pours in one's heart upon one's repentance, and so on with the other beautiful attributes of God.

Now, we know that there are three types of God's knowledge:

a. The intellectual knowledge; which alone is not sufficient.

b. The experienced knowledge; attained through one's communion with God.

c. The revealed knowledge. In this type God reveals Himself to those who love Him in various ways. The Lord Himself gave this promise, saying, *"he who loves Me will be loved by My Father, and I will love him and manifest Myself to him"* (Jn. 14: 21). These last words are the holiest of the holy, they need us to put off our shoes while approaching, and to kneel down in gratitude and say to the Lord: You gave me to learn to know You.

It is noteworthy that our knowledge of God starts here on the earth, but does not end or reach its perfection here. It continues in the eternity.

To know God is not an easy or a slight matter; for as Paul the apostle says, *"For now we see in a mirror, dimly ... Now I know in part"* (1 Cor. 13: 12). How strange is this for Paul the apostle who enjoyed *"the abundance of revelations"* (2 Cor. 12: 7, 1), and who *"was caught up into Paradise and heard inexpressible words, which it is not lawful for a man to utter"* (2 Cor. 12: 4)! How strange for such a person as this great St. Paul to say that he knew only in part! How strange it is for him to say that he had struggled and gave everything in order to know, *"What things were gain to me, these I have counted loss for Christ. Yet indeed I also count all things loss for the excellence of the knowledge of Christ Jesus my Lord ... that I may know Him and the power of His resurrection, and the fellowship of His resurrection"* (Phil. 3: 7, 8, 10)

It is clear then that even the apostles did not attain perfect knowledge.

This is clear from the preceding words quoted from St. Paul, as well as from the words of the Lord Christ, "*I have declared to them Your name, and will declare it*" (Jn. 17: 26). But what will You, O Lord, declare to those whom You entrusted with teaching the whole world? Is there any other knowledge You will give them? Yes, indeed, much knowledge still, for which the whole life on earth was not sufficient! That is why the Lord said, addressing the Father, "*And this is eternal life, that they may know You, the only true God*" (**Jn. 17: 3**)

More knowledge in eternity:

As long as we are in this world within the mist of the present material body, we will not attain perfect knowledge of God. We only see in a mirror, dimly, but when we put off this body, our transparent spirits that are made in the image of God, will know more. When we come into the kingdom prepared for us which no eye has seen, nor ear heard, nor ever occurred to a human heart (1 Cor. 2: 9), then we will know more and more. But shall we know everything about God when we will attain such a glory? Certainly not, for we are limited creatures whereas God is unlimited.

The limited cannot know everything about the Unlimited.

How can a limited mind or heart know everything about God the Unlimited? This reminds us of a verse in a poem compiled by us entitled "A Love Whisper", which says:

The Universe could not contain You;

How can then the heart do?

The only possible thing is that God will widen our hearts and minds to hold more knowledge about Him. We will be so overwhelmed with such marvelous knowledge that we will say:

enough, enough, we cannot bear more! We will remain dazzled for some time by what was revealed to us before we come to ourselves (we do not know when?). After enjoying what we had known and contemplated on it, and after enjoying the taste and sweetness of it, God will widen our hearts and minds again to be able to hear more knowledge, because the mind and the heart are lovesick (Song 2: 5). Yet the mind and the heart, being limited, will not be able to hold and contain the **Unlimited, Him who is unsearchable and incomprehensible, blessed be His name!**

When then shall we have such a perfect knowledge of God, if we ever will have? Our Good Teacher gives the answer in His words to the Father, *"And this is eternal life, that they may know You, the only true God"* (Jn. 17: 3)

If this is our state when we will go to heaven, when we will have that heavenly spiritual body raised in glory (1 Cor. 15), what can be said of our knowledge while on the earth? Should we not be ashamed of the words of the Lord to one of the eleven holy apostles, *"Have I been with you so long, and yet you have not known Me, Philip?"* (Jn. 14: 9)? And if this is the extent of the apostle's knowledge of the Lord Incarnate, How far would be his knowledge of God in the glory of His divinity?

Actually God grants us an amount of His knowledge sufficient to make us believe on Him and love Him.

This is sufficient for us here on the earth. We cannot guess how far we will know Him in eternity. Most probably we will grow in the knowledge of God so far as our human nature can bear in the glory that will be granted it.

Through inspiration many things have been revealed to us by God, and many more by His incarnation. As St. John the apostle said, *"No one has seen God at any time. The only begotten Son, who is in the bosom of the Father, He has declared Him"* (Jn. 1: 18). The Son, actually, declared to us much about the Father, and there is more still to be declared. That is why the Lord said, "*I have declared to them ... and will declare*".

Believe me, our whole life is not sufficient to make us know just one attribute of God! What can we say about all His attributes?

Even God's attributes are not well known by us; we have not yet gone deep into them. David the prophet thus said, "*I have seen the consummation of all perfection, but Your commandment is exceedingly broad*" (Ps. 119: 96). This great prophet David used to implore God with respect to His ways, "*Show me Your ways, O Lord, teach me Your paths*" (Ps. 25: 4)

In this life on earth, we try to know the things pertaining to God, that we may attain some knowledge of God Himself. We try to know about His Scriptures, His Law, His Commandments that enlighten the eyes (Ps. 19: 8), and about His angels, the spirits sent to minister, and who are a flame of fire (Heb. 1: 14) (Ps. 104: 4). We try to meditate on His heavens, and on the heavenly Jerusalem which is God's dwelling place with the people (Rev. 21). However, the most wise among us would say 'I do not know', or "*I know in part*" (1 Cor. 13: 12).

If we have not yet known everything about the universe created by God, how could we know God, the Creator of this universe?

We have not yet known all the galaxies, planets and stars. When we find a small piece of the moon rocks brought by the spacemen, we engage ourselves on examining it to know its constituents, how can we then know Him who created the moon?

Even the earth on which we live, is full of mysteries underground and in the depths of waters which we know nothing of. We keep digging or diving that we may know, and the result is partly knowledge. How far then is our knowledge of God?

May the reader pardon me if I say that we have not even known ourselves! What do we know, for instance about the spirit, its nature, and how it quits the body? What do we know about the spiritual body in which we will be raised? If we do not know man himself, nor the secrets of the universe in which we live, how dare we say that we know God?

However, we can say that on the earth we grow in knowledge.

Through our fellowship with God and experiencing Him in our life, our knowledge of Him grows. This is exactly what Job the righteous said to Him, "*I have heard of You by the hearing of the ear, but now my eye sees You*" (Job 42: 5). The same applies to the people of Samaria. When the Samaritan woman called them to see Christ, and said, "*Come, see a Man who told me all things that I ever did*" (Jn. 4: 29). But when they saw Him and believed, they said to the woman, "*Now we believe, not because of what you said, for we ourselves have heard Him ...* " (Jn. 4: 42). What they saw was much deeper in effect than what they heard from her. It resembles – though incomparable – the feeling of the queen of Sheba when she saw Solomon, as the Scriptures describe it, "*there was no more spirit in her*" (1 Kgs. 10: 5)

Stupor and abstemiousness:

If you know God you will be in a sort of stupor, drunken with His love! It is a state of stupor – as some may call it – in which one knows things that have not entered into the heart of man (1 Cor. 2: 9), or perhaps words which it is not lawful for a man to utter (2 Cor. 12: 4). Such knowledge will create in one's heart feelings and emotions so sublime that no one can describe. Such knowledge will make one scorn any other knowledge which is described as "foolishness" (1 Cor. 3: 19). In this case your mind will be elevated and your soul filled.

If you really knew God, you would renounce all things of the world, whether the lust of the flesh, the lust of the eyes, or the pride of life (1 Jn. 2: 16). On the other hand, if you loved the worldly things, the love of the Father would not be in you (1 Jn. 2: 15), and you will not have known Him. See how Paul the apostle counted all things loss for the excellence of the knowledge of Christ (Phil. 3: 8)

A person who knows God will certainly have satisfaction in Him, and will say with David the prophet, *"There is none upon earth that I desire besides You"* (Ps. 73: 25); *"It is good for me to draw near to God"* (Ps. 73: 28). If you attain such a spiritual level, you will have known God, I mean known Him in part. God's knowledge is in fact based on taste and vision "Taste and see" (Ps. 34: 8).

There still remains the important question in this topic:

How can we know God, here, on the earth?

Pardon me, for this is probably a main issue which needs a whole book.

THE ENCOUNTER WITH GOD

Everyone should have some relationship with God; an attitude towards Him or with regard to Him. But complete passivity or isolation from Him is not easy for anyone. There are various sorts of relationship with God:

The relationship of some people with God may be one of ideology.

God to those is a mere thought which they examine and discuss. They argue about God's existence, attributes, and work. God to them is part of a philosophy to be discussed, and their relationship with Him is a relationship with God as presented in books and by theology professors or scholars. God to them is a mere idea taught and read, or perhaps understood and discussed!

Some others have a formal occasional relationship with God.

Those remember God only in His feasts (such as the Christmas or Easter), or on some occasions as in funerals where one remembers some friend or relative taken by God.

The relationship of some persons with God may be a formal one without spirit. It is a sort of practice where one does what one should do in due time without feeling God's presence in that. One may pray in the fixed times, read the Holy Bible regularly, and may even feel remorse for not doing that (spiritual) duty:

All such people, actually have no relationship with God.

None of these matters constitute a spiritual relationship with God: neither arguing about God and theological matters, nor remembering Him formally and on occasions, nor even the practices that are void of spirit and are mere duties.

The relationship with God is a heart-to-heart relationship.

In such a relationship one feels God's presence in his heart, and feels his presence in God's heart.

This sort of relationship may be called the meeting with God. Through this meeting a fellowship and a sentiment are created. Through it one comes to know God truly and practically, and comes to experience Him, love Him, and be attached to Him, becoming one with Him in love and will.

Many people have religious practices, but they do not feel God's presence in their life, they do not touch Him or see Him, as if He is in one place and they in another, or as if He were a stranger to them or they strangers to Him, or as if there are walls or spaces between them and Him which cannot be traversed!

Speak to the Lord then; say to Him: I want to see You.

Say: I want to feel Your presence in my life; I want to have a fellowship with You and love You. O Lord, I want my sentiments to be inflamed with Your love. As You have entered my mind, may You, O Lord, enter my heart also, that as my mind is convinced with You, I may experience You in my life as Job the righteous said, "*I have heard of You by the hearing of the ear, but now my eye sees You*" (Job 42: 5).

Unless we meet with God here on the earth, we will not meet with Him there in heaven; for here is the taste of the kingdom.

Here starts the relationship with God, in the heart according to the request of God Himself, "*My son, give Me your heart*" (Prov. 23: 26). Thus God sanctifies the heart, fills it with love and lays His head therein. This is the pledge of the kingdom as the Gospel says, *"the kingdom of God is within you"* (Lk. 17: 21)

Hence, before attaining the kingdom of heavens, one should experience God's kingdom within oneself.

But how could one attain this pledge of the kingdom? How could one attain communion with God? And how could one be always with Him?

My advice to you is to be occupied always with God; to read about Him and about His work in the church. Read about His relationship with His saints, and about His beautiful attributes, and read about His hand in any events. Thus your heart will be moved with His love, and will be always ready to His encounter.

A ready heart is the heart that longs to God and to the life with Him.

That heart says in his prayer, *"As the deer pants for the water brooks, so pants my soul for You, O God. My souls thrists for God, for the living God. When shall I come and appear before God"* (Ps. 42: 1, 2); *"O God, You are my God; early will I seek You; my soul thirsts for You"* (Ps. 63: 1)

Truly, one cannot be with God unless one loves Him.

Through love one gets close to God, and the closer one gets the more one's heart enjoys His love and the more His name be on one's mouth all the time, as the psalmist says, *"In Your name they rejoice all day long"* (Ps. 89: 16), and as we sing, [Your name is sweet and blessed on the mouths of Your saints]. It is indeed an encounter between two hearts. Many are those who preach, who build houses for God, and who explain His laws, but where are they who love Him?

God does not only want those who get close to Him, but rather those who abide in Him.

For one may get close to God some day then separates from Him for months, or may taste and love Him then leaves one's first love (Rev. 2: 4). One may also be attracted by the world and becomes occupied with it and tepid in God's love. Therefore the Lord wants us to abide in Him, *"Abide in Me, and I in you"* (Jn. 15: 4), exactly as the branch is in the vine, or the head in the body. What a great mystery this is (Eph. 5: 32)!

It is not then a mere meeting, but a dwelling; the dwelling of God in you.

The Scriptures say, *"Do you not know that you are the temple of God and that the Spirit of God dwells in you?"* (1 Cor. 3: 16). Yea, God, seeing your clean loving heart, says, *"This is My resting place forever; Here I will dwell, for I have desired it"* (Ps. 132: 14). It is permanent dwelling without separation. Whenever one says, *"Amen, Even so, come, Lord Jesus!"* (Rev. 22: 20), come, O Lord, dwell in me and I will open all the doors for You, then He will respond in love as He did to Zacchaeus the tax-collector, saying, *"today I must stay in your house"* (Lk. 19: 5)

One should then meet with God within oneself, not outside, for many seek Him here or there while He is within them and they are not aware. He is everywhere inside and outside you! When Augustine became aware of this, he said his famous words [O Lord, You were with me all the time, but, for my great misery, I was not with You]!

The meeting with God then is the feeling that God is in one's life.

So one says: You, O Lord, are within me, and with me. But I lack the feeling and the awareness; I lack the exercised senses by which I could see You and feel You in my life! I pray open my eyes that I may see (2 Kgs. 6: 17). The Lord was with many people and even talked with them, but they were not aware, nor even knew Him! This happened, for instance, to the two disciples from Emmaus (Lk. 24: 15, 16)

The indisputable fact is that God is present in your life. He often draws near you, but you are not aware.

He may visit you with His grace and works in you with His Holy Spirit, yet, you are not aware. He may inflame your spirit some times, awaken your conscience other times, take part in what you do many times, while you think yourself working alone, by yourself! This is because your senses are not exercised to feel God's presence. Try then to train yourself to have this awareness of God's hand in your, and in others' life as well as in the events that take place. Only then you can say: Lo, I found Him ... I saw Him ... I met Him in everything that happened.

How could one meet with God?

To meet with God one should have the desire for this.

However, this is not the general rule; for our father Adam feared the meeting with God after eating from the tree. He even hid from God's face. But God Himself sought him and met with him!

Another amazing example is Saul of Tarsus who was on his way to persecute the church of God very hardly and very violently; he was on his way with letters, and bringing men and women bound to be put in prison (Acts 9: 1), yet God met him on his way to Damascus, attracted him to Himself, and made of him an apostle to the Gentiles!

The Samaritan woman also, whom the Lord met at the well, and who knew Him not, nor was even ready to meet Him or to drink from the living water, this woman the Lord met with, talked to, led to repentance and faith, and made her call her people to believe on Him.

Many more wonderful meetings took place between the Lord God and His children.

He met with the three young men in the furnace of fire, walked with them in the midst of the furnace, and prevented the fire from hurting them, so the hair of their head was not singed, nor their garments affected (Da. 3: 25-27)

He met with Jonah the prophet in the belly of the fish. When Jonah prayed to the Lord, the Lord heard his voice and ordered the fish, and it vomited Jonah onto dry land (Jn. 2: 1, 10).

God met also with Moses the prophet and the children of Israel in the midst of the Red Sea and the waters were a wall to them on their right hand and on their left (Ex. 14: 22).

He met with the thief at His right hand on the cross. He accepted the thief's faith and promised that he would be with Him that same day in Paradise (Lk. 23: 43).

Many more wonderful innumerable meetings took place which imply God's love as well as many signs and wonders, and faith and prayer on the part of the people.

If you really want to meet with God, never let another love take you from God's love

As the Scriptures say, "*Do not love the world or the things in the world. If anyone loves the world, the love of the Father is not in him*" (1 Jn. 2: 15); "*friendship with the world is enmity with God*" (Jas. 4: 4).

How beautiful the words of Peter the apostle to the Lord are "*we have left all and followed You*" (Mt. 19: 27)! Have you also left all things for Him and He became everything to you. If so, God will meet you.

God works with His grace to clear your heart so that you might be for Him. Then He meets with you. This clearing comes through renunciation.

When one feels that everything is trivial compared to God, one renounces every lust or desire that stands between one and God. And no one can renounce the world and the worldly things unless the world becomes of no value in one's sight as St. Paul the apostle says:

"I have suffered the loss of all things, and count them as rubbish, that I may gain Christ" (Phil. 3: 8)

St. Paul did not only gain Christ but he also was found in Him. Abraham the father of the fathers also –for the sake of the Lord- left his country, his family, and his father's house to the land that the Lord showed Him (Gen. 12: 1). There Abraham met the Lord and lived with Him, for he said: O Lord, I have no family, no house, and no land, You are everything to me, You alone; since I have met You I had no one but You. In this way one empties one's heart of everything that the heart may be a dwelling place for God.

Is your heart also a dwelling place for God? Or have you subleased it to others?

I wonder if God says to you, *"My son, give Me your heart"*, would you say to Him; O Lord, You have come late, for others came and occupied it. So and so has taken my heart, and such and such lust and desires have taken it. If my heart were empty, I would offer it to You, but regretfully it is occupied!

When God created man, God was to him everything. But other types of love soon entered the heart of the man and occupied it. From that time man's meeting with God decreased, and he even began to escape from the sight of God!

Hence, we need to reevaluate matters so as to be aware of the value of living with God, which is worth forsaking everything.

If you really want to meet with God, your objective and will should conform to His.

As the saying goes: companionship requires concordance. Be sure then if your will concords with God's will or you have other thoughts and attitudes. See also the beautiful words of St. Paul the apostle, *"We have the mind of Christ"* (1 Cor. 2: 16). Therefore we pray the Lord continually, saying, *"Let Your will be done"*, for in this will we meet with God.

We meet with God also in prayer and in the readings of the Scriptures.

Prayer should nevertheless be spiritual and with love, for one may pray but does not enjoy the prayer for not meeting with God! The sign of enjoying the meeting with God in prayer is that once a person starts prayer, he cannot stop it. Mar Isaac said of such people:

The word in the prayer on their mouths is so sweet that they cannot leave it to another word!

One can also meet with God in His Scriptures if one's delight is in the law of the Lord and he meditates in His law day and night (Ps. 1)

ABIDING IN GOD

It is not sufficient for one to know God, for one should abide in Him. Nor is it sufficient to love Him, but one should moreover abide in His love.

In this chapter we will talk about abiding in God, the reasons leading to it or shaking it.

The importance of abiding in God:

The Lord did not only say, *"you (are) in Me, and I in you"* (Jn. 14: 20), but He furthermore said, *"Abide in Me, and I in you"* (Jn. 15: 4).

He gave us the example of the vine and the branches.

The branch that abides in the vine as part of it without separation or deviation will be fed with its sap and becomes one with it.

Without this abiding one's spiritual life ends like the branch that does not abide in the vine. The Lord Himself said, *"If anyone does not abide in Me, he is cast out as a branch and is withered; and they gather them and throw them into the fire, and they are burned."* (Jn. 15: 6).

St. Paul the apostle gives us as example the branch that became a partaker of the root and fatness of the olive tree (Rom. 11: 17), and he says, *"you stand by faith ... Therefore consider the goodness and severity of God ... toward you, goodness, if you continue in His goodness. Otherwise you also will be cut off"* (Rom. 11: 21, 22)

As the believer is likened to the branch that abides in the vine, he is also likened to the house built on the rock (Mt. 7)

The house built on the rock: the rain descended, the floods came, and the winds blew and beat on that house, and it did not fall, for it is founded on the rock. The house built on the sand, on the contrary, was not stable; and it fell, and great was its fall.

Another example the Lord gave us is that of the sower and the good ground (Mt. 13)

The seed sowed on the ground, having strong root, produced fruit a hundredfold, sixty, or thirty. Whereas the seed that had no root withered away. The seed that fell by the wayside was devoured by the birds, and that which fell among thorns was chocked by the thorns.

The children of God, on the other hand, are always stable; no birds can prevail over them nor thorns nor dryness. No stumbling blocks nor temptations can shake them.

Examples and causes:

A wonderful example is given us by Paul the apostle; for he wonders in astonishment and objection:

"Who shall separate us from the love of Christ? Shall tribulation, or distress, or persecution, or famine, or nakedness, or peril, or sword? ... Yet in all these things we are more than conquerors through Him who loved us" (Rom. 8: 35-37).

Such tribulations then do not shake our abiding in the Lord, but rather make us conquerors! The apostle therefore continues, *"For I am persuaded that neither death nor life, nor angels nor principalities nor powers, nor things present nor things to come, nor height nor depth, nor any other created thing, shall be able to separate us from the love of God which is in Christ Jesus our Lord"* (Rom. 8: 38, 39)

The lesson can be taken from the lives of the martyrs and confessors; for they underwent all kinds of torment and passions and remained steadfast in faith and unshaken.

The harsh torturing whether skinning, whipping, pulling off nails and teeth, burning or scraping off, all this could not shake their strong firm hearts. They rather faced this joyfully and sang while in prison. It is said about the father apostles after their being imprisoned and whipped, *"So they departed from the presence of the council, rejoicing that they were counted worthy to suffer shame for His name"* (Acts 5: 41)

A person who is steadfast in the Lord is firm in His love, and his attachment to the Lord is not mere formality or practices, nor even obedience or submission.

The love of a steadfast person is a zealous love which is described as one that never fails (1 Cor. 13: 8), or as strong as death which many waters cannot quench (Song 8: 6, 7). Such love gives steadfastness in the Lord.

To abide in the Lord is to abide in His love.

For the Lord said, *"Abide in My love"* (Jn. 15: 9). And the apostle explains, *"God is love, and he who abides in love abides in God, and God in him"* (1 Jn. 4: 16)

The surroundings, home, or outer circumstances might be the cause behind not abiding in the Lord. However, firm persons remain steadfast whatever were the causes.

For instance our father Noah lived in very sinful surroundings, which the Lord destroyed by the flood, but Noah remained steadfast in the Lord worshipping Him alone with his family!

Another example is the Lord's twelve disciples to whom He said, *"you are those who have continued with Me in My trials"* (Lk. 22: 28). He said this because many others did not continue with Him as those who went back and walked with Him no more when He was speaking about His flesh and blood (Jn. 6: 66). He even said to the twelve, *"Do you also want to go away?"*, but Peter answered Him, *"Lord, to whom shall we go? You have the words of eternal life"*. Other examples are the spiritual children of John the beloved to whom he said in his Epistle, *"I have written to you, young men, because you are strong, and the word of God abides in you, and you have overcome the wicked one"* (1 Jn. 2: 14).

A person who is steadfast in the Lord is a steadfast person not shaken.

Such person's love never fails in spite of hindrances, for these cannot shake him. Therefore the apostle says, *"Therefore, my beloved brethren, be steadfast, immovable, always abounding in the work of the Lord, knowing that your labor is not in vain in the Lord"* (1 Cor. 15: 58)

The Lord Christ wants His children to be strong, steadfast and conquerors always, for such persons know their aim, and fix their eyes on it, not faltering between two ways or two opinions, as said about the Lord, *"He steadfastly set His face to go to Jerusalem"* (Lk. 9: 51)

One who has the aim clear before him, finds his way easily, never hesitates or reconsiders.

The church history is full of strong examples of persons who remained steadfastly abiding in the Lord.

Among those are the martyrs who prevailed over all kinds of torturing and over the cruelty of Niro, Deucletian, Irian and the other human monsters. Some others prevailed over the doubts spread by philosophies or adversary thoughts. In all this they kept, *"bringing every thought into captivity to the obedience of Christ"* (2 Cor. 10: 5)

A person abiding in the Lord does not return back, but is rather reaching forward to things ahead. He is always in growth, and such growth gives him fervence and zeal pushing him forward that he never looks around but sets his face steadfastly towards Jerusalem.

The aim is clear and fixed before such a person. He never deviates from it, for the aim is God, and his love increases his steadfastness in Him, and is in turn inflamed more and more. Such a person is like a glass full of hot liquid, if left on a table it will cool, but if put on a stove the hot liquid will never cool.

Be therefore kindled with the fire of the Spirit, or be like the burnt offering which fire was always burning on the altar.

In the Books of the Leviticus we read about the burnt offering which was usually put on the hearth upon the altar all night until morning. The fire was kept burning on the altar and never put out. The priest had to burn wood on it every morning and burn on it the fat of the peace offerings, *"A fire shall always be burning on the altar; it shall never go out"* (Lev. 6: 13)

If you want then to abide in the Lord keep kindled with the fire like the burnt offering to which burning wood is always added and like peace offerings. Neglect not any of the means of grace.

Be steadfast in faith and love and worship God even though you were alone as Noah had done amidst a generation that God destroyed with flood.

Some others did the same: Moses was steadfast amidst a stiff-necked people; Joseph amidst sin and temptation; and Jeremiah amidst a generation of which God said, *"do not pray for this people, nor lift up a cry or prayer for them, nor intercession to Me; for I will not hear you"* (Jer. 7: 16)

The relationship of such a person with God is not one of duties or commands but a personal relationship of love and trust between a child and his father.

Such a relationship is not affected by other relationships with other people.

One should not say: since the majority of people do this, can I stand alone? No, brother, what have you to do with the majority? If this majority crucify Christ, would you do like them? The majority were destroyed by the flood, would you drown like them? Let your first and greatest example be the life of the Lord Christ, then the lives of the saints who were perfected in the faith.

It is not proper for you to go with the current, rise when the people rise, fall when they fall, and stumble with their sins. Be rather steadfast in the Lord and stumble not with anyone.

Do not be influenced by the fall of the others, but say rather, *"as for me and my house, we will serve the Lord"* (Josh. 24: 15). Do not stumble when someone stumbles on the Lord's way, for he might have certain circumstances or temptations different from yours.

Do not stumble by the fall of the others, but pray for them, and be yourself steadfast.

Flee from anyone who might bring you down or weaken your spirituality, for the Gospel says, *"If your right hand causes you to sin, cut it off and cast it from you"* (Mt. 5: 30)

The Parable of the Sower presents us types of steadfastness and non steadfastness.

Some seeds sprang up but soon was choked up by the thorns, others had no root nor depth and soon withered away. Some others did not continue either for outer causes or because the ground was not good. But the good ground certainly yields good fruit while bad fruit comes from a bad ground.

An autumn wind cannot shake a strong or a deep-rooted oak; only dead dry leaves fall

The wind cannot make the firm branches, nor even the green leaves, fall because they have life in them that enables them to resist. The Belshevists said to Patriarch Sergi: [Belshevism has destroyed Christianity]. But the Patriarch answered them:

Belshevism has not destroyed Christianity, but it rather purified Christianity from formal or unreal Christians.

Likewise the dead fish only float on the water surface, but the strong fish plow through the waves of the sea and resist the current.

Hence a person who abides in God's love, cannot be shaken by any power, whereas a weak person finds a plea in outer causes because these could shake him.

A strong person is not shaken by anything; he is like the house built on the rock (Mt. 7). But what are the means by which one may abide in God. And what about those who did not abide and turned back or faltered between two ways? What are the causes of that?

How to abide in God:

If one wants to abide in God and God in him, let the relationship be that of love, a heart-to-heart relationship.

The relationship of some persons with God is one of benefit or request. They follow God so that He might respond to their requests and facilitate everything to them. If God does not respond to their wishes they get angry and may even separate themselves from Him! Those are like children, for a child loves whoever pampers him and gives him what he wants and thus can never abide in God. But a person who is spiritually mature, and who in love gives and sacrifices, holds to God as an aim not a means.

Let your relationship with God be one of love, growing to giving and sacrifice. In this way you can give God your heart and emotions, and can give Him your time and everything, even yourself, and be delighted in that. Thus you will abide in God, and God in you without being shaken.

Our father Abraham is an example of such relationship of love and sacrifice.

The first call he received from God was to leave his family, his home, and his father's house, and to go to the mountain God was going to show him (Gen. 12: 1). Thus, starting with this renouncing and sacrifice, God lifted him to a higher level; to give his only son whom he loved and to offer him as a burnt offering! In his deep faith, Abraham did not object or argue, but went immediately to do as he was asked! Nothing hindered our father Abraham, who was steadfast in faith, from obeying God even to give his only son!

So the love that abides in God is that which does not love anyone else or anything else besides or more than God.

He Himself said, *"He who loves father of mother more than Me is not worthy of Me. And he who loves son or daughter more than Me is not worthy of Me."* (Mt. 10: 37). And the first commandment is, *"You shall love the Lord your God with all your heart, with all your soul, and with all your mind"* (Mt. 22: 37) (Deut. 6: 5)

In this way God will have no rival in one's heart or mind.

In this way God will be all in all, alone, and such a relationship continues and never shakes. Some would say: Does this mean that I love no one but God only? Nay. One can love all people but through God's love, not to rival His love in one's heart. Let your love to the people be part of your love to God. Love them because they are loved by God. Love them and call them to His love. Love them in purity and righteousness, thus you might abide in God in spite of being fought by the devil.

Who wants to conquer in the wars of steadfastness makes his only aim God alone, not the good things He gives him.

One should love God for Himself alone not for His good things; for if one loves God for the good things one receives from Him, one's attachment to God will shake if these good things decrease. Suppose such a person fails in the exams, or have a sick relative not healed, or undergoes a temptation, his faith will shake and he will be in trouble. So, let God's love be your food and drink as the psalmist says,

"Oh, taste and see that the Lord is good" (Ps. 34: 8)

Thus one's soul lives by every word that proceeds from the mouth of God (Mt. 4: 4). In one's love, one addresses God, saying, *"I sat down in His shade with great delight"* (Song 2: 3); *"His left hand is under my head, and his right hand embraces me"* (Song 2: 6). It is not then a formal relationship or love in appearance only, for such love or relationship fails and cannot continue.

Who is God for you? Is He that remote God?

Is He that very distant God in the heaven of heavens that is separated from you with long long distances and partitions? Do you not feel His presence deep within you? You will abide only in God in whom you feel that you live, exist, and move (Acts 17: 28), and of whom you can say, *"I am my beloved's, and my beloved is mine, He feeds His flock among the lilies"* (Song 6: 3). You feel that it has been a long relationship through which you walked with God, experienced Him, and tasted His sweet love.

If not a long relationship, it has been at least a deep one.

Augustine for example did not have a long relationship with God, for he said [I delayed much in Your love, O You unattainable beauty]. But since he knew God, his relationship with Him has been very deep and far deeper than that of many of his predecessors. Such is the firm love and the firm knowledge.

Some people repent their former life before knowing God.

Some others repent knowing Him because they suffered under a cross which they felt very heavy. Those lived only the words, *"In the world you will have tribulation"* (Jn. 16: 33). Perhaps they found some difficulty in complying with the commandment or in conquering the ego, and this made them feel God as a burden on them!

Such people carried the cross on their shoulders, not in their hearts.

They did not experience the words of the Lord, *"My yoke is easy and My burden is light"* (Mt. 11: 30). So they grumbled and refused the life with God. They could not abide in Him, and they turned back.

Some others had a formal superficial relationship with God and thus could not abide in Him.

Such is a Pharisee relationship, mere obedience to commands, without spirit or love. Like the Pharisees and lawyers, they could not abide, for they just carry out the commandment like a servant obeying his master. They may do this without conviction, not from their heart, and may continue for some time then stop. Such people have their relationship with the law not with God.

Would that you rise above the lawful and the unlawful, the good and the evil, and above the law and the commandment. Then you could enter the circle of the divine love.

The link of love that attaches you to God is above law and commandment. Therefore it is included by the apostle as the first fruit of the Holy Spirit (Gal. 5: 22). Moreover the virtues acceptable to God are those based on love, whereas those lacking love are hateful to God. God said about them to the Jews, *"they are a trouble to Me, I am weary of bearing them"* (Isa. 1: 14)

It is not proper to start with the surface and forget inner love. We should rather love God first, then these virtues will be an expression of such love, an outcome, or an element thereof and not separate from it.

Hence the Lord Christ focused in His reproach to the angle of the Church in Ephesus on one thing, *"I have this against you, that you have left your first love"* (Rev. 2: 4).

If you want to abide in God's love, beware love of the world, for St. James the apostle says, *"friendship with the world is enmity with God"* (Jas. 4: 4). And St. John the apostle also says, *"Do not love the world or the things in the world. If anyone loves the world, the love of the Father is not in him"* (1

Jn. 2: 15). As an example Demas the assistant of St. Paul the apostle could not withstand, for St. Paul says, *"Demas has forsaken me, having loved this present world"* (2 Tim. 4: 10). Some people, like Demas, forsake God's love for the love of the present world. You should therefore be steadfast and immovable.

Some, being unsteady, forsook even the Lord Himself, they *"went back and walked with Him no more"* (Jn. 6: 66). The steady, on the other hand, said to Him, *"to whom shall we go? You have the words of eternal life"* (Jn. 6: 68). Lot's wife was of that unsteady type because she looked back behind her (Gen. 19: 26). Her heart was not completely away from Sodom, so she looked back. Therefore the Lord says to us, *"No one having put his hand to the plow, and looking back, is fit for the kingdom of God"* (Lk. 9: 62)

Some people are unsteady, being by their nature hesitating and changeable or weak and irresolute.

Such people cannot withstand long. One may resist sin for a day or a couple of days or even for months, but afterwards gets weary and submits. The nature of such a person is unsteady and irresolute, or may be wavering and changeable. So such a person fails soon, gets desperate soon, and also returns soon!

Do not be moved by the diabolic wars but be immovable.

You may face wars raised against you by Satan. He may fight you with thoughts, lusts, temptations, money, fame, or with pride.

He may raise against you visible or invisible wars, quick or long lasting, but in all this he has no power over you. It is you who are given the authority to trample on serpents and scorpions, and over all the powers of the enemy (Lk. 10: 19). Be firm then and heartened in the wars you undergo. It is the will of our Lord to be steadfast to the end; for He says,

266

"But he who endures to the end shall be saved" (Mt. 24: 13)

The words "to the end" signify that the spiritual life is not for one or a couple of days, or is temporary exercises, but is rather the whole life. And man should endure to the last moment, which matter requires steadfastness. The same meaning is repeated in other words, *"Be faithful until death, and I will give you the crown of life"* (Rev. 2: 10). The words "until death" refer also to the whole life and requires one to be steadfast.

We shall therefore present here the elements required for abiding in God as stated in the Holy Bible, thus establishing the spiritual rules for abiding in the Lord:

* Partaking of the Lord's flesh and blood; for He says, *"He who eats My flesh and drinks My blood abides in Me, and I in him"* (Jn. 6: 56)

* Keeping the commandment and sound spiritual conduct; for the Lord says, *"If you keep My commandments, you will abide in My love, just as I have kept My Father's commandments and abide in His love"* (Jn. 15: 10). St. John the apostle also said about the Lord, *"He who says he abides in Him ought himself also to walk just as He walked"* (1 Jn. 2: 6).

* **Remembering the readings which previously had an influence on you, or the contemplations, sermons, liturgies and hymns which had affected you before.**

* Examining oneself and finding out what things are capable of strengthening oneself to be attached with. Never leave yourself without fuel kindling you.

* **Avoid slackness and neglect for this leads to recklessness and indifference after a while.**

When the Lord Christ was speaking about the end of the days, He probable meant to draw the attention to steadfastness. He said that in those last days, "*Satan will be released from his prison and will go out to deceive the nations*" (Rev. 20: 7, 8). The great apostasy will happen and Satan will deceive, if possible, even the elect, but God's mercy will shorten those days; for, "*unless those days were shortened, no flesh would be saved*" (Mt. 24: 22). How fearful this is!

The Church requires her children to be steadfast in faith so that when Satan is released and apostasy comes, the church remains firm.

In those days Satan will work with all power, signs, and lying wonders, and with all unrighteous deception among those who perish (2 Thess. 2: 9, 10). As the Lord said to His disciples, "*Satan has asked for you, that he may sift you*" (Lk. 22: 31). Therefore be steadfast and immovable (1 Cor. 15: 58)

FLEEING FROM GOD

Fleeing from God is very old, since the beginning of creation; since our father Adam.

Causes of Fleeing:

* Adam fled from God because of fear when he sinned.

He hid from God behind the tree, and said to Him, *"I heard Your voice in the garden, and I was afraid because I was naked; and I hid myself"* (Gen. 3: 10). When Adam was attached to God in love, he did not fear nor flee, and even longed to this meeting with God. But after sinning, it was hard for him to meet God, so he fled.

* Jonah the prophet also fled from God when his thoughts were not in conformity with God's.

The cause was Jonah's pride and dignity. When God ordered him to go to Nineveh and call against it for destruction, he knew that in case they repented God would forgive them, thus his word will fail because of God's forgiveness. Therefore he fled from the Lord and he said so expressly to Him (Jon. 4).

* Elijah the prophet, while fleeing from Jezebel, was in fact fleeing from God. The cause was the troubles and the threats which he faced. When God met him on his way and said to him, *"What are you doing here, Elijah?"*, Elijah said, *"I have been very zealous for the Lord God of hosts; because the children of Israel have forsaken Your covenant, torn down Your altars, and killed Your prophets with the sword. I alone am left; and they* *seek to take my life"* (1 Kgs 19: 14). Elijah ought to have laid his trust in God's protection instead of fleeing.

Some people thus flee from God because of troubles surrounding them.

Those are involved in such troubles and their minds are so occupied with them that they keep away from God. But in case of troubles one should turn one's eyes to God, open one's heart before Him, reveal one's troubles, and let Him take part instead of fleeing from Him.

* Some people may flee from God, feeling that He neglects them.

Such a person feels offended and feels himself alone amidst the troubles, no one helping or saving him, and God stands afar off. He should rather say to God, *"Why do You stand afar off? Why do You hide in times of trouble?"* (Ps. 10: 1); *"Lord, how they have increased who trouble me! ... Many are they who say of me: There is no help for him in God"* (Ps. 3)

* Others may flee from God because of lust.

Such people think that their relationship with God will deprive them of the lusts which they do not want to forsake. The existionalists and atheists are examples of this type. They think that God's commandments hinder the fulfillment of their lusts and prevent their self-assertion. A person of this type says to himself! It is good that God exists not, so that I may exist! Such people are satisfied with their condition though they say they are worried!

Some may think if they walk with God they will divide against themselves and there will be struggling between the spirit and the body and between good and evil. So they avoid such strifes.

Those do not like to face the real fact because they fear it, such as a person contracting a serious disease; he avoids the physician and avoids examination, X ray or analysis. Such a person thinks he comforts himself by this, even false comfort, to escape from the reality which worries him.

Some may flee from God because of being entrusted by Him some heavy mission.

Such a person, not willing to trouble himself, sees that God's yoke is hard and His burden is heavy though the Lord Christ Himself said, *"My yoke is easy and My burden is light"* (Mt. 11: 30). St. John the beloved also said, *"His commandments are not burdensome"* (1 Jn. 5: 3).

This type of people may evade ministry with its various requirements, burdens, and responsibilities. This person is in fact evading God.

Examples of this type are Moses and Jeremiah the prophets.

When Moses was sent by God to meet Pharaoh, Moses tried to evade this mission, and said to God, *"I am not eloquent, neither before nor since You have spoken to Your servant; but I am slow of speech and slow of tongue"* (Ex. 4: 10).

Jeremiah also, when called to ministry, apologized and said, *"I cannot speak, for I am a youth"* (Jer. 1: 6)

God, however, refused the execuse of both, and promised to give them power.

Others may flee from God because the gate is narrow and the way is difficult (Mt. 7: 14)

Such a person thinks that as soon as he proceeds in the way of God he will undergo difficulties, so he evades God and His cross. People in fact want others to be like them and to approve their ways, to laugh at their laughing and be pleased by their behaviour even though against the law. They want someone to cover their stealing and their lies even if he himself lies to save them! Unless a person does this, they will persecute him and cause him troubles. Therefore such a person evades God.

* A person may notice that those who are far away from God are in comfort whereas God's children are in trouble and humiliation, so he prefers to keep away from God like those.

The children of this world can save themselves by many wiles, and can obtain what they want through many ways and by various means, whether a lie to cover a fault, a false certificate evidencing illness to cover their absence from work, a bribery or a favor to attain some end, lenience by which they can win friends, words of flattery by which they can win seniors to their side or deceive them, a little hypocrisy to gain esteem, or a hard blow or plot by which they can get rid of adversaries!

God's children, on the other hand, have blocked ways and little devices, and often fail.

That is why many flee from God; for He has become not fit for this age and His means are not always successful! This made a great prophet like Jeremiah cry out, *"Righteous are You, O Lord, when I plead with You; Yet let me talk with You about Your judgments. Why does the way of the wicked prosper? Why are those happy who deal so treacherously?"* (Jer. 12: 1)

* Some person may flee from God so as not to bear the responsibility of his own sins.

Such a person does not want to face the consequences of his sin or fulfill the requirements of repentance. He wonders: What do you mean by repentance? Should I remember my sins, reprimand myself and suffer the humilitiation of reproach, weeping, and remorse? What have I to do with all this? Do you want me to suffer the sense of guilt? Leave me alone; this is better and more comfortable for me. This person is like one with an abscess which he does not want to open or clean and bandage, but to leave it as it is so as not to suffer!

Such people find repentance difficult, and the ways of the world sweet, gentle and easy because they comfort and please them even though for a while.

Those are spiritually tranquilized and live unconsciously. They flee from reality, from facing themselves, and from repentance and its requirements.

A person may flee from God due to despair!

One may say: Whatever I do, I cannot please God for He requires us to be holy and perfect (Mt. 5: 48)! God even says, *"So likewise you, when you have done all those things which you are commanded, say, 'We are unprofitable servants'"* (Lk. 17: 10). So, if even saints weep for their sins, and the way is long and unattainable, it is better for me to evade it!

Someone else may flee from God, being covetous to keep something he has.

Some person may be covetous to keep what he has whether wealth, dignity, lusts, or even a trivial thing. A youth may flee from God, being desirous to keep his hair long, or a girl for being desirous to have long colored nails! It seems as if they put God in a scale and such trivialities in another scale of the balance of more weight!

A serious thing is that those who flee from God flee also from everything related to Him.

Those flee from the church, from the meetings, from the holy communion, from the father confessor, from the Holy Bible, and from whatever reminds them of God!

A piece of advice to those who flee:

To those I have a word to say:

First: Wherever you go, God will seek you, and you will no more be able to flee.

Second: The way of God is not depressing, nor difficult as you may think.

See how David said, *"Where can I go from Your Spirit? Or where can I flee from Your presence?"* (Ps. 139: 7). Neither Adam nor Jonah could flee. You likewise will not be able to flee. It is not even good for you. You should face the reality, plainly and bravely.

The first reality one should face is the eternal life.

Does the way leading to eternal life conform with one's way or not? Where will one's conduct lead him? And how long? Suppose one is able to put one's conscience to sleep, will it remain asleep for ever? And when it wakes up what can be done about the whole past? Hence, one should face the reality.

What profit is it to a man if he gains the whole world, and loses his own soul?

One should then meet with God. But to meet with God, one should meet with himself i.e. to sit to himself.

Do as the lost son did when he came to himself and found the solution. Be frank with yourself and do not evade the reality. Do not call things with other names than theirs, deceiving yourself. Do not think that God is awesome, or that He will refuse you. Remember that the lost son was received warmly in the father's arms on his return. The father even killed for him the fatted calf!

The big problem with the people is that how they would forsake the sin which they love!

Mistaken is the person who thinks that he will keep the same heart with its desires when he forsakes sin. Nay, for God will give him a new heart and a new spirit. The new heart will not love sin but will rather reject it, and will not find difficulty in evading it.

In the beginning, one may feel that the commandment is heavy and burdensome, but this is due to being still far off from God's love. This will not continue.

The struggle is existing between the flesh and the spirit, *"For the flesh lusts against the spirit, and the spirit against the flesh"* (Gal. 5: 17). This struggle is in the beginning only, for the beginners. Afterwards, when the body is elevated, purified, and sanctified, it will not lust against the spirit, nor there will be any struggle but the peace of God's children.

The narrow gate we are called by the Lord to enter is not narrow to the end. Its beginning only is narrow but it gets broader as we go through it.

The narrow part is a test of our will, whether we are ready to endure for God's sake or not. If we show readiness, if we be patient, and if we struggle, the Lord's grace will visit us and remove the burden. Even the cross, we will be able to carry joyfully and walk with to the Golgotha. Even if we fall down under the cross, the Lord will send us a Cyrenean to carry it instead of us along the way.

The devil tries to deceive you by convincing you that the way is hard and long, and the repentance is not easy if not impossible.

By the grace a sinner can turn into a saint, not only to a repentant. This happened to Mary the Copt, Pelagia, Moses the black as well as to others. God will take care of you, and you will find joy in the commandment and pleasure in God's way.

Think not that God's children are sorrowful whereas the children of the world are joyful. Be sure that the worldly matters are sweet in the beginning and bitter at the end, whereas God's ways start with bitterness and turn sweet at the end.

Though God's children seem troubled outwardly, they are happy and joyful inwardly, as Paul the apostle says, *"as sorrowful, yet always rejoicing; ... as having nothing, and yet possessing all things"* (2 Cor. 6: 10)

More about fleeing:

The person who flees from God is a person who has not known Him, nor has tasted how sweet He is and has not tried to have communion with Him.

One who flees from God is either ignorant of God, or afraid of Him, one who is not attached to Him with love and far from spiritual experiences.

For one who has tasted God can never flee from Him. Such a person may keep away for some time but cannot dispense with Him. God to him is more than the blood running in his veins, more than the air filling his lungs, and even more necessary for him than himself. One who has tasted God and how sweet He is, says with the bride in the Song, "*I held Him and would not let Him go*" (Song 3: 4). He seeks Him everywhere, to be found in Him, to have life in Him, and abide in Him. God becomes to him solely everything.

Whoever tastes God's communion even for a while, will have such taste in his heart and mind for ever.

If such a person keeps away, he longs to return, and if his love cools off, he longs to kindle it. Those who met Christ on the earth were much influenced by Him. Even those who resisted Him, such as Judah Scariot who accompanied the Lord for some time. When Judah betrayed the Lord, he suffered much and gave back the money, saying, "*I have sinned by betraying innocent blood*" (Mt. 27: 3), then he hanged himself.

Whoever lives with Christ, will find that Christ is the essence of his whole life, and will say, "*For to me, to live is Christ*" (Phil. 1: 21).

It means as if one says: If I kept away from Christ, I would be away from life i.e. my life in Him; for I live by Him, with Him, and in Him, "*in Him we live and move and have our being*" (Acts 17: 28).

The Lord Christ said, "*I am the vine, you are the branches*" (Jn. 15: 5). As the branches abide in the vine, so we do in Christ. And as the sap of the vine runs in every branch, in every fruit, in every flower and in every leaf, otherwise it withers and dies, so is man with regard to Christ.

Christ is present in the whole life of man, within man's heart, mind, senses, and emotions, filling him all.

One who has experienced the life with God and the work of God's Spirit in him, loves always to be filled by the Spirit of

God, and loves to have his heart, his mind, and his whole life filled with the Spirit. Th Spirit works fully in such a person, and when he speaks the Spirit speaks by his mouth. Unlike this type of people are those who flee from God. They do not taste Him truly, nor experience the life with Him or His dwelling and work in them. Therefore the Psalmist calls upon them to taste and see how good God is (Ps. 34: 8), and calls them to try to have communion with Him.

Do not look to God as a preventive power that prevents you from fulfilling your goals. Do not see only the words: you shall not murder. You shall not commit adultery. You shall not steal. You shall not bear false witness. You shall not covet anything your neighbor has.

On the contrary, God is the giving power, He gave you existence and gifts.

He gave you also everything, as well as the commandment which says "you shall not". But His purpose is to protect you from yourself, from your lusts, from corruption, and from loss. You should take God as a friend, a companion, a beloved, a support, a helper, a keeper, and a shepherd. Do not consider Him a mere authority giving orders, but rather a great heart flowing with love. Even His commands are due to His flowing love.

Do not flee from God; for even if you do, where will you go. He will follow you.

His words will run after you everywhere, and His commandment will ring in your ears wherever you go. So try to meet with God, and if you have fled, return to Him.

FALTERING BETWEEN TWO WAYS

Some people have no steadfastness in God. They want to keep God's love and the love of the world together. They follow a famous saying which says: Give an hour to your heart, and an hour to your God!

Examples of this type of people:

Those remind me of the people who lived at the times of Elijah the prophet and king Ahab. They belonged to God, but they worshipped Baal also! Therefore Elijah the prophet rebuked them, saying, *"How long will you falter between two opinions? If the Lord is God, follow Him; but if Baal, follow him"* (1 Kgs. 18: 21)

It is the same way the Jews followed in the wildernessss of Sinai.

They were under the spiritual leadership of Moses the prophet, but at the same time they longed for the material good things they enjoyed while in the servitude of Pharaoh. Their hearts were not with God though He protected them with the cloud by day and guided them with the pillar of fire by night.

Though they ate the holy Manna which God sent them from heaven, they longed for the melons, the leeks and the garlic of Egypt.

They faltered between both, and they neither gained Egypt nor God. Neither did they love manna, nor ate the leeks. They did not live with Pharaoh, nor obeyed Moses, neither lived in the land of servitude, nor entered Canaan. As the saying goes: They kept an eye on Paradise and the other on Hades.

It is the condition of many, of whom Christ said, *"No one can serve two masters"* (Mt. 6: 24). However, many still say to themselves:

Would that I keep God's love and the love of the world together! I would have been happy here in this world and in the other life! But this of course is impossible.

Another example is Ananias and Sapphira.

These two wanted to keep their love of money and at the same time enter the new life of fellowship. On the other hand, the saints at that time sold their possessions and laid the proceeds at the apostles' feet. But Ananias and his wife Sapphira sold a possession and kept back part of the price, and what was the result? They lost everything as well as their life (Acts 5: 1-10).

Balaam the son of Beor was of this type.

He wanted to please Balak by cursing the people, and at the same time to please God by blessing them. He had the outward righteousness, but his heart was subject to the work of the devil. By the tongue he said beautiful words, *"Though Balak were to give me his house full of silver and gold, I could not go beyond the word of the Lord my God, to do less or more"*; *"The word that God puts in my mouth, that I must speak"*; *"How shall I curse whom God has not cursed? And how shall I denounce whom the Lord has not denounced?"* ; *"All that the Lord speaks, that I must do"* (Num. 22: 18, 38; 23: 8, 26)

Beautiful words indeed, showing outward submission and obedience to the Lord, but the heart was lusting for money and for secret violation that could not be found out.

Secretly, at the same time, Balaam gave Balak an advice by which he could destroy the people while the cause seems to be their own sin not Balaam (Num. 25: 1-3). That is why Balaam perished, and the Revelation tells us about the false doctrine of Balaam (Rev. 2: 14)

Balaam represents those who keep the outward formality of religion whereas the heart is attached to the world, loves to indulge in sin but not to appear as sinner.

Thus did the rich young man; he came to the Lord Christ seeking eternal life. But with this love of eternal life he kept the love of money in his heart. So he went sorrowful (Mt. 19: 16-22)

Such a person faltered between two ways. With respect to his relationship with God, he kept all the commandments from his youth, but he loved money also. He lacked that one thing: to sell his possessions and give the poor. All his desire was to follow Christ and to attain eternal life, besides keeping his possessions. And of course he could not.

Another one who faltered between two ways is Simon the Pharisee.

Simon invited Christ to his house, showing love to the Great Master. In front of the people he was the friend of Christ, and in his heart he suspected Christ and condemned His behavior. When he saw the woman anointing the Lord's feet with the fragrant oil and wiping them with the hair of her head, he said to himself, *"This man, if He were a prophet, would know who and what manner of woman this is who is touching Him, for she is a sinner"* (Lk. 7: 36-47)!

The scribes and Pharisees –described as hypocrites- were also among those who faltered between two ways (Mt. 23)

Outwardly they kept precisely the commandments; fasting two days every week, paying tithe of mint and anise and cummin, but neglecting the weightier matters of the law: justice and mercy and faith.

They were like whitewashed tombs which indeed appear beautiful outwardly, but inside are full of dead men's bones. They kept the formalities of the tithes and Sabbaths, but neglected the spirit and essence of the commandment.

Those who faltered between two opinions or two ways include also the people mentioned in the prophesy:

"This people honors Me with their lips, but their heart is far from Me" (Mk. 7: 6)

They offered sacrifices and burnt offerings, raised incense in the temple, celebrated the New Moons and feasts, the assemblies and Sabbaths. They fasted, prayed and held sacret meetings, but their hearts were far away from God (Isa. 1: 11-18)

The formality with this type of people is fulfilled but spirituality is lacking.

The Lord God therefore rebuked them hardly on the mouth of Isaiah the prophet, saying, *" 'To what purpose is the multitude of your sacrifices to Me?' says the Lord. 'I have had enough of burnt offerings of rams and the fat of fed cattle. I do not delight in the blood of bulls, or of lambs or goats. When you come to appear before Me, who has required this from your hand, to trample My courts?* '" (Isa. 1: 11, 12).

*"**Bring no more futile sacrifices; incense** is an abomination to Me".*

By incense the Lord meant that lacking the purity of heart and repentance. He furthermore referred to their faltering between two ways, saying, *"I cannot endure iniquity and the* sacred meeting. *Your New Moons and your appointed feasts My soul hates; they are a trouble to Me, I am weary of bearing them*" (Isa. 1: 13, 14)

"When you spread out your hands, I will hide My eyes from you; even though you make many prayers, I will not hear. Your hands are full of blood" (Isa. 1: 15)

To this extent, Lord, they contradict themselves? Yea, to this extent. But how can the hands be raised in prayer though full of blood? How can one combine between prayer and hard heartedness and lack of love? How can one combine between worship and sin? It is an outward appearance, faltering between two ways, and formality.

Some others falter between two ways through taking the middle course.

Such a middle course may be through keeping away from both the right and the left ways, or through slackening and negligence. This middle course may take the appearance of non extremism while actually it represents lack of power to resist.

Samson also faltered between the two ways; he kept his hair long as a Nazirite to God, and at the same time he was attached to Delilah.

Part of the time he spent in Gaza, and some other time he spent in Jerusalem. At a time he saved God's people and another time he was with adulterers! (Jud. 13-16). But Samson could not continue long in this dual position, for soon he lost his vow, had his hair cut, and lost his sight, his freedom, his dignity, and his power (Jud. 16: 16-22).

King Saul is another example. He wanted to keep the blessing of Samuel the prophet and to disobey him at the same time. Therefore the Lord rejected him and he was forsaken by the Spirit.

Even the angel of the church in Sardis faltered between two ways. And the Lord said to him, *"you have a name that you are alive, but you are dead"* (Rev. 3: 1)! This angle combined between life in appearance and hidden death. He was an angle of a church, having outward piety but his words were not perfect in God's sight.

Not to forget the Jews also, they had the appearance of being God's people, and another appearance as murderers of the prophets (Mt. 23: 37)

They were Abraham's children but they did not do Abraham's deeds (Jn. 8: 39). They were children by descent, but their conduct took another direction. They combined between taking pride in God and disobeying Him. They took pride in being the disciples of Moses, but when Moses was on the mount, they asked Aaron to make for them a golden calf, and they worshipped it! (Ex. 32: 1-7)

This faltering is clear also in the words of our father Isaac to his son Jacob; for he said to him, *"The voice is Jacob's voice, but the hands are the hands of Esau"* (Gen. 27: 22). It is a word to those who combine between two personalities; that of Jacob, and the other of Esau. As Jacob the father of the fathers fell in this fault, Peter the apostle also fell in. Peter denied the Lord, then said to Him, *"Lord, You know all things; You know that I love You."* (Mt. 26: 69-74; Jn. 21: 15-17)

Once more Peter fell in the same fault and Paul the apostle rebuked him.

He faltered between the truth and pleasing the Jews. Before the Jews he behaved in a certain way, and away from them he behaved in another. Therefore Paul said that he was to be blamed and that he played the hypocrite. Paul said it to him frankly, *"If you, being a Jew, live in the manner of Gentiles and*

not as the Jews, why do you compel Gentiles to live as Jews?"
(Gal. 2: 11-14).

Among those who faltered between two ways and failed are Lot's wife, and the righteous Lot himself in some way!

Lot's wife came out of Sodom the sinful city burnt with God's fire. She put her hand in the angel's hand, leaving everything behind. This was in the appearance. But while she was out of Sodom by the body, she was with her whole heart inside Sodom. That is why she looked behind her toward the city, and thus lost everything, being turned into a pillar of salt! (Gen. 19: 26).

Is it not hard that the angel holds your hand while your heart holds to Sodom? Is it not hard to have your legs outside the city while your eyes directed towards it? (Gen. 19: 23, 30).

Lot also, in some way but in a lesser degree, was of this type. He combined between his love to God and his dwelling in the sinful Sodom, being a watered plain like the garden of the Lord, though with the company of its wicked people! Therefore Peter the apostle said about Lot, *"and delivered righteous Lot, who was oppressed by the filthy conduct of the wicked; for that righteous man, dwelling among them, tormented his righteous soul from day to day by seeing and hearing their lawless deeds"* (2 Pet. 2: 7, 8)

Many hearts are not completely faithful to God. Part of their hearts is given to Him, and another part to the world. They say, as mentioned before, "An hour to the heart, and an hour to the Lord". Therefore do not waver in your spiritual life, because you cannot keep in one place Sarah and Hagar. One cannot consult Samuel and the fortuneteller, nor keep the vow, and Delilah. One cannot hold to the hand of the angel and to the sight of Sodom.

Pieces of advice:

If you want to be steadfast in your relationship with God and not to falter between two ways, follow these pieces of advice:

1. Let there be a fixed aim before you, and a firm intent to hold to this aim in spite of all external wars.

2. Be steadfast in practicing the spiritual means which are capable of strengthening God's love in your heart and strengthening your will so as not to accept sin.

3. Keep away from bad company that takes your heart away from God's love as the foreign women had turned Solomon's heart after other gods (1 Kgs. 11: 4). The Psalmist therefore warns us not to stand in the path of sinners, nor to walk in the counsel of the ungodly, nor to sit in the seat of the scornful (Ps. 1: 1)

4. Return quickly if you find yourself astray toward the other way, and chasten yourself prudently correcting your conduct.

5. Keep to continual prayer asking God's help to support you.

Pray for me also that God may be with us all to guide our steps towards fulfilling His good will.

FELLOWSHIP WITH GOD

What is the spiritual life but a fellowship with God and people. For St. John the apostle says, *"that which we have seen and heard we declare to you, that you also may have fellowship with us; and truly our fellowship is with the Father and with His Son Jesus Christ"* (1 Jn. 1: 3)

This fellowship God initiated when He created us.

God was alone from eternity, but, not willing to be alone, He brought us also into existence. He granted us the gift of existence, and furthermore He made us in His image, after His likeness.

A large step was further taken by God in the Incarnation.

He took our nature and shared in the flesh and blood (Heb. 2: 14). He sanctified also this human nature in Himself, shared our passions and pains, tempted in everything like us except for sin.

The most beautiful aspect of this fellowship is the Eucharist Sacrament.

When we partake of the Lord's flesh and blood, He abides in us and we in Him (Jn. 6: 56). Therefore this Sacrament is known also by the church as the Communion Sacrament. Thus Paul the apostle said, *"The cup of blessing which we bless, is it not the communion of the blood of Christ? The bread which we break, is it not the communion of the body of Christ?"* (1 Cor. 10: 16)

This holy communion is one of companionship.

Suffice that the most beautiful name of God is "Immanuel" which means "God with us" (Mt. 1: 23). However, the picture represented in the Book of Revelation is that of God in the midst of His people, and the heavenly Jerusalem His tabernacle, or dwelling place, with them (Rev. 21: 3). Another picture is that of the Lord in the midst of the seven golden lampstands, i.e. the seven churches (Rev. 2: 1).

In this communion the Lord says, "*where two or three are gathered together in My name, I am there in the midst of them*" (Mt. 18: 20). Another prominent example of this communion is the picture of the tent of meeting in the midst of the tents of the people, and the ark of testimony in the midst as well. See also how the Lord said: Do not be afraid, for I am with you. See how Jacob the father of the fathers was on his way afraid of his brother, but the Lord appeared to him and said, "*Behold, I am with you and will keep you wherever you go, and will bring you back to this land*" (Gen. 28: 15). And God went with Jacob along the whole way.

The Lord wants this communion and this companionship or fellowship to continue here and in heaven.

The Lord therefore says, "*I, if I am lifted up from the earth, will draw all peoples to Myself*" (Jn. 12: 32); "*And if I go and prepare a place for you, I will come again and receive you to Myself; that where I am, there you may be also*" (Jn. 14: 3). And He prays to the Father, saying, "*I desire that they also whom You gave Me may be with Me where I am*" (Jn. 17: 24)

He furthermore says, "*I in them, and You in Me*"(Jn. 17)

The Lord says about Himself, "*I am the vine, you are the branches*", and He calls us, "*Abide in Me, and I in you*" (Jn. 15: 4, 5)

Through such communion we share one body.

The Lord being the head and we are the members as the apostle says, "*Do you not know that your bodies are members of*

Christ?" (1 Cor. 6: 15). We become the temple of God and the Spirit of God dwells in us (1 Cor. 3: 16; 6: 19). What a type of communion this is!

It is not that communion of fellowship only, but rather of love.

It is exchanged love where man loves the Lord God with all his heart, with all his soul, and with all his strength (Deut. 6: 5). On the part of the Lord, it is written, *"God so loved the world that He gave His only begotten Son"* (Jn. 3: 16); *"having loved His own who were in the world, He loved them to the end"* (Jn. 13: 1)

The communion with God is a fellowship with Him in work.

We work with Him in building the kingdom, and in making ready a people prepared for Him with repentance. He also works with us in whatever we do in conformity with His good will. It is necessary that He shares work with us, because He said, *"without Me you can do nothing"* (Jn. 15: 5). The Psalmist therefore said, *"Unless the Lord builds the house, they labor in vain who build it. Unless the Lord guards the city, the watchman stays awake in vain"* (Ps. 127: 1). The building and the guarding are shared between God and man. We therefore pray the Lord in the Litanies, saying, [Take part, O Lord, with your servants, in every good work].

God's Spirit takes part with the people in work. This is called "the communion of the Holy Spirit"

Therefore we say in the blessing, *"The grace of the Lord Jesus Christ, and the love of God, and the communion of the Holy Spirit be with you all"* (2 Cor. 13: 14). Hence we pray for the believers to have the work of the Holy Spirit with them, the love of the Father, and the grace of His only begotten Son. Without this communion they cannot do anything.

This communion in work is what the apostle means by the words *"partakers of the divine nature"* (2 Pet. 1: 4)

We take part with the divine nature in work, and not partake of the essence or the Godhead, otherwise we would be gods, God forbid! Besides, what we do for the restoration of people and for reconciling them with God cannot be a pure human work; for it is necessary that the Spirit of God works with us. He puts the word on our mouths, and we utter it. This is the meaning of partaking of the divine nature.

It is also God's humbleness that makes Him work with us.

It is His humbleness that permits us to work with Him, and it is His love that makes Him work with us. He supports our weakness by His power, or entrusts us to work with Him.

Fellowship in work is however preceded by sharing the same will.

It means that one has the Lord's will in his life. Therefore the Lord taught us to say in our prayer "Let Your will be done". We should have only what God wills us to have.

Through this sharing of work by God, man is saved from condemnation.

Since God shares work, there could be no fault, and consequently no condemnation. We are condemned only when we separate ourselves from God in work. This happens through sin.

Sin is separation from God and breaking of the communion with Him.

For as St. Paul the apostle says, *"what communion has light with darkness? And what accord has Christ with Belial?"* (2 Cor. 6: 14). And St. John the beloved also says, *"if we say that we have fellowship with Him, and walk in darkness, we lie and do not practice the truth"* (1 Jn. 1: 6)

Communion with God in work leads to communion with Him in glory, for we will be glorified with Him.

We will be with Him *"Fellow heirs"* (Eph. 3: 6). He will take us with Him on the clouds, and we shine with His light like Moses and Elijah on Mount Tabor (Phil. 3: 21). Before that we will also rise in the likeness of His glorious body, sit with Him, and be crowned with crowns of righteousness (2 Tim. 4: 8), sanctifying our nature.

To be glorified with Him, we should first suffer with Him (Rom. 8: 17), and have fellowship of His sufferings as St. Paul says (Phil. 3: 10)

The Lord Christ carried His cross, and we also should bear ours and follow Him. He was nailed to the cross, and you also say with Paul the apostle, *"I have been crucified with Christ; it is no longer I who live, but Christ lives in me"* (Gal. 2: 20). Thus we die with Christ to rise with Him, not only to be buried with Him through baptism (Rom. 6: 4), but to be always carrying about in the body the dying of the Lord Jesus, *"that the life of Jesus also may be manifested in our body"* (2 Cor. 4: 10).

Our communion with God results in a fellowship with the brethren.

For the Lord said, *"By this all will know that you are My disciples, if you have love for one another"* (Jn. 13: 35). Another factor is the fellowship and cooperation among us, as well as fellowship with the head.

The believers share one faith, one table, and one common salvation. They share love, and are co-workers for the edification of the kingdom, and the edification of this one body whose head is Christ.

Who are the members of this one body?

Those are the saints struggling on the earth, as well as the saints who had departed to heaven, in addition to the hosts of angels. From all those is formed the holy universal church.

As we have communion with the living, we have also communion with the departed.

Death does not separate us from the other members of Christ; for we remember them in our congregational prayers and in our private prayers. They also pray for us that we may complete our days of sojourning in peace and join their holy company. St. John the beloved says concerning this holy fellowship among the believers, *"If we walk in the light as He is in the light, we have fellowship with one another, and the blood of Jesus Christ His Son cleanses us from all sin"* (1 Jn. 1: 7).

It is then fellowship in light, that is in the life of righteousness.

It is fellowship in Christ Jesus, fellowship among a group of holy temples in each of them the Holy Spirit dwells. The church used to put away whoever walks in the darkness, as the Scriptures say, *"put away from yourselves the evil person"* (1 Cor. 5: 13); *"And have no fellowship with the unfruitful works of darkness, but rather expose them"* (Eph. 5: 11)

This fellowship of the believers aim at achieving unity.

For the apostle says, *"... endeavoring to keep the unity of the Spirit ..."*, *"There is one body and one Spirit, just as you were called in one hope of your calling"* (Eph. 4: 3, 4). Therefore, the believers had one mind and one soul.

If you have communion with God in love, you will have fellowship with his children. On this love of God and love of the brethren hang all the law and the prophets.

RECONCILIATION WITH GOD

Sin is controversy with God:

When you sin, you lose fellowship with God and enter into controversy with Him.

This controversy with God is the most serious result of sin.

Sin, actually, has two results; perdition of one's soul, and making God angry. Hence the sacrifices of the Old Testament were offered for both purposes as indicated in the Book of Leviticus.

The purpose of the burnt offering was to reconcile with God and to satisfy His justice.

Therefore, the burnt offering was often described as "*a sweet aroma to the Lord*" (Lev. 1). It was the first sacrifice mentioned in the Book of Leviticus. No one was allowed to eat from it because it belongs to God alone. Moreover, fire was to be kept burning on it to consume it and turn it to ashes as a symbol of satisfying God's justice (Lev. 6)

The sin offering and the trespass offering both were a symbol of man's salvation from the penalty of sin. The passover lamb was another symbol as well.

The Lord Christ on the cross undertook both deeds. As a burnt offering, He reconciled God with people, and as a sin offering He bore their sins, redeemed, and saved them.

The only thing you should be concerned with is the reconciliation with God. Do not be like the servant who wants only to be freed from the punishment, but rather be like the son who is concerned first with pleasing his father's heart. Say to Him: It is most important to me to please You and to have Your blessing. I want to reconcile with You and to have You again in my heart. I am not concerned only about being freed from the punishment, but what avails to me is Your love and the fellowship with You. I am not worried only about my salvation or perdition, but rather more about Your love. I seek to be reconciled with You, and You do whatever You want to me.

Do not think that Adam's sin was just eating from the forbidden tree, but mainly separation from God. Adam loved himself more than he loved God, and obeyed his wife rather than God, and finally submitted to the serpent's counsel instead of God's. Thus Adam separated himself actually and practically from God.

Adam hid from God's presence behind the tree on hearing the Lord's voice, and fear replaced love in his heart. This fleeing from God is the aspect of the controversy between Adam and God.

The problem is that when you sin you think that you are sinning against the others, against yourself, or against the principles. But the fact is that your sin is addressed against God. Therefore David the prophet said:

"Against You, You only, have I sinned, and done this evil in Your sight" (Ps. 51: 4)

David did not sin against Uriah the Hittite, nor against his own chastity, but mainly against God. This annoyed him so much that he said the preceding words.

Sin is always addressed against God. So when Joseph the righteous was tempted to sin, he said, *"How then can I do this great wickedness, and sin against God?"* (Gen. 39: 9). Sin is disobedience, resistance, rebelling against God and lack of love, for He said, *"He who has My commandments and keeps them, it is he who loves Me"* (Jn. 14: 21, 23, 15; 15: 15)

More serious still is the fact that sin is enmity with God, as the apostle said, *"friendship with the world is enmity with God"* (Jas. 4: 4). It is separation from God.

"What communion has light with darkness? And what accord has Christ with Belial?" (2 Cor. 6: 14). When you sin, you lose that communion with God. You cannot say that you have communion with the Holy Spirit or with the divine nature so long as you are in sin! That is why it is said of the lost son that he left his father's house.

Sin is loss of familiarity and fellowship with God and loss of God's love in the heart. Thus The Lord, blaming the angel of the Church in Ephesus, said, *"I have this against you, that you have left your first love"* (Rev. 2: 4)

Reconciliation is the mission of Christ and His apostles:

The main work of the Lord Christ was to reconcile humanity with God.

This is what we say in the Reconciliation Prayer in the Liturgy of St. Gregory: [You have reconciled the heavenly with the earthly]. Christ made reconciliation with the blood of His crucifixion. He made peace with God, *"He Himself ... has broken down the middle wall of separation, having abolished in His flesh the enmity"* (Eph. 2: 14-16)

The ministry of reconciliation is the mission of the holy father apostles.

It became also the mission of the pastors and all ranks of the holy orders that came after them. Hence the apostle said in his Second Epistle to the Corinthians, *"God, who has reconciled us to Himself through Jesus Christ, and has given us the ministry of reconciliation, that is, that God was in Christ reconciling the world to Himself, not imputing their trespasses to them, and has committed to us the word of reconciliation"* (2 Cor. 5: 17-20).

He further said:

"Now then, we are ambassadors for Christ, as though God were pleading through us: we implore you on Christ's behalf, be reconciled to God" **(2 Cor. 5: 20)**

Yea, indeed. The reconciliation ministry or word is the work of the church that gives the people of the blessings of the reconciliation made by Christ on the cross. This ministry of reconciliation is represented in all the church sacraments. The Lord Christ paid for it, but after our reconciliation with God, we sinned again.

The words [You have reconciled the heavenly to the earthly] imply another meaning; that,

Sin is not a controversy with God only, but also with all the heavenly creation.

When we sin we annoy God, and all the heavenly host and spirits of the saints; we make them angry. See what God says about the angels, *"The angel of the Lord encamps all around those who fear Him and delivers them"* (Ps. 34: 7). It is also said about them, *"Are they not all ministering spirits sent forth to minister for those who will inherit salvation?"* (Heb. 1: 14). But what about those who will not inherit salvation?

Sin is awful, and the angels cannot bear to see it. The angels support man so as not to accept sin, but if man accepted it and fell in impurity, thus betraying the Lord, the angels could not bear it and they leave him to the devils his friends!

When man repents and returns with his heart to God, he reconciles with God and His angels, *"likewise there will be more joy in heaven over one sinner who repents"* (Lk. 15: 7).

The ministry of reconciliation was so important that the Lord undertook it on Himself and paid His blood for it. However, after getting reconciled to God, we returned to sin and to controversy with Him. Therefore He sent us His ministers – with all their ranks- to call us to reconcile to God.

Reconciliation is the ministry of the prophets, the apostles, the pastors, as well as the bishops, the priests, the deacons, and all the ministers. All of those have this ministry as their only task.

God seeks to reconcile you to Himself; He knocks at the doors of your soul, saying, *"Open for Me, My sister, My love, My dove, My perfect one; for My head is covered with dew, My locks with the drops of the night"* (Song 5: 2). Yet, we slacken, we refuse the work of the grace within us, we resist the ministry of reconciliation, then we repent and say, *"my beloved has turned away and was gone ... I sought Him, but I could not find Him, I called Him, but He gave me no answer"* (Song 5: 6). It is the controversy with God.

God wants to reconcile you to Himself through the various means of grace, but He gives one condition: He says, *"My son, give Me your heart"*.

Reconciliation is not mere practice or formal worship, prayers, or fasting, but it is rather the giving of the heart to God. The Jews offered these practices to God but He refused them, and said blaming, *"these people draw near with their mouths and honor Me with their lips, but have removed their hearts far from Me"* (Isa. 29: 13)

The Lord God therefore said to them, *"When you spread out your hands, I will hide My eyes from you; even though you make many prayers, I will not hear"* (Isa. 1: 15). Why, O Lord, is this controversy? It is because they had not given the heart to the Lord. But what if the heart is far away? The Lord says' *"I will give you a new heart and put a new spirit within you"* (Ezek. 36: 26). That is why we say in our prayers,

"Create in me a clean heart, O God" (Ps. 51: 10)

The word "create" in this verse has a deep significance. It is not only a restoration of the old heart, but the creation of a new heart.

Reconciliation starts within the heart not outwardly.

If you say to Him: I shall fast to You twice a week, give the tithes of all my money, give the firstlings, the vows, the increase, and the offerings, or I shall give my body to be burned, He will say, *"My son, give Me your heart"* (Prov. 23: 26)

Is it then the heart only that God requests in reconciliation? Nay, for He requests also the will. Love is not merely in word or in tongue, but in deed and in truth (1 Jn. 3: 18)

God does not compel people to love Him, for He wants their will to move. He once said, *"How often I wanted ... but you were not willing"* (Lk. 13: 34). And St. Augustine says:

[God, who created you without your interference, does not will to save you unless you are willing]

The Lord Christ used to say to those who asked to be healed: *"Do you want to be made well?"*; *"Do you want to be cleansed?"* One's will is important as evident from the words of the Lord, "*If anyone hears My voice and opens the door, I will come in to him and dine with him*" (Rev. 3: 20). If one opens ... if one's will moves ... It is not sufficient that you love God and desire to be reconciled to Him, but you should also offer your will.

Is there a third condition besides giving the heart and the will? Yea. It is faith.

Your heart may lack love and your will fail, in this case your faith interferes. You trust that God is capable of saving you, and of working within you that you may will and act, so, pour yourself before God with all determination. Wrestle with Him, and say,

Even though I do not love You, O Lord, nor give You my heart, You are able to pour Your love in my heart by the Holy Spirit (Rom. 5: 5)

Even if my faith is weak, You can strengthen my weak belief (Mk. 9: 24). If my will is weak, my strength is from You. In the reconciliation, You will give me a new nature, "*renew a steadfast spirit within me*" (Ps. 51: 10); "*if anyone is in Christ, he is a new creation*" (2 Cor. 5: 17)

This renewal is the outcome of reconciliation, which gives also sanctification, justification, and forgiveness.

In the reconciliation, God blots out our sins and remembers them no more (Jer. 31: 34). He accepts them who are reconciled to Him, not imputing their trespasses to them (2 Cor. 5: 19). And as one of the saints said: Repentance make the adulterers celibate. It means that they become as chaste as if they have never sinned nor been defiled!

WRESTLING WITH GOD

God wants to reconcile you to Himself:

He Himself wants you to be reconciled to Him.

He wants this reconciliation, He requests and seeks it with all His power, with all His grace, and with the action of His Holy Spirit. You should at least respond.

God rebukes man, saying, *"Come now, and let us reason together"* (Isa. 1: 18). He says also, *"Return to Me, and I will return to you"* (Mal. 3: 7). He stands at the door, knocking, waiting who will open to Him, and says, *"the one who comes to Me I will by no means cast out"* (Jn. 6: 37). He further says reproaching, *"All day long I have stretched out My hands to a disobedient and contrary people"* (Rom. 10: 21)

Can you imagine God stretching out His hands to you all day long, all the life, desiring you to be reconciled to Him? Can you imagine Him willing to wash you that you may be whiter than snow, and to dwell in your heart and you in His, and to establish with you a covenant and a relationship?

He, the owner of the heavens and the earth, the Creator of the heavens and the earth, the Almighty, who has all the perfections, the Holy whose holiness has no limits, He says that His delight is with the sons of men (Prov. 8: 31)! He looks to your heart and says, *"This is My resting place forever; Here I will dwell, for I have desired it"* (Ps. 132: 14). And the Spirit, addressing your soul, says, *"Listen, O daughter, consider and incline your ear; forget your own people also, and your father's house; so the king will greatly desire your beauty; because He is your Lord, worship Him"* (Ps. 45: 10, 11)

For this reconciliation God sent the prophets, the pastors, the priests, the teachers, and the preachers. All of those call, "be reconciled to God". And for this reconciliation He sent also His grace and His Holy Spirit.

God wants to reconcile you to Himself, to correct you under any condition and in any way. He may even send you temptations, tribulations, or diseases if this would restore you to Him.

All this He does for your sake so as not to perish.

He wants your salvation, and He desires all men to be saved and to come to the knowledge of the truth (1 Tim. 2: 3). He has no pleasure in the death of the sinner but that he turns and lives (Hez. 18: 32). There is even joy in heaven over one who repents.

God is concerned about you, knowing that if you go astray you will be lost. Therefore He draws you near so that you may not be lost.

He knows that if you go astray from Him, you will lose your ideals and your divine image and will return to dust (Gen. 3: 19). He knows that you will become again an earthly creature; you will be lost and you will be separated from the kingdom. Knowing that you will also lose the wedding dress, the holiness, chastity, and faith which you have, therefore God, out of His deep love, cares for you and is concerned about you.

Even the Holy Scriptures are inspired by God for your sake. The Holy Scriptures tell the story of God with mankind, the story of their fall, and the story of their salvation.

The Holy Bible is not the story of God with the angels, nor with nature, but God's story with the people.

The heavenly Jerusalem, the place of everlasting death, is called in the Holy Bible *"the tabernacle of God with men"* (Rev. 21: 3). What a divine care! and what an opportunity for reconciliation! Seize the opportunity of the Lent to make this reconciliation. Let nothing hinder you.

Obstacles that hinder reconciliation:

Sometimes the cause is unawareness, as when a person is unaware of his condition or of the change that happened to Him. Such a person does not have God in his mind, being busy with other things.

The issue of reconciliation never occurs to the mind of such a person, for his relationship with God is not the object of his concern or interest. He does not feel at all God's presence in order to be reconciled to Him!

In order to be reconciled to God, give yourself the chance to think of Him. Try to repeat frequently God's name in your mind, on your tongue and with your emotion that you may be busy with Him for some time. Escape, even for a little time, from your involvements, and think of God.

Be sure that if you think of God, you will think of reconciling with Him.

Involvements often distract man from God and from himself. Therefore the Scriptures say, *"Consecrate a fast, call a sacred assembly"* (Joel 2: 15). This would give a chance for thinking of God. Do this, then, as far as possible, and in a spiritual way.

Among the things that hinder reconciliation with God is love of the world, or love of sin. One may say: I do want to reconcile with God, but I could not!

Such a person finds himself unable to reconcile with God so long as sin is standing before him. This means that God is put in the scale before sin and the scale of sin is more weighty. As if one says: O Lord, if only You agree that I continue in this sin while I love You, this will be the best solution!

My advice to you in this case is to wrestle with God until He delivers you of this sin.

Wrestling with God:

Say to God: I want to live with You, but deliver me of this obstacle. Save me; give me power.

Pour yourself before God. Even if you love sin deeply from your heart, ask God, also deeply from your heart, to save you from it.

Say to Him clearly: I wish, O Lord, to stop this sin, but I love it. I desire to be rid of it, but my heart is fully involved with it.

If my heart loves sin, O Lord, You are able to change this heart.

You can make me hate this sin which I love.

Pour yourself before God, and take power from him over sin. Say to Him: O Lord, You saved saints whose life had been much worse than mine. You saved Moses the black, Augustine, Mary the Copt, Irianos the governor of Ensena, and many others, save me also as You have done to those.

Say to Him: Consider me, O Lord, among the complex cases which Your divine wisdom has healed.

Say: I am a problem standing before Your omnipotent divinity, make me subject to the work of Your Holy Spirit.

Wrestle with God to save you from the love of sin. But a piece of advice I give you, blessed son, on the way of your repentance:

You cannot prevail over sin with your human effort alone.

The Scriptures say about sin, *"She has cast down many wounded, and all who were slain by her were strong men"* (Prov. 7: 26). So, if all who were slain by it were strong men, no one but God can overcome it. Remember that Joshua with his great army could not defeat Amalek except with the raised hands of Moses (Ex. 17: 11). Therefore, wrestle with God, and say to Him:

If I have no power, You, O Lord, have all the power.

If I do not desire to live with You, suffice that You, O Lord, desire to live with me. If I am not serious about my own salvation, You, O Lord, are very serious about saving this soul of mine.

If my own will cannot attain the salvation of my soul, no doubt, Your grace, O Lord can realize it for me.

If my own struggle is of no avail, perhaps my prayer avails.

Blessed child, who struggles for the salvation of your soul, be always a friend of the Holy Spirit; be in fellowship with the Holy Spirit; let the Holy Spirit share always in your life and in your struggle.

WAITING FOR THE LORD

God promised Adam and Eve that the woman's seed would bruise the serpent's head (Gen. 3: 15). However, the serpent continued lifting up its head for thousands of years, causing harm to mankind in faith and spirituality. Mankind remained waiting when the Lord would come and fulfill His promise.

Then the Lord said to our father Abraham, "*In your seed all the nations of the earth shall be blessed*" (Gen. 22: 18). And this promise was repeated to Abraham's sons. Yet, more than two thousand years passed and the sons of Abraham have been waiting the fulfillment of this blessing. And the Lord was still waiting for the fullness of time to come (Gal. 4: 4)

Humanity expected the salvation of the Lord all these years, trusting that He will come, and save, and fulfill His promise.

When that was to take place, no one knew. Many holy persons waited all their life, yet, "*These all died in faith, not having received the promises, but having seen them afar off were assured of them, embraced them ...*" (Heb. 11: 13). And the Lord came indeed, after this long waiting. But let us talk about this waiting:

The Psalmist says, "*Wait for the Lord; be strong, and let your heart take courage; wait for the Lord*" (Ps. 27: 14)

This psalm gives us a beautiful hint about how to wait for the Lord. We should not wait in despair, in mean-spiritedness, or in weakness, but strongly, with trust, and with our hearts strengthened with faith. Isaiah the prophet explains this when describing those who wait for the Lord. He says,

"But those who wait for the Lord shall renew their strength; they shall mount up with wings like eagles, they shall run and not be weary, they shall walk and not faint" (Isa. 40: 31)

Unlike this the person who has not experienced the waiting for the Lord, he is always confused and troubled, fearing that no help will come to him from the Lord. He requests, but gets very annoyed if his request is not quickly given. Any delay in response increases his trouble and makes him lose his peace.

He who waits for the Lord never loses peace, nor feel concerned

God had promised Elijah the prophet that heaven would give rain, and Elijah prayed, but it did not rain! Elijah prayed again a second, a third, and a fourth time, yet it did not rain! However, Elijah never felt worried, for he trusted the Lord's promise and waited. At the seventh prayer, he saw *"a cloud as small as a man's hand"* (1 Kgs. 18: 44). He knew then that the Lord responded, and heavy rain came.

The waiting for the Lord is a test of our faith: will our faith shake if the Lord delays? will it remain firm?

A person who experiences the life of faith, will put all his affairs in the hands of the Lord and leave them there. He will not be worried or troubled, nor demand a quick response. Such a person trusts that God will interfere in the most perfect way and in suitable time to solve any problem. True are the deep words of the Lord to His disciples:

"It is not for you to know times or seasons which the Father has put in His own authority"(Acts 1: 7)

We wait for the Lord; we wait for Him in hope, confidence, and joy. We trust that He will come, we do not know when, but we are sure that He will come and will work for our salvation.

We do not know if He will come morning, noon, midnight, or in the fourth watch! We leave the time to His wisdom.

Whoever waits for the Lord must be sure of two main things: God's exceeding love towards mankind, and His unlimited wisdom.

During the period of waiting, do not seek human means.

Do not do as Rebekah did. Having lost hope that God would bless Jacob, she sought her human intelligence using craft and deceit (Gen. 27). Nor do you do like Abraham who, despairing that God would give him Isaac, took Hagar (Gen. 16: 3, 4). Truly, human means are a painful result of despair during waiting for the Lord, and they reveal concern as the period extends. But see what the Psalmist says,

"My soul waits for the Lord more than those who watch for the morning"(Ps. 130: 6)

Do not feel worried then, thinking that God tarries in coming; for God never delays even through you think He has delayed in responding.

God knows the proper time very accurately and does not delay even for a moment.

What one thinks delay is in fact an error in your valuation due to being concerned about when God will respond. Trust then God's wisdom in choosing the suitable time, and trust before anything else God's love towards you.

God, the lover of mankind, loves you more than you love yourself. He works for your benefit more than you do.

He gives you even if you do not ask, or before you ask. How much rather will He give you when you ask. He cares to give what benefits you rather than what you ask for. Indeed, how do you know that the things you ask for is more useful or suitable to you? Even the time which you think fit, perhaps God sees unsuitable or unuseful to you due to circumstances He knows before their taking place.

Be humble then, and let God's wisdom act, and wait for the Lord.

It is not shameful and painful that we trust our intelligence more than we trust God, and His wisdom and good dispensation?! God –while you think He had delayed- is managing all matters with such a wisdom which you can only recognize afterwards when things are revealed before you.

The story of Pharaoh and Moses raises much wonder:

The Lord God tarried for more than four hundred years to save His children from their humiliation. The reason is that the cup of the sinful people whom He was going to remove from their face was not yet full. He tolerated Pharaoh ten times correcting him with heavy successive blows giving him the chance to repent or submit! Those who were waiting were bored and worried, wondering for what was happening. But when they saw the wonder of dividing the Red Sea they could realize the wisdom and depth of the long time God left them to wait.

Had God destroyed Pharaoh and his men in the first blow, the matter would not have been so strong as when He divided the Red Sea!

Some would have exclaimed why God had not tolerated much longer and given Pharaoh another chance. God's longsuffering for over four hundred years does not mean that He forgot or neglected His children. It shows that He was planning and choosing the most powerful way and the most suitable time. Let us then trust God's wisdom while we wait.

Waiting may also teach us prayer.

Waiting can be a school in which we learn earnestness in prayer and holding to the Lord. We can learn also to depend on

Him, and get deeply attached to Him. What we call "delay" of the Lord, may urge us to pour ourselves before Him imploring. The longer the time of waiting extends, the more we add to our prayers fasting, prostration, and perhaps vows also. God delayed to respond to the request of Hanna, the wife of Elkanah to have a child, for He had closed her womb, so she prayed to the Lord and wept in anguish. She even made a vow to give her child to the Lord all his life, and it happened so (1 Sam. 1: 9-11)

Moreover, if the response was quick, one would not recognize its value.

Not recognizing its value, we are not urged to show love, thanks, or gratitude. Besides, being not aware of its value, we may lose it. The bride of the Song could not find her groom, and suffered much for him, sought him and could not find him, called him but found no answer, asked the daughters of Jerusalem to tell him she was lovesick, so when she found him, she held him and would not let him go (Song 5: 6-8; 3: 4). That is why God may delay a little, but with wisdom and love that you may hold to Him, long for Him, and say to Him, *"With my whole heart I have sought You"* (Ps. 119: 10)

Whoever waited for the Lord, found wonderful results.

The children who were granted to their mothers after being barren for long years, those became a blessing to their generations. Among those are:

* **John the Baptist**, who was born after long waiting, became the angel that prepared the way before the Lord (Mk. 1: 2). He even became the greatest among those born of women (Mt. 11: 11).

* **Samuel**, whose mother was barren and gave prayers and vows to have him, became the great prophet who had the flask of oil with which he anointed Saul and David.

* **Joseph**, who was given by the Lord to Rachel after being barren responding to the intercession of Jacob for her, became a blessing to Egypt and to his own family, and got a double portion among his brothers.

* **Samson**, who was born also after long years, became the strongest man in his time.

You also, wait for the Lord, trusting that your waiting will end with blessing and grace.

You should not wait with displeasure, anxiety or worry, doubting God's response, or suspecting the effectiveness of prayer. Nay, this is not spiritual. You should rather wait with full hope and confidence, and with faith. If you feel weak, pray that the Lord may strengthen your faith.

God's promises are true and faithful and we trust them. Whatever hindrances we face that fight our faith, we should not doubt.

We should believe, not only that God will act, but also that He is now working, and has begun to work before we ask. For example, the ministry in some church is in shortage, and they pray to the Lord to give them quickly a holy, active and loving priest. But the ordination may be postponed for some months or years, and the people cry out why the Lord delayed. Here the Lord says to them: I have not delayed, on the contrary, I have been preparing for you this priest thirty or forty years. I have been preparing him with a special heart, high spiritualities, and a special mind. I have been preparing him through temptations, and experiences so as to be fit for your church and your congregation in particular. I have been preparing him long before you asked and before you needed a priest!

Therefore, God's children are happy and in peace. Whenever they are fought with doubts, they say, "*The voice of my beloved! Behold, he comes leaping upon the mountains, skipping upon the hills*" (Song 2: 8). And certainly He who leaps upon the mountains never delays.

The passengers on a plane think sometimes that it is standing still, whereas it is actually flying with great speed!

Likewise, when one looks at an electric fan, he thinks it is still, though it may be working with its full speed. In the same way one may look God working but thinks He is not. So do not depend on your vision, nor your senses, nor your human mind and understanding, but rely rather on faith. For so many things God does for us, but we are not aware of their consequences except very late.

REJOICING IN THE LORD

We do not rejoice over the world, for the world has nothing to satisfy us.

As St. John says, *"the world is passing away, and the lust of it"* (1 Jn. 2: 17). All the material things passing away do not satisfy us spiritually; nor do they fill a life which has been sanctified by the Lord. Such things cannot please hearts that have become temples of the Holy Spirit and dwelling place for God.

We do not rejoice over the world because the world always takes and does not give; for whatever the world gives is *"vanity of vanities"* (Eccles. 1). Whatever the world gives is unstable, even the worldly relationships. The souls which are attached to the everlasting life and have begun the way from now cannot find joy in such things.

We put our trust in none but God, and we rejoice in Him alone.

Rejoicing in God is the real joy and the continuous joy. It is a pure joy in which the spirit takes the greater part. This joy starts when we find God, get acquainted with Him, taste how sweet He is, love Him, and live with this love seeking nothing else.

To this holy joy the Psalmist calls us, saying, *"Oh, taste and see that the Lord is good"* (Ps. 34: 8). For when we taste the Lord, we come to the beauty of the real life and forget all our past one. We remember only the Lord filling our heart, mind, and spirit.

How great was the joy of Nathanael when Philip called him, saying, *"we have found Him of whom Moses ... wrote"* (Jn. 1: 45). And how great was the joy of the Samaritan woman when she got acquainted with Messiah and proclaimed Him to her people (Jn. 4). Great also was the joy of Saul of Tarsus who met with the Lord, and therefore said, *"I have suffered the loss of all things and count them as rubbish, that I may gain Christ and be found in Him"* (Phil: 3: 8, 9)

To know God is a great treasure, which taste is inexpressible joy. It is the treasure which the Lord mentioned, saying, *"... treasure hidden in a field, which a man found and hid; and for joy over it he goes and sells all that he has and buys that field"* (Mt. 13: 44). And you, have you found this treasure? Have hidden it in your heart? Have you counted all things rubbish for the excellence of His knowledge? Augustine rejoiced in Him more than over the worldly philosophy and the lusts of the body. And Solomon rejoiced in Him more than over all riches and enjoyment. The disciples as well were glad when they saw the Lord (Jn. 20: 20)

This joy is the only joy that is never taken away from us.

It is a joy that starts here, on the earth, and continues in eternity also. It grows continually as the Lord reveals Himself to us, and as He pours His love into our hearts.

Any joy which does not have its source in God will certainly come to an end.

Solomon tasted all the joys of the world, but he got bored of them. They lost their first delight, so he· left them to seek something else more profound and more sublime.

Lot also was glad with Sodom and the well watered plain, and so it was like the garden of the Lord, like the land of Egypt (Gen. 13: 11). But this ended with a disaster!

Ahab rejoiced at the field of Naboth the Jezreelite, but his joy ended with his destruction (1 Kgs. 21)!

Amnon was very happy with Tamar and loved her with all his heart, then he hated her exceedingly (2 Sam. 13: 14, 15).

And Samson was very happy also with Delilah, but his happiness led to his disaster (Judg. 16).

The joys of the world are not true joys, but can be called temporary sensual delight, enjoyment or pleasure, and do not rise to the level of the real joys.

Man's heart is superior to the world and more sublime than the material because it is made in God's image and likeness.

When a person rejoices over the world, or feels sad over something worldly lost, it means that he has forgotten who he is, and deviated from the divine image; in other words, he got lost. When such a person returns to himself, he will be aware of the triviality of what he did. He will weep bitterly as David the prophet did when he, forgetting himself, responded to moments of vain lust (Ps. 6)

One's spirit will find its peace only in God, and will rejoice only in Him if one really lives according to the spirit. He who esteems the joys of the world has in fact strayed from his own spirit. Therefore, the apostle says to us, *"rejoice in the Lord"* (Phil. 3: 1).

"Rejoice in the Lord always. Again I will say, rejoice!" (Phil. 4: 4) (1 Thess. 5: 16).

How beautiful it is the repetition of the word "always", for God is the source of all joy. He is with you always, He works for you all the time, and does not ignore you even for a moment. Therefore nothing prevents you from rejoicing always, even in the moments when afflictions surround you.

The apostle says, *"as sorrowful, yet always rejoicing"* (2 Cor. 6: 10)

That is why the apostles were singing spiritual hymns and songs while in the inner prison with their feet fastened in the stocks (Acts 16: 24, 25). Their joy was derived from God not from external circumstances. With respect to these circumstances they were "sorrowful", and with respect to God they were "always rejoicing". When one puts all his concern in the external circumstances, one will be distressed. In this case one actually has stopped being occupied with God and interested in Him, and began to be involved with the world. Thus the world makes of him a plaything, gives him sometimes and deprives him other times, thus causing him worry and trouble. As for you, God made you His followers and members of His household (Eph. 2: 19). He wants you, therefore, to hand Him all your affairs and be concerned about nothing. See what the apostle says:

"Be anxious for nothing, but in everything by prayer and supplication, with thanksgiving ..."(Phil. 4: 6)

He says also, *"I want you to be without care"* (1 Cor. 7: 32). And the Lord says, *"Therefore do not worry about tomorrow"* (Mt. 6: 34); for the heavenly Father takes care of us.

Since the Lord cares for you, you should be joyful and have no concern.

To have any concern means that you have begun to bear the responsibility instead of God who had promised to bear it. For He said, *"Come to Me, all you who labor and are heavy laden, and I will give you rest"* (Mt. 11: 28). And instead of seeking Him, you sought yourself, and put all your concerns on yourself, thus increasing your own troubles. It means also that you look no more with hope to the future, nor look in trust to God's work for you! Would that you cast all your troubles at the Lord's feet and rejoice in Him!

You will certainly rejoice in the Lord if you take Him as the Good Shepherd who cares for His sheep.

When David remembered this fact, he rejoiced in the Lord, and sang, *"The Lord is my shepherd; I shall not want. He makes me to lie down in green pastures; He leads me beside the still waters ... though I walk through the valley of the shadow of death, I will fear no evil; for You are with me"* (Ps. 23). Have you also taken the Lord as your Shepherd? Have you relied on His care? Do this, and you will rejoice.

You will rejoice also if we remember all God's beautiful attributes, and all His promises to you and to His church. This will give you comfort and peace.

Who is like God? There is none like Him. He does not frighten us with His divinity, nor terrifies us with His greatness, but attracts us with His love.

We rejoice in Him as a Shepherd giving Himself for the sheep; we rejoice in Him as a Father with all the fatherly kindness; and we rejoice in Him as the beloved of our souls.

For He says, *"No longer do I call you servants ... but I have called you friends"* (Jn. 15: 15); therefore we rejoice and are glad because He has loved His own who are in the world, He loved them to the end (Jn. 13: 1). He is not an ordinary friend; for He says, *"I am with you always, even to the end of the age"* (Mt. 28: 20); *"Can a woman forget her nursing child ... they may forget, yet I will not forget you. See, I have inscribed you on the palms of My hands"* (Isa. 49: 15, 16)

How glad we are with this loving God who is meek and humble hearted!

With the Song, we say, *"I sat down in his shade with great delight"* (Song 2: 3). He made man's relationship with Him extend beyond formalities and become all love and emotions, even the prayers and the worship. The whole life of holiness has become concentrated in one commandment:

"You shall love the Lord your God with all your heart, with all your soul, and with all your mind" (Mt. 32: 27)

We are no more charged with many commandments in our spiritual life, but only with one commandments involving everything, that is "love"; *"he who abides in love abides in God, and God in him"* (1 Jn. 4: 16)

We rejoice in God likewise because He does not leave us to ourselves, but supports us with His grace.

We rejoice because He knows our nature and our weakness, that we are dust (Ps. 103: 4). And He does not leave us to the weakness of our nature, but supports us with His grace and the work of His Holy Spirit. With the commandment He gave us the power to implement it, and forgiveness in case we break it and repent.

We rejoice in God whom David experienced and said, *"Please let us fall into the hand of the Lord, for His mercies are great; but do not let me fall into the hand of man"* (2 Sam. 24: 14). He is the loving God who redeemed and saved us, and who turned the punishment into salvation. He is the real physician of our souls and bodies.

We rejoice over His work with us, His protection, and His promises to us. We rejoice in His communion and love, and we feel glad when we are with Him.

In our joy we feel no distress at all, for peace reigns over our hearts always. We derive our joy not from the circumstances surrounding us, but from the deep faith and trust in Him and in His work for us.

This is how the church has lived all the past generations, and will continue to live for the end of times. The church is always happy with God Almighty, who walks in the midst of the seven candlesticks, holding the seven stars in His right hand (Rev. 2: 1). The church is happy with Him who shines over all people with His light and who numbers all the very hairs of our heads (Mt. 10: 30)

Blessed be the Lord, and let us rejoice always in Him and sing to Him a new song!

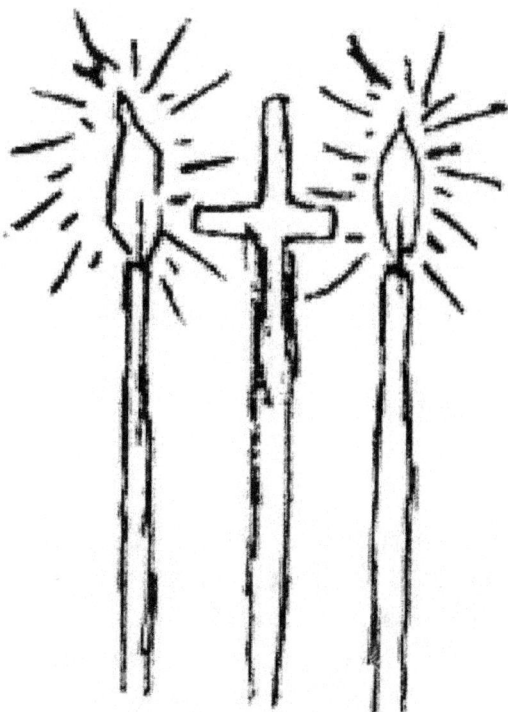

AMEN. COME, O LORD JESUS (Rev. 22: 20)

This verse comes at the end of the last chapter of the Holy Bible. In this chapter the word "come" is repeated many times. So what is our contemplation on this call with regard to man's relationship with God?

1. This call may be an expression of longing for Christ's second coming.

This desire inflamed the hearts of the believers in the first church in the apostolic epoch. Their eyes were fixed towards heaven from where Christ will come again. Their messages often contained the words *"Maran Atha"* i.e. our Lord come (1 Cor. 16: 22)

The longing for the coming of the Lord meant also that they longed for their eternal life when all will be caught up in the clouds to meet the Lord in the air, and will be always with the Lord. (1 Thess. 4: 17). We therefore say, "Amen. Come, O Lord Jesus", that you may take us with You. Then we will change, putting on the spiritual body in the general resurrection that will accompany the Lord's coming (1 Cor. 15: 51)

How delightful it is to be with the Lord always, with spiritual bodies, on His second coming! So, we say to Him, *"Come, O Lord Jesus"*.

But only the righteous should say so, being ready for His coming, whereas the wicked will say to the mountains: Fall on us!, and to the hills: cover us from the rage of the Lord (Lk. 23: 30) (Rev. 6: 16). Yea, this second coming we describe in the divine liturgy as "frightful and full of glory".

2. The words, *"Amen. Come, O Lord Jesus"* can be said when one is dying.

When one is dying he may say: O Lord, come and receive that which You have committed me, *"Into Your hand I commit my spirit"* (Ps. 31: 5). St. Stephen the first deacon, while being stoned, said, *"Lord Jesus, receive my spirit"* (Acts 7: 59)

Only a righteous person can say at the time of death, "Amen. Come, O Lord Jesus". Thereupon the Lord receives that soul and sends an angel to carry it as we know from the story of poor Lazarus, *"so it was that the beggar died, and was carried by the angels to Abraham's bosom"* (Lk. 16: 22). See what beautiful words are said about death, *"Let me die the death of the righteous, and let my end be like his!"* (Num. 23: 10). For the death of the wicked is different from that of the righteous. Some of the wicked, at the time of their death, see terrible scenes, and the devils take his spirit with them to Hades.

Those who can say at the time of their death, *"Come, O Lord Jesus"* are only those like Paul the apostle who said, *"... having a desire to depart and be with Christ, which is far better"* (Phil. 1: 23), or like Simon the elderly who said, *"Lord, now You are letting Your servant depart in peace, ... for my eyes have seen Your salvation"* (Lk. 2: 29, 30)

Among those who received death joyfully are the martyrs and confessors who certainly had in mind the words: Amen. Come, O Lord Jesus.

Their hearts certainly said: O Lord, come, that we may conclude with You this life which we started with You, spent with You, and offered to You. Come, and receive our passions and blood.

These words are also said by those who suffered much and long from incurable diseases. They say: Come, O Lord Jesus that our pains may end in Your hands.

3. Humanity, while waiting for salvation, said the same: Amen. Come, O Lord.

In the Old Testament, they did not know Jesus but "Messiah" whom they waited for and asked to come. Even the Samaritan woman said, "*I know that Messiah is coming – who is called Christ – when He comes, He will tell us all things*" (Jn. 4: 25). The whole humanity were saying, "Amen. Come" to Him of whom the prophecies came, the symbols given, and the sacrifices told.

Even now, humanity can say, "*Amen. Come, O Lord Jesus*" to save the world from materialism and corruption, and from heresies, heterodoxies, and atheism. Come, O Lord Jesus, and save the world from dissentions and make reconciliation between the world and God.

Those who lived under the communist rule with all its pressures and cruelty, cried out: Come, O Lord Jesus. And He did come to them and saved them, whether in Russia, Romania, or the Soviet Union countries. Therefore they began to worship God again with all confidence and no one forbidding them.

4. The words: Amen. Come, O Lord Jesus, may also be an appeal for help asking for repentance.

Many desire to repent but could not. They may rise from their fall, then fall again and they seem to say everyday, "Amen. Come, O Lord Jesus", or "*Restore me, and I will return*" (Jer. 31: 18). They would say: Of our own selves we are not able. We need Your divine help. We ask You to grant us willpower, to change the desires of our hearts, and to save us from the spiritual captivity which overwhelms us. All attempts of repentance have failed, and there is no hope but in the Lord to come and pick us up.

5. The words, "Amen. Come, O Lord Christ", can be said also in times of worry and troubles.

These words can be uttered in times of great troubles of which the Lord said, "*Call upon Me in the day of trouble; I will deliver you, and you shall glorify Me*" (Ps. 50: 15). Therefore David said in the psalm, "*If it had not been the Lord who was on your side, when men rose against us, then they would have swallowed us alive, when their wrath was kindled against us; then the waters would have overwhelmed us, the stream would have gone over our soul*" (Ps. 124: 2-4). But what did happen when you called upon the Lord, David? As he says, "*Our soul has escaped as a bird from the snare of the fowlers; the snare is broken, and we have escaped. Our help is in the name of the Lord, who made heaven and earth*" (Ps. 124: 7, 8).

In the troubles, the heart cries out, "*Lord, how they have increased who trouble me! Many are they who rise up against me. Many are they who say of me: There is no help for him in God*" (Ps. 3: 1, 2), "*For strangers have risen up against me, and oppressors have sought after my life; they have not set God before them*" (Ps. 54: 3). But I have nothing to do except to say, "*Amen. Come, O Lord Jesus*", for the Lord is my strength and song, and He has become my salvation (Ps. 118: 14). Let God arise then, let His enemies be scattered before Him (Ps. 68: 1), and "*Make haste, O God, to deliver me! Make haste to help me, O Lord*" (Ps. 70: 1)

Yea, come, O Lord. These words were said by many saints and prophets.

They said them with all their hearts. Daniel said these words while in the lions' den, so God sent His angel and shut the lions' mouths (Da. 6: 22). And Jonah said them while in the belly of the fish, so God ordered the fish to cast him out (Jon. 2). The three lads also said them while in the furnace of the fire, so God sent a fourth like the sons of gods to walk with them in the fire (Da. 3: 25)

All those were in great trouble which no human power could save them from.

There remained nothing but their hearts crying out, "*Come, O Lord Jesus*". And the Lord responded as the psalmist says, "*I cried to the Lord with my voice, and He heard me from His holy hill*" (Ps. 3: 4). This reminds us of the words of the Lord, "*Behold I send you out as sheep in the midst of wolves*" (Mt. 10: 16). O Lord, what can the sheep do in the midst of wolves? They can do nothing but cry out, "*Amen. Come, O Lord Jesus*". This was what actually happened; for He came and king Constantine became Christian and issued the Milan Decree in 313 A.D. which gives freedom of creed. He came and Irianos the Governor of Insena, who was hard-hearted and violent, turned into a believer and martyr. Thus He turned the wolves into sheep. Likewise, He turned Saul of Tarsus into an apostle that labored for the ministry more than all the other apostles (1 Cor. 15: 10)

6. The words, "*Amen. Come, O Lord Jesus*" can also be said while in the midst of problems seeming to have no solution; for the Lord always has many solutions.

It was in the heart during the hardship caused by Haman who threatened Mordecai and the whole people with destruction. And behold Haman was crucified on the cross which he had prepared for Mordecai (Esther 7: 9, 10)!

The same cry arose also when the emperor ordered that Arius be permitted to communion and prayer. And before such an authority of the emperor there was no solution but to cryout, "*Amen. Come, O Lord Jesus*", come, for You are the Powerful, the Savior, and the Helper. Come, for You are the only One who opens and no one shuts (Rev. 3: 7). When these words were said in the days of the heretics, God saved the church, and faith has been kept since then.

7. The same words, *"Amen. Come, O Lord Jesus"* will be said by the people in the last days when Satan will be released from his prison (Rev. 20: 7)

In those days Satan will go out to deceive the nations which are in the four corners of the earth (Rev. 20: 8). Then the anti-Christ, or the lawless one, will come with all power, signs, and lying wonders, according to the working of Satan, and with all unrighteous deception among those who perish (2 Thess. 2: 9, 10). And unless those days were shortened, no flesh would be saved (Mt. 24: 22). When the people cryout to the Lord, for the elect's sake, those days will be shortened.

In those days, the seven angels will sound with their terrible trumpets, and awful plagues will come that have never happened before (Rev. 8, 9). The people will have nothing to do but to cry to the Lord.

8. The words, *"Amen. Come, O Lord Jesus"* should also be said for the church and the ministry.

We should say: You, Lord, have set the foundation, may You complete the building and watch over it! For, *"Unless the Lord builds the house, they labor in vain who build it; Unless the Lord guards the city, the watchman stays awake in vain"* (Ps. 127: 1)

O Lord, we serve, preach, speak, and watch, but it is You who works in the hearts. You give the word influence, and You turn the people's will towards good to do it. Tend then, O Lord, this vine which Your right hand has planted. Yea, Come, O Lord Jesus, and give the Spirit to the speaker, and the will to him who hears. We ask You also, O Lord, to send laborers to the harvest.

9. They are words signifying faith and acceptance.

When you say, *"Amen. Come, O Lord Jesus"*, this means that you have believed in Him as Lord, and have accepted to receive Him. And the Gospel says, *"But as many as received Him, to them He gave the right to become children of God, to those who believe in His name"* (Jn. 1: 12). Those who believe in the Lord accept Him as God and leader of their life. Remember also the words of the apostle, *"For as many as are led by the Spirit of God, these are sons of God"* (Rom. 8: 14)

10. In some cases the words, *"Amen. Come, O Lord Jesus"* signify responding to the call.

This happened with Saul of Tarsus who persecuted the church, but when the Lord appeared to him and called him, he responded and became an apostle to the Gentiles. The Samaritan woman also responded and her heart said, *"Amen. Come, O Lord Jesus"*

11. The words, *"Come, O Lord Jesus"* can be a prayer of love and longing.

They are uttered by one longing for God as the thirst land longs for water. Such a person says to Him: Come, O Lord Jesus. Dwell in my heart, in my mind, and in all my emotions. You seek a place to lay Your head, lo, I open my heart to You. With all my heart I seek You and I say to You: Come, O Lord. Come, leaping on the mountains, and skipping upon the hills, for my soul feels You coming, and says, *"The voice of my beloved"* (Song 2: 8). You stand at the door, knocking and saying, *"If anyone hears My voice and opens the door, I will come in to him and dine with him, and he with Me"* (Rev. 3: 20). Lo, I open to You, and I say: Amen. Come, O Lord Jesus. You knocked my door, and my door is open to You. Come, and let me be attached to You and establish a relationship with You.

12. Come, that I may have fellowship with You.

Let Your will be mine, Your intention be my intention, and Your work be my work, that You may be in me, and I in You and that I may say with the apostle, *"For to me, to live is Christ"*

(Phil. 1: 21); *"it is no longer I who live, but Christ lives in me"* (Gal. 2: 20). Thus I may become a temple for Your Spirit, and Your Holy Spirit dwells in me (1 Cor. 3: 16)

Let these words be a prayer for us throughout all our life.

These words do not express temporary, but permanent emotions which we acquired since we have been born of God through faith and baptism, and since we have become a dwelling place for Him through the holy chrism. Since then we are saved by His life in us (Rom. 5: 10).

So, Amen. Come, O Lord Jesus, that we may be saved by Your life in us!

✤

ENGLISH TRANSLATIONS OF BOOKS BY
HIS HOLINESS POPE SHENOUDA III

Among 103 books written by His Holiness Pope Shenouda III in Arabic Language, 47 have been translated into English, namely :

1. Release of the Spirit.
2. Words of Spiritual Benefit.   (Vol. 1).
3. Words of Spiritual Benefit.   (Vol. 2).
4. Words of Spiritual Benefit.   (Vol. 3).
5. Words of Spiritual Benefit.   (Vol. 4).
6. Contemplations on the Ten Commandments   (Vol. 1).
.7. Contemplations on the Ten Commandments.   (Vol. 2).
8. Contemplations on the Ten Commandments.   (Vol. 3).
9. Contemplations on the Ten Commandments.   (Vol. 4).
10. Contemplations on the Sermon on the Mount.
11. The Seven Words of Our Lord on the Cross.
12. Thine is the Power and the Glory.
13. Contemplations on Jonah the prophet.
14. Priesthood.
15. Salvation in the Orthodox Concept.
16. The Heresy of "Salvation in a moment".
17. Diabolic wars.
18. Spiritual warfares.
19. Lord, how ? .
20. Discipleship.
21. The Holy Zeal.

✝

✳ ✳ ✳